MW01226940

Lab Manual
The Culinary Professional

Second Edition

David Ross, CCC
Chef Instructor, Le Cordon Bleu Culinary Arts Atlanta

Text by

John Draz, CEC, CCE
Christopher Koetke, MBA, CEC, CCE

Publisher
The Goodheart-Willcox Company, Inc.
Tinley Park, Illinois
www.g-w.com

Introduction

The *Lab Manual* is designed for use with **The Culinary Professional** textbook. The activities in the *Lab Manual* guide you through applying and practicing the key concepts and techniques presented in the text. Completing these activities will help you build the confidence and skills needed to succeed in the culinary field.

Many of the activities include both *Chef's Journal* and *Performance Review* components. The *Chef's Journal* encourages you to reflect on your performance and identify areas for improvement. Successful chefs pursue continuous improvement in the quality and efficiency of their work. Developing this habit will help you achieve your goals. Your instructor can use the *Performance Review* to evaluate your proficiency of the core skills and knowledge required for completion of the various activities. As a culinary professional, learning to accept and use feedback is essential.

Many of the lab activities include recipes. These recipes can also be found on **The Culinary Professional** Companion Website. Recipe yield conversion worksheets and blank recipe forms are located on the Companion Website as well.

Contents

Chapter 15 Using Recipes

Chapter 16 Basic Preparations—Mise en Place

Chapter 18 Cooking Principles

Chapter 19 Salads and Dressings

Chapter 21 Fruit Preparation

Chapter 22 Cold Sandwiches

Chapter 23 Stocks

Chapter 24 Sauces

Chapter 25 Soups

Chapter 27 Vegetable Cookery

Chapter 29 Starch Cookery

Chapter 32 Dry-Heat Cooking Methods for Meat and Poultry

Chapter 33 Moist-Heat and Combination Cooking Methods for Meat and Poultry

Chapter 35 Fish and Shellfish Preparation and Cookery

Chapter 36 Hot Sandwiches and Pizza

Chapter 38 Breakfast Cookery

Chapter 41 Quick Breads and Batters

Chapter 42 Cookies

Chapter 43 Yeast-Raised Products

Chapter 44 Pies and Tarts

Chapter 45 Cakes

Chapter 46 Custards, Foams, and Buttercreams

Chapter 47 Dessert Sauces and Frozen Desserts

Chapter 48 Table Service

Lab Activity 4-1: **The Brigade System**

Name _____ **Date** _____ **Period** _____

Group Members _____

Designed in the early 1900s to organize the work in professional kitchens, the traditional brigade system was based on the structure used by the military. The brigade uses a chain of command—each workstation has a leader and each leader reports to the head chef—to complete a task. Today's professional kitchens still employ this method of organization to varying degrees. Workers are assigned to workstations with specific tasks and products assigned to the workers in each station, making the modern kitchen highly efficient, organized, and productive.

Objectives

After completing this lab, you will be able to

- recognize the workstations in the brigade.
- explain how tasks for producing a food order are distributed to workstations.
- understand how workstations and positions coordinate to complete a food order.

Preparation

1. Review the sections *The Brigade* and *Organization of Modern Kitchens* in text Chapter 4.

2. Write the names of each position in Figure 4-2 on a separate 3″ × 5″ card. (***Note:*** *Your instructor may already have these cards prepared.*) Place the cards in a basket face down and in no particular order.

3. In small groups, write three sample food orders typically received by waitstaff in a full-service restaurant. Make sure the food orders are complete and contain an interesting variety of dishes. Include garnishes and methods of preparation in the description. A sample food order might include the following: *spring salad greens with balsamic vinaigrette, grilled chicken breast topped with sautéed mushrooms on a bed of rice pilaf, dinner rolls, and raspberry mousse.*

Lab Procedure

1. Each student draws a position from the basket and proceeds to the appropriate workstation in the kitchen where that position works.

2. Once everyone is in their workstation, line up by title in the correct brigade order and hierarchy.

3. The executive chef reviews the brigade to ensure that each position is in the correct workstation and place in the line up according to hierarchy.

4. The executive chef selects and announces a sample food order. After the order is read, the executive chef calls on each workstation to explain its role (if any) in completing the order. If there is more than one position in a workstation, each position should explain his or her responsibilities.

(Continued)

Observations/Questions

1. Explain how the brigade system makes the professional kitchen more efficient, organized, and productive.

    _____

    _____

    _____

    _____

2. Were there any workstations or positions that had more work than another? What suggestions would you make to reorganize the workstations and even out the workload?

    _____

    _____

    _____

Lab Activity 7-1: **Using Material Safety Data Sheets (MSDS)**

Name _____ **Date** _____ **Period** _____

Group Members _____

A material safety data sheet (MSDS) is designed to provide both workers and emergency personnel with the proper procedures for handling or working with a particular substance. MSDS include information such as physical data, toxicity, health effects, first aid, reactivity, storage, disposal, protective equipment, and spill or leak procedures. MSDS vary in length from 1 to 10 pages. By law, these sheets must be displayed in a visible and accessible place in the kitchen.

Objectives

After completing this lab, you will be able to

- recognize the information on a material safety data sheet that is important to your job.
- recall the location of protective equipment in the kitchen lab.

Lab Procedure

Part 1: Reading an MSDS

Use the material safety data sheet that follows to answer these questions.

1. What is the product name?

   _____

2. What is the intended use for this product?

   _____

3. What is the physical state (for example, liquid or powder) and color of this product?

   _____

4. What are the potential acute health effects of this product?

   _____

   _____

5. What first aid measures should be taken in the event of eye contact?

   _____

   _____

6. What personal protection is recommended when using this product?

   _____

   _____

(Continued)

Material Safety Data Sheet

OASIS146 MULTI-QUAT SANITIZER Use Solution (0.25- 0.67 oz/gal)

Section 1. Chemical product and company identification

Trade name	: OASIS146 MULTI-QUAT SANITIZER Use Solution (0.25- 0.67 oz/gal)
Product use	: Sanitizer.
Supplier	: Ecolab Inc. Institutional Division
	370 N. Wabasha Street
	St. Paul, MN 55102
	1-800-352-5326
Code	: ut910787
Date of issue	**11-June-2008**

EMERGENCY HEALTH INFORMATION: 1-800-328-0026
Outside United States and Canada CALL 1-651-222-5352 (in USA)

Section 2. Composition, information on ingredients

To the present knowledge of the supplier, this product does not contain any hazardous ingredients in quantities requiring reporting, according to local regulations.

Section 3. Hazards identification

Physical state	: Liquid.
Emergency overview	: CAUTION !
	MAY CAUSE EYE IRRITATION.
	Avoid contact with eyes. Wash thoroughly after handling.

Potential acute health effects

Eyes	: Slightly irritating to the eyes.
Skin	: No known significant effects or critical hazards.
Inhalation	: No known significant effects or critical hazards.
Ingestion	: No known significant effects or critical hazards.

See toxicological information (section 11)

Section 4. First aid measures

Eye contact	: In case of contact, immediately flush eyes with plenty of water. Remove contact lenses and flush again. Get medical attention if irritation persists.
Skin contact	: In case of contact, immediately flush skin with plenty of water. Wash clothing before reuse.
Inhalation	: If inhaled, remove to fresh air.
Ingestion	: Do not induce vomiting. Never give anything by mouth to an unconscious person. If irritation persists, get medical attention.

Section 5. Fire fighting measures

Flash point	: > 100°C
Hazardous thermal decomposition products	: No specific data.
Fire-fighting media and instructions	: Use an extinguishing agent suitable for the surrounding fire.
	Dike area of fire to prevent runoff.
	In a fire or if heated, a pressure increase will occur and the container may burst.
Special protective equipment for fire-fighters	: Fire-fighters should wear appropriate protective equipment and self-contained breathing apparatus (SCBA) with a full face-piece operated in positive pressure mode.

(Continued)

OASIS146 MULTI-QUAT SANITIZER Use Solution (0.25- 0.67 oz/gal)   **Page: 2/3**

Section 6. Accidental release measures

Personal precautions	:	Use suitable protective equipment (section 8). Do not allow to enter drains or watercourses.
Environmental precautions	:	Avoid dispersal of spilled material and runoff and contact with soil, waterways, drains and sewers. Inform the relevant authorities if the product has caused environmental pollution (sewers, waterways, soil or air).
Methods for cleaning up	:	For small spills, add absorbent (soil may be used in the absence of other suitable materials), scoop up material and place in a sealable, liquid-proof container for disposal. For large spills, dike spilled material or otherwise contain it to ensure runoff does not reach a waterway. Place spilled material in an appropriate container for disposal.

Section 7. Handling and storage

Handling	:	Avoid contact with eyes. Wash thoroughly after handling.
Storage	:	Keep out of reach of children. Keep container in a cool, well-ventilated area. Keep container tightly closed.

Section 8. Exposure controls/personal protection

Engineering measures	:	Good general ventilation should be sufficient to control worker exposure to airborne contaminants.

Personal protection :

Eyes	:	No protective equipment is needed under normal use conditions.
Hands	:	No protective equipment is needed under normal use conditions.
Skin	:	No protective equipment is needed under normal use conditions.
Respiratory	:	A respirator is not needed under normal and intended conditions of product use.

Consult local authorities for acceptable exposure limits.

Section 9. Physical and chemical properties

Physical state	:	Liquid.
Color	:	Red.
pH	:	7.04 [Conc. (% w/w): 100%]
Boiling/condensation point	:	100°C (212°F)
Specific gravity	:	1.002

Section 10. Stability and reactivity

Stability	:	The product is stable. Under normal conditions of storage and use, hazardous polymerization will not occur.
Hazardous decomposition products	:	Under normal conditions of storage and use, hazardous decomposition products should not be produced.
Hazardous polymerization	:	Under normal conditions of storage and use, hazardous polymerization will not occur.

Section 11. Toxicological information

Potential acute health effects

Eyes	:	Slightly irritating to the eyes.
Skin	:	No known significant effects or critical hazards.
Inhalation	:	No known significant effects or critical hazards.
Ingestion	:	No known significant effects or critical hazards.

(Continued)

Section 12. Ecological information

Section 13. Disposal considerations

Waste disposal   : The generation of waste should be avoided or minimized wherever possible. Avoid dispersal of spilled material and runoff and contact with soil, waterways, drains and sewers. Disposal of this product, solutions and any by-products should at all times comply with the requirements of environmental protection and waste disposal legislation and any regional local authority requirements.

Consult your local or regional authorities.

Section 14. Transport information

See shipping documents for specific transportation information.

Section 15. Regulatory information

HCS Classification   : Not regulated.

U.S. Federal regulations : **SARA 302/304/311/312 extremely hazardous substances**: No products were found.

SARA 302/304 emergency planning and notification: No products were found.

TSCA 8(b) inventory   : All components are listed or exempted.

California Prop. 65   : No products were found.

Section 16. Other information

Hazardous Material   :
Information System (U.S.A.)

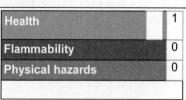

Health	1
Flammability	0
Physical hazards	0

Date of issue   : **11-June-2008.**
Responsible name   : **Regulatory Affairs**
Date of previous issue   : **08-January-2007.**

Notice to reader

The above information is believed to be correct with respect to the formula used to manufacture the product in the country of origin. As data, standards, and regulations change, and conditions of use and handling are beyond our control, NO WARRANTY, EXPRESS OR IMPLIED, IS MADE AS TO THE COMPLETENESS OR CONTINUING ACCURACY OF THIS INFORMATION.

(Continued)

Name _____

Part 2: MSDS in Your Kitchen

Find a chemical used in the kitchen and locate its MSDS. Answer these questions using the MSDS.

1. What is the product name?

    _____

2. What is the intended use for the product?

    _____

3. What does the product look like?

    _____

4. What are the potential acute health effects of this product?

    _____

    _____

5. What protective equipment is recommended when using this product?

    _____

    _____

6. Locate the protective equipment mentioned in the previous question in your kitchen lab. If the MSDS does not require any protective equipment, find the following equipment: goggles or face shield, impervious gloves, synthetic apron, eyewash.

Additional Instructor's Comments

Lab Activity 7-2: **Preventing Chemical Hazards**

Name _____ **Date** _____ **Period** _____

Group Members _____

Incorrect chemical storage, use, dilution, and labeling are important concerns in kitchens. Foodservice professionals are responsible for safe handling of chemicals to protect themselves and their customers.

Objective

After completing this lab, you will be able to

- apply safety precautions to prevent chemical contamination.

Preparation

1. Review the section *Chemical Hazards* in text Chapter 7.
2. Locate the MSDS folder in the kitchen lab.

Key Terms

Define the following terms used in this activity. Some may have been defined in previous chapters.

1. contamination _____
_____

2. material safety data sheets (MSDS)_____
_____

3. chemical hazard_____
_____

Lab Procedure

1. Working in small groups, locate all the chemical products in your kitchen lab. As you find each chemical, write it on the attached Chemical Inventory sheet. Complete the inventory sheet by placing a (✔) in the column of each safety precaution that is being followed. If the safety precaution is not being followed, the potential for a chemical hazard exists. Write the corrective action needed to avoid a chemical hazard on the lines at the bottom of the sheet.

2. Discuss your findings as a class.

(Continued)

Name _____ **Date** _____ **Period** _____

Group Members _____

Chemical Inventory			
Chemical Name	**Safety Precautions**		
	In original or clearly labeled container?	Stored separate from food prep or storage?	MSDS available for chemical?
1.			
2.			
3.			
4.			
5.			
6.			
7.			
8.			
9.			
10.			
11.			
12.			
13.			
14.			
15.			

Corrective action:

_____

_____

_____

_____

_____

Lab Activity 7-3: **Calibrating a Thermometer**

Name _____ **Date**_____ **Period** _____

Group Members _____

The bimetallic stem thermometer is commonly used for testing internal temperatures of hot and cold foods including raw and cooked product. The calibration, use, and understanding of the bimetallic stem thermometer are essential for safe food handling. Two methods are commonly used for correct calibration—ice water and boiling water. Thermometers should be calibrated periodically, as well as, after being knocked or dropped.

Objectives

After completing this lab, you will be able to

- recognize the parts of a bimetallic thermometer.
- calibrate a bimetallic stem thermometer using the ice water method.
- calibrate a bimetallic stem thermometer using the boiling water method.

Preparation

1. Read Lab Procedure and gather the following supplies:
   - bimetallic stem thermometer with sheath
   - 12-16 oz. (or larger) container
   - crushed ice
   - suitable tool for adjusting hex nut on thermometer (sheath or small wrench)
   - small saucepan
2. Review the section *Burns* in text Chapter 9.
3. Review the effect of altitude on boiling point in *Science & Technology: The Atmosphere for Moist Cooking* in text Chapter 18.
4. Review the following diagram of a bimetallic stem thermometer.

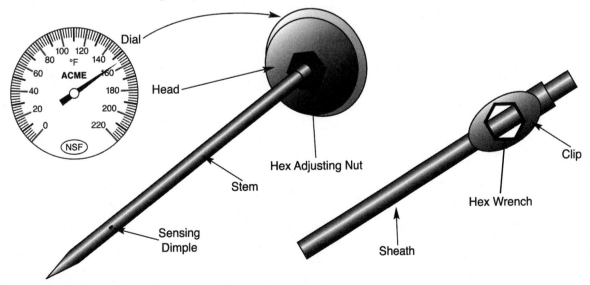

(Continued)

Lab Procedure

Part 1: Ice Water Method

1. Fill a container with crushed ice. Add clean cold tap water to cover ice and stir well.

2. Slide the stem of the thermometer through the clip portion of the sheath for ease and safety when handling. *Note: Often this part of the sheath has a hexagon-shaped hole that serves double duty when calibrating a thermometer—it can be used to hold, as well as, adjust the thermometer.*

3. Immerse the thermometer stem a minimum of two inches (sensing dimple should be immersed) into the mixture. Make sure it is not touching the sides or bottom of the container.

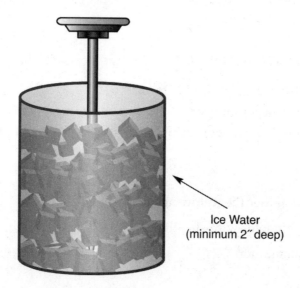

Ice Water
(minimum 2″ deep)

4. Hold the thermometer in the water for one minute before adjusting.

5. While continuing to hold the thermometer in the ice water, read the temperature on the dial. If the reading is 32°F (0°C), the thermometer is calibrated. If the reading is different, adjust the hex nut located under the dial until it reads 32°F (0°C). *Note: 32°F (0°C) is freezing temperature.*

6. Remove the thermometer from the water and repeat steps 1 through 5 to confirm thermometer is calibrated.

(Continued)

Part 2: Boiling Water Method

1. Bring a saucepan of clean tap water to a full rolling boil.

2. Slide the stem of the thermometer through the clip portion of the sheath for ease and safety when handling. *Note: Often this part of the sheath has a hexagon-shaped cutout that serves double duty when calibrating a thermometer—it can be used to hold, as well as, adjust the thermometer.*

3. Immerse the thermometer stem a minimum of two inches (sensing dimple should be immersed) into the boiling water. Make sure it is not touching the sides or bottom of the container.

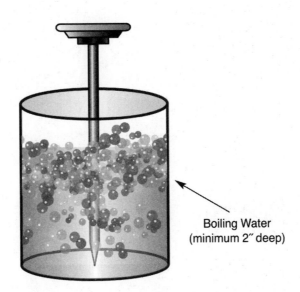

Boiling Water
(minimum 2″ deep)

4. Carefully hold the thermometer in the water for a minimum of 30 seconds before adjusting.

5. While continuing to hold the thermometer in the boiling water, read the temperature on the dial. If the reading is 212°F (100°C), the thermometer is calibrated. If the reading is different, adjust the hex nut located under the dial until it reads 212°F (100°C). *Note: This temperature may vary due to differences in atmospheric pressure at altitudes above sea level.*

6. Remove the thermometer from the water and repeat steps 1 through 5 to confirm thermometer is calibrated.

Additional Instructor's Comments

Lab Activity 8-1: **Avoiding Cross-Contamination**

Name _____ **Date**_____ **Period** _____

Group Members _____

Cross-contamination of food or food-contact surfaces with biological hazards is one of the greatest causes of foodborne illness. Biological hazards cannot be seen or smelled, but they exist in many foods and in all kitchens. Understanding how to prevent the transfer of biological hazards is critical for avoiding cross-contamination and foodborne illness.

Objectives

After completing this lab, you will be able to

- explain how employees' hands and food-contact surfaces contribute to cross-contamination.
- apply effective hand-washing procedure.
- understand the need for sanitizing equipment after cleaning.

Preparation

1. Read Lab Procedure and gather the following supplies:
   - fluorescent cream or gel
   - fluorescent powder
   - ultraviolet light
   - chef knife
   - two potatoes
   - cutting board
2. Review the section *Hand Washing* in text Chapter 8.

Key Terms

Define the following terms used in this activity. Some may have been defined in previous chapters.

1. bacteria _____

   _____

2. contamination _____

   _____

3. biological hazard _____

   _____

4. cross-contamination _____

   _____

5. foodborne illness _____

   _____

(Continued)

6. pathogen _____
   _____

7. sanitary _____
   _____

8. food-contact surface _____
   _____

Lab Procedure

Part 1: Simulation of Bacteria on Hands

1. Rub fluorescent cream or gel on hands until absorbed. The cream or gel is used to simulate bacteria such as *salmonella*.
2. Turn off room lights and scan hands and fingernails with ultraviolet (UV) light. The "bacteria" will glow in the UV light. This represents contamination of your hands with a "bacteria."
3. Wash hands thoroughly using the technique described in the text.
4. Turn off the room lights and scan hands and fingernails with (UV) light again.
5. Any "bacteria" that remains on your hands after washing will glow when examined with the UV light. This indicates that hands have not been washed correctly and are carrying a potential biological hazard. In the kitchen, unclean hands can result in cross-contamination of food or equipment and possibly foodborne illness.
6. Wash hands again, paying close attention to those areas harboring the "bacteria."

Observations/Questions

1. Did you see any "bacteria" remaining on your hands after washing? If so, what areas of your hands harbored the most "bacteria?" _____
   _____

2. How could you improve your handwashing technique?_____
   _____

Part 2: Simulation of Bacteria on Equipment

1. Dust a chef knife and potato (A) with the fluorescent powder to simulate chicken juice containing "bacteria."
2. Place potato A on a cutting board and slice it several times with the chef knife.
3. Place the sliced potato A in a bowl.
4. Select another potato (B) and place it on the same cutting board. Use the chef knife to slice potato B several times as well. Place the sliced potato B in a different bowl.
5. Use the UV light to examine potato A, potato B, your hands, the knife, and the cutting board. Record your observations in the table that follows.
6. Wash the chef knife and cutting board. Wash your hands.
7. Turn off the room lights and pass the UV light over the chef knife, cutting board, and your hands again. Observe if any traces of "bacteria" from the simulated chicken juice are still present. Record your observations in the table that follows.

(Continued)

Name _____

Observations/Questions

Observations		
	Step 5	**Step 7**
potato A		
potato B		
knife		
your hands		
cutting board		

1. Did the chef knife and cutting board look clean after you washed them?

   _____

2. Based on the UV light inspection of the washed chef knife and cutting board, would you consider them sanitary? Explain.

   _____

   _____

3. According to the text, what should be the next step to rid the food-contact surfaces (chef knife and cutting board) of the "pathogens" still present after cleaning?

   _____

   _____

Additional Instructor's Comments

Lab Activity 8-2: **Preparing Sanitizing Solutions**

Name _____ **Date**_____ **Period** _____

Group Members _____

Chlorine and quaternary ammonium compounds (quats) are the two most commonly used sanitizers in commercial kitchens. Each has its advantages and disadvantages. Whichever sanitizer you use, it is most important that you use it properly.

Objectives

After completing this lab, you will be able to

- produce a proper sanitizing solution for food-contact surfaces.
- recognize factors that impact the effectiveness of a sanitizing solution.

Preparation

1. Read Lab Procedure and gather the following supplies:
   - volume measuring equipment
   - thermometer
   - sanitizer
   - 3 buckets for sanitizing solution
   - test strip appropriate for sanitizer being used
   - detergent
   - wiping cloths
2. Read and follow manufacturers' directions for chemicals when preparing sanitizing solutions.
3. Wear any protective equipment recommended in manufacturers' directions.
4. Locate and read the MSDS sheet for the sanitizing product.

Lab Procedure

Part 1: Preparing and Using Solution

1. Measure one gallon of tap water. Read manufacturers' directions to learn the optimal water temperature for their product. Use a thermometer to measure the water temperature. Many sanitizers require water temperatures between 75°F (24°C) and 100°F (37.8°C). ***Note:*** *Some sanitizers lose effectiveness in temperatures outside this range.*
2. Add enough sanitizer to the water to create a sanitizing solution for food-contact surfaces. Check manufacturers' directions for the recommended amount to add.
3. Mix sanitizing solution and check concentration with test strip. (Be sure you are using the correct test strip for the sanitizer you are using.) Test strips should be used to recheck the concentration periodically. ***Note:*** *Some sanitizers dissipate and lose effectiveness.*

(Continued)

4. Adjust dilution if needed. If test strip indicates concentration is low, add sanitizer. If test strip indicates concentration is high, add water. Record the amount of any water or sanitizer you must add to achieve the accurate concentration. *Note: Some sanitizers lose effectiveness in hard water.*

5. Clean food-contact surface with a detergent solution to remove any food or grime before sanitizing. *Note: Some sanitizers lose effectiveness in the presence of food residue, oil, or organic material.*

6. Rinse food-contact surface with clean water to remove detergent residue. Be sure to remove any excess water from surface after rinsing is complete. *Note: Some sanitizers lose their effectiveness in the presence of detergents.*

7. Dip a clean wiping cloth in sanitizing solution. Lightly wring out excess solution. Wipe the food-contact surface with sanitizing solution and allow it to air-dry.

Observations/Questions

1. Did you need to adjust the dilution by adding any additional water or sanitizer? If so, how much did you add?

_____

_____

2. What factor(s) might cause the need to add more water or sanitizer than the manufacturers' directions recommend?

_____

_____

Part 2: What Impacts Effectiveness?

1. Divide the sanitizing solution you made in Part 1 into three plastic buckets.

2. Label the first bucket "A." Test this sanitizing solution with a test strip every hour over four hours at room temperature. Record any changes in concentration in the table that follows.

3. Label the second bucket "B." Add approximately 8 fluid ounces of diluted pot and pan detergent to this bucket and mix. Record any change in concentration in the table that follows.

4. Label the third bucket "C." Use a wiping cloth to clean a heavily soiled food-contact surface, pot, or pan. Rinse the soiled wiping cloth in the bucket C solution. Record any changes in concentration in the table that follows.

(Continued)

Name _____

Observations/Questions

Observations				
		Change in Concentration		
	Time Elapsed	**No Change**	**Increase**	**Decrease**
Bucket A	1st hour			
	2nd hour			
	3rd hour			
	4th hour			
Bucket B				
Bucket C				

1. Based on your observations, are the solutions in buckets A, B, and C still effective sanitizing solutions? If not, which solution(s) is no longer effective?

   _____

   _____

2. What action(s) could you take to ensure that you maintain an effective sanitizing solution in your daily work?

   _____

   _____

   _____

   _____

Additional Instructor's Comments

Lab Activity 8-3: **Sanitation Self-Inspection**

Name _____ **Date**_____ **Period** _____

Group Members _____

Professional culinarians have a moral obligation to prepare and serve wholesome, safe food. Food safety and sanitation procedures must become second nature. Routinely performing sanitation self-inspections helps you identify areas that are not meeting standards so corrective action can be taken.

Objectives

After completing this lab, you will be able to

- identify unsafe food-handling practices.
- plan corrective action.

Lab Procedure

1. Carefully read self-inspection checklist before starting.
2. For each standard on the list, indicate whether it has been met.
3. Write a corrective action for standards which are not met.

Chef's Journal

After completing the self-inspection, reflect on your findings. Were you surprised by anything you found? What suggestions do you have to improve the checklist?

_____

_____

_____

_____

_____

_____

_____

_____

_____

_____

_____

_____

_____

(Continued)

Name _____ **Date** _____ **Period** _____

Group Members _____

Sanitation Inspection Checklist

Place a "✔" in the box if the standard is met. For any standards that do not have a "✔," note the number and corrective action in the space provided at the end of the checklist.

Employee Dress and Hygiene

❑ 1. Uniform and apron are clean and shoes are nonskid

❑ 2. Hair is neat and restrained

❑ 3. Nails are short, clean, and unpolished (no artificial nails)

❑ 4. Jewelry on hands and arms is restricted to a watch and plain ring

❑ 5. Hands are washed using proper technique at critical points

❑ 6. Gloves are changed at critical points or when torn

❑ 7. Open sores, cuts, and bandages on or near hands are covered

❑ 8. Personal items such as jackets and backpacks are not stored in food preparation and storage areas

❑ 9. An employee with a Food Service Manager's certification is on premises

Food Purchasing and Storage

❑ 10. Food is obtained from sources that are in compliance with the law

❑ 11. Foods are checked for appropriate temperature, spoilage, and contamination at delivery

❑ 12. Foods are dated and rotated upon receipt to facilitate first in, first out usage

❑ 13. Food that is removed from original packaging and held in approved containers must be clearly labeled with the common name of the food

❑ 14. Food is not stored under exposed sewer or water lines

❑ 15. Food must be stored at least 6 inches from the floor

❑ 16. All storage surfaces and floors are clean

❑ 17. Dry storage is well ventilated and kept cool and dry

❑ 18. Chemicals are stored separate from food and food-related supplies

❑ 19. Refrigerators and freezers have working thermometers located in the warmest part of the refrigerator

❑ 20. Refrigerator and freezer temperatures are regularly checked and recorded

❑ 21. Raw foods are not stored above ready-to-eat foods to avoid cross-contamination

❑ 22. Foods are appropriately wrapped, labeled, and dated

(Continued)

Name _____

Food Preparation

❏ 23. Foods are cooked to proper temperatures

❏ 24. Foods are held below 41°F or above 135°F and temperatures are checked regularly

❏ 25. Foods are thawed in the refrigerator or in cold, running water

❏ 26. Work surfaces are cleaned and sanitized before and after each task

❏ 27. Buckets of sanitizing solutions are present in food prep areas and at proper concentrations

❏ 28. Cutting boards and utensils are cleaned and sanitized for each food preparation task

❏ 29. Vegetables and fruits are washed prior to cutting, peeling, or cooking

❏ 30. Employees do not eat in the food preparation area (tasting with a single-use utensil is allowed)

Cleaning and Sanitation

❏ 31. Three-compartment sink setup includes wash, rinse, and sanitizing sinks

❏ 32. Three-compartment sanitizing sink contains an approved sanitizing solution at appropriate concentrations (Test kits are used)

❏ 33. Dishmachine water temperatures are appropriate and regularly recorded

❏ 34. Dishes, utensils, and smallwares are allowed to air-dry

❏ 35. Clean dishes, smallwares, and utensils are stored properly to protect them from contamination

❏ 36. Large equipment is clean to sight and touch

❏ 37. Handwashing sinks are stocked with soap and paper towels or other approved drying device

❏ 38. Cleaning supplies are properly labeled and stored separate from food and other supplies

❏ 39. Material safety data sheets (MSDS) are readily accessible to employees

Facilities, Waste, and Pest Control

❏ 40. Bathrooms are stocked and clean

❏ 41. Floors, walls, and ceilings are in good repair and clean

❏ 42. Exhaust hood and filters are clean

❏ 43. Garbage cans in kitchen are clean and covered

❏ 44. Outdoor dumpsters are clean and lids are closed

❏ 45. Screens, walls, and ceilings are in good repair to discourage entrance of pests

Recommended Corrective Action

_____

_____

_____

(Continued)

Name _____

Lab Activity 8-4: **Identifying CCPs**

Name _____ **Date** _____ **Period** _____

Group Members _____

Critical control points (CCP) are steps in food handling at which improper practice may result in unwholesome food. Culinary professionals must be able to identify CCPs and ensure that safe food-handling practices are applied at these critical stages.

Critical control points exist as food flows from the farm to the table. In the commercial kitchen, CCPs occur in receiving, storage, preparation, cooking, holding, service, cooling, and reheating. To limit or prevent most threats to wholesome food:

- Avoid holding food in the temperature danger zone for too long
- Cook foods to proper temperatures
- Protect food from cross-contamination

Objectives

After completing this lab, you will be able to

- identify critical control points in a foodservice operation.
- determine appropriate corrective action.

Lab Procedure

For each of the following scenarios, underline any examples of food being handled at a critical control point (CCP). If the food was handled improperly, write the correct procedure for handling the food in the space that follows.

1. Receiving

One hot summer day, the receiving clerk had to leave work unexpectedly due to a family emergency. After the lunch rush was over, the kitchen manager asked her new dishwasher Liam to finish receiving the delivery of fresh meat and poultry that was sitting at the dock. Liam had never worked in foodservice before, but was anxious to impress the manager. Liam went back to the receiving dock, loaded the cases of meat and chicken onto a cart, and pushed it into the walk-in refrigerator.

_____

_____

_____

(Continued)

2. Storage

Once in the walk-in refrigerator, Liam noticed the thermometer read 45°F which felt good after being on the hot receiving dock. He proceeded to place the cases of meat and poultry on the open shelf space above some cases of cantaloupe. Liam returned the empty cart to the receiving area and went back to washing dishes.

_____

_____

_____

3. Preparation

The cold foods prep cook, Juanita, needed to prepare some cantaloupe for the next meal. She took her cart into the walk-in refrigerator to get the case of cantaloupe. Juanita removed the melons from the case, placed them in a colander in a sanitized sink, and placed them under running water. Using a clean, sanitized cutting board and knife, she proceeded to peel and cut the cantaloupe into wedges. She then covered the cut cantaloupe, labeled it with the date, and placed it in the reach-in refrigerator in her prep area.

_____

_____

_____

4. Cooking

The evening cook, Mattie, needed to prepare chicken for the dinner meal. She retrieved a case of chicken breasts from the walk-in refrigerator and brought it back to her workstation. She quickly placed the chicken breasts on a sheet pan, seasoned them, and placed them in the preheated oven. Customer orders for chicken were beginning to back up. When Mattie checked the temperature of the chicken with her thermometer, it read 158°F. She quickly pulled the chicken out of the oven and began plating it.

_____

_____

_____

5. Holding

After Mattie finished plating up the orders, she covered the remaining chicken and placed it in a 150°F warmer.

_____

_____

_____

(Continued)

Name _____

6. Service

Due to an employee calling off sick, Tony was trying to do two jobs. He was working as cashier taking the customers' money and making change. In between customers, Tony would run to the service window and check the customers' orders for accuracy as the cooks finished them. He would then place the garnishes on the plates and let the waitstaff know their orders were ready to serve. Tony did not have time to wash his hands in between each task, so he wore gloves when handling the money and putting the garnishes on the plates.

_____

_____

_____

7. Cooling

As prep cook, one of Lena's jobs is to prepare 2 gallons of refried beans for the next day. When the refried beans are done cooking, she covers the stockpot of beans, labels and dates it, and moves it onto a cart. She then rolls the cart into the walk-in refrigerator to cool and moves on to her next task.

_____

_____

_____

8. Reheating

Malcolm is getting ready for the lunch shift. He retrieves the chili that was prepared the day before from the refrigerator. Malcolm places the chili on the stovetop to reheat and notes the time is 10:30 a.m. As he performs his other tasks, he frequently stops and stirs the chili. At 11:15 a.m., Malcolm uses his thermometer to check the temperature of the chili. It is 168°F.

_____

_____

_____

Additional Instructor's Comments

Lab Activity 11-1: Identifying Knives and Hand Tools

Name _____ **Date**_____ **Period** _____

Identify each knife or hand tool pictured and give a brief description of its use.

1. Name _____

   Uses _____

   _____

2. Name _____

   Uses _____

   _____

3. Name _____

   Uses _____

   _____

4. Name _____

   Uses _____

   _____

5. Name _____

   Uses _____

   _____

(Continued)

6.   Name _____

Uses _____

_____

7.   Name _____

Uses _____

_____

8.   Name _____

Uses _____

_____

9.   Name _____

Uses _____

_____

10.   Name _____

Uses _____

_____

11.   Name _____

Uses _____

_____

(Continued)

Name _____

12.

Name _____

Uses _____

_____

13.

Name _____

Uses _____

_____

14.

Name _____

Uses _____

_____

15.

Name _____

Uses _____

_____

16.

Name _____

Uses _____

_____

17.

Name _____

Uses _____

_____

(Continued)

18.

Name _____

Uses _____

_____

19.

Name _____

Uses _____

_____

20.

Name _____

Uses _____

_____

21.

Name _____

Uses _____

_____

22.

Name _____

Uses _____

_____

23.

Name _____

Uses _____

_____

Lab Activity 11-2: **Sharpening a Knife**

Name _____ **Date**_____ **Period** _____

Group Members _____

For generations, chefs have closely guarded their personal knives. Chefs know the value of a well-maintained, sharp knife and are reluctant to let others use their knives. The most important characteristic of a sharp knife is having an even and equal beveled edge on both sides of the blade. This is critical because the cutting edge—not you—dictates how straight your cuts are. Most chefs prefer a 20-degree angle on both sides of the blade.

Objectives

After completing this lab, you will be able to

- use a steel to maintain an edge on a knife.
- use a whetstone to sharpen a knife.
- understand how the angle on the knife edge impacts the cut it makes.

Preparation

1. Read Lab Procedure and gather the following supplies:
   - whetstone (double- or triple-sided is preferred)
   - mineral oil
   - steel
   - cutting board
   - chef knife
   - serrated knife
   - piece of paper
   - raw potato
   - paper towels
2. Review the section *Cuts* in text Chapter 9.
3. Review the *Mix In Math: Measuring Angles* in text Chapter 11.

Key Terms

Define the following terms used in this activity. Some may have been defined in previous chapters.

1. steel _____

_____

2. whetstone _____

_____

(Continued)

Lab Procedure

Part 1: Using the Steel

Method One

1. Begin by holding the steel in front of you and parallel to your body. Place the heel of the knife blade at the top end of the steel, being sure the edge of the knife is at a 20-degree angle to the steel.

2. By rotating the wrist of your knife hand downward, gently draw the length of the blade across the steel, ending with the tip.

3. Repeat the process several times on each side of the blade until the edge has a fine finish.

Method Two

1. Place the tip of the steel on the cutting board and grasp the handle so the steel is vertical, butt side up.

2. Place the heel of the blade at the top of the steel keeping the edge of the knife at a 20-degree angle to the steel.

3. With even pressure, draw the blade across the steel to the tip maintaining the 20-degree angle.

4. Repeat the process several times on each side of the blade until the edge has a fine finish.

Part 2: Using a Whetstone

1. Place the sharpening stone on a wet towel or rubber mat to prevent it from slipping during the sharpening process. Begin with the coarsest side of the stone.

2. If you are using a lubricant, saturate the surface of the stone with an even layer of water or mineral oil.

3. Hold the knife at a 20-degree angle to the surface of the stone.

4. Maintain a 20-degree angle as you begin with the heel of the blade in the upper left-hand corner of the stone.

5. Draw the knife down and across the stone until the tip of the knife is on the lower right-hand corner of the stone. Be sure to maintain even pressure on all parts of the blade throughout the process.

6. Repeat the process on the other side of the blade. Begin with the heel in the upper-right corner of the stone and finish with the tip in the lower-left corner.

7. Repeat the process 5 to 10 times depending on the dullness of the blade. Apply equal pressure to all parts of the blade and an equal number of strokes to each side of the blade.

8. Turn the stone to its finer side, lubricate it, and repeat steps three through six.

9. To finish the edge, hone it on the steel.

10. Wipe the knife blade carefully with a paper towel. Observe the metal filings on the paper towel. Knives must be properly cleaned and sanitized after sharpening.

11. To test the sharpness of your knife blade, hold a piece of paper by one corner and attempt to cut the paper with your knife. A well-sharpened knife should be able to cut the paper easily.

(Continued)

Name _____

Part 3: The Angle of a Knife's Edge

1. Look closely at angles on the edge of your chef knife. Next, look at the angles on the edge of your serrated knife.

2. Try cutting a piece of paper with the serrated knife as you did with the chef knife.

3. Using the cutting board, try cutting a potato with the chef knife. Next, try cutting it with the serrated knife.

Chef's Note: A serrated blade cannot be sharpened. Once the blade is damaged, throw the knife away.

Observations/Questions

1. Based on your observations, how do the edges of the chef knife and serrated knife blades compare?

    _____

    _____

    _____

2. Did both knives cut the paper? If so, were the cuts similar? Explain.

    _____

    _____

    _____

3. Did the knives make similar cuts in the potato? Were you able to make a straight cut with the serrated knife? Explain.

    _____

    _____

    _____

4. Would your understanding of this activity help in a professional kitchen? Explain.

    _____

    _____

    _____

Additional Instructor's Comments

Lab Activity 12-1: **Basic Knife Cuts I**
Batonnet, Tourné, and Dices

Name _____ **Date**_____ **Period** _____

Group Members _____

To perform the basic knife cuts correctly requires great skill. The knife must be held correctly, hand-eye coordination is essential, and consistency must be the goal. Mastery of the basic knife cuts is a trademark of an accomplished, professional chef. You will use these knife cuts throughout this class and your career. Only constant practice will ensure that you understand and master these key skills.

Chef's Note: Uniform knife cuts are necessary to ensure even cooking. For this reason, you would never cook a large dice with a small dice—the large dice would be undercooked or the small dice overcooked.

Objectives

After completing this lab, you will be able to

- organize a proper workstation.
- execute correct cutting technique.
- execute the following knife cuts: batonnet, tourné, small dice, medium dice, and large dice.

Preparation

1. Read Lab Procedure and gather the following supplies:

    - chef knife
    - paring or tourné knife
    - damp towel
    - cutting board
    - ruler
    - 4 potatoes
    - peeler
    - lemon or lemon juice
    - 5 bowls

2. Review the sections *Basic Knife Cuts* and *Using the Paring Knife* in text Chapter 12.

3. Sharpen knife if needed.

Sanitation and Safety Reminders

1. Clean and sanitize the workstation before beginning to work.

2. Wash hands properly and as often as needed.

3. Wash potatoes.

(Continued)

Key Terms

Define the following terms used in this activity. Some may have been defined in previous chapters.

1. batonnet _____

   _____

2. small dice _____

   _____

3. medium dice_____

   _____

4. large dice_____

   _____

5. tourné _____

   _____

Lab Procedure

Part 1: Set Up the Workstation

1. Select a cleaned and sanitized cutting board.

2. Place a damp towel between the cutting board and worktable to keep the cutting board from shifting during knife work.

3. Assess the height of the worktable and cutting board. If the cutting board is too low, a series of sheet trays can be used to elevate the cutting board. Place the sheet trays right side up on the worktable and nest the cutting board inside the top sheet tray. If the cutting board is too high, it may be necessary to stand on a step stool. Some worktables have height-adjustable legs.

Chef's Note: Working at a station that is not at a comfortable height can be dangerous and cause excessive fatigue.

4. Select the appropriate knife and make sure the edge is sharp.

5. Stand facing the worktable. Feet should be shoulder-width apart with weight evenly distributed on both feet.

Part 2: Preparing Stick Cuts

1. Mix approximately 1½ Tbsp. of lemon juice with 1½ qt. of water. Divide lemon water into 5 small bowls and set aside.

Chef's Note: Potatoes brown very quickly when exposed to air. Holding the cut potatoes in lemon water slows the browning process.

2. Peel a potato and trim it so it is flat on one side. This keeps the food steady while you are cutting and forms the first side of a rectangle.

3. Trim the other five sides of the potato to create a rectangular box.

4. Cut lengthwise slices ¼-inch thick to prepare the batonnet stick cut. Use the ruler for a reference if needed.

(Continued)

5. Stack two or three of these slices and cut them lengthwise into ¼-inch thick sticks or batonnets. (Cut the sticks into 2-inch lengths for batonnets only.)

6. Place about half of the sticks into one of the bowls of lemon water and label with the type of knife cut. (Skip this step for ½- and ¾-inch dimensions and proceed to Part 3.)

7. Reserve the remaining sticks and proceed to Part 3.

Part 3: Preparing Dices

1. Turn the reserved sticks perpendicular to the knife and cut across the sticks every ¼ inch to form cubes or dice.

2. Place these in a bowl of lemon water and label it with the type of knife cut.

3. Return to Part 2 and repeat steps 1–7 substituting ½-inch and then ¾-inch dimensions whenever it calls for ¼ inch.

Part 4: Preparing Tournés

1. Select the appropriate knife for the task.

2. Peel a large potato and cut into quarters lengthwise. This will be the approximate desired length of the tourné.

3. Hold a potato quarter in the guiding hand.

4. Place the thumb of the knife hand on or near the end of the potato. Starting at the top, draw the paring knife toward the bottom of the potato in a slightly rounded fashion. It is important that one continuous cut is made so the tourné does not look jagged.

5. Turn the potato $1/7^{th}$ revolution and make another cut. Right-handed cooks turn the potato counterclockwise, while left-handed cooks turn clockwise. The finished tourné should have seven equal sides.

6. Place tourné in a bowl of lemon water and label.

Performance Review

Ask your instructor to review your performance using the form on the next page.

Performance Review: **Basic Knife Cuts I**
Batonnet, Tourné, and Dices

Name _____ **Date**_____

Core knowledge/skills: setting up a workstation, knife skills; batonnet, tourné, small, medium, and large dices

Culinary Proficiency	Expectations	Instructor's Review
Professionalism: Demonstrate appropriate workplace hygiene and appearance.	Hair neat and restrained	
	Clean chef uniform and apron; nonslip, closed-toe shoes	
	No nail polish or jewelry	
Sanitation: Wash hands properly. Demonstrate safe food handling.	Display correct handwashing at beginning and throughout production	
	Clean, peel, and trim potatoes	
	Clean and sanitize workstation before and after work	
Preparation: Set up workstation properly. Review lab.	Position cutting board at a comfortable height, secure so it does not slip during cutting	
	Needed equipment available and ready	
Knife Skills: Demonstrate correct cutting technique.	Select appropriate knife for each cut	
	Use a sharp knife	
	Use appropriate knife grip	
	Position guiding hand properly	
	Use correct cutting motion	
Product Evaluation: Demonstrate correct knife cuts.	Accurate knife cut dimensions	
	Uniform, neat cuts. ____batonnet ____tourné ____small dice ____medium dice ____large dice	

Lab Activity 12-2: **Basic Knife Cuts II**
Julienne, Brunoise, Rondelles, and Paysanne

Name _____ **Date**_____ **Period** _____

Group Members _____

This activity uses carrots; however, these techniques and basic cuts can also be used on other vegetables. Carrots represent a challenge because of their round shape, which makes them a little more difficult to work with. You will find these same techniques used each day in kitchens around the world.

Objectives

After completing this lab, you will be able to

- organize a proper workstation.
- execute correct cutting technique.
- execute the following knife cuts: julienne, brunoise, rondelles, and paysanne.

Preparation

1. Read Lab Procedure and gather the following supplies:
   - knife
   - damp towel
   - cutting board
   - ruler
   - carrots
   - 4 small plates
   - peeler
2. Review the section *Basic Knife Cuts* in text Chapter 12.
3. Sharpen knife if needed.

Sanitation and Safety Reminders

1. Clean and sanitize workstation before beginning to work.
2. Wash hands properly and as often as needed.
3. Wash, peel, and trim carrots.

(Continued)

Key Terms

Define the following terms used in this activity. Some may have been defined in previous chapters.

1. julienne _____

_____

2. brunoise _____

_____

3. rondelles _____

_____

4. paysanne _____

_____

Lab Procedure

Part 1: Set up the workstation

1. Select a cleaned and sanitized cutting board.

2. Place a damp towel between the cutting board and worktable to keep the cutting board from shifting during knife work.

3. Assess the height of the worktable and cutting board. If the cutting board is too low, a series of sheet trays can be used to elevate the cutting board. Place the sheet trays right side up on the worktable and nest the cutting board inside the top sheet tray. If the cutting board is too high, it may be necessary to stand on a step stool. Some worktables have height-adjustable legs.

Chef's Note: Working at a station that is not at a comfortable height can be dangerous and cause excessive fatigue.

4. Select the appropriate knife and make sure the edge is sharp.

5. Stand facing the worktable. Feet should be shoulder-width apart with weight evenly distributed on both feet.

Part 2: Preparing Julienne

1. Peel and trim a carrot so it is flat on one side. This keeps the food steady while you are cutting and forms the first side of a rectangle.

2. Trim the other five sides of the carrot to create a rectangular box.

3. Cut carrot into 2-inch lengths.

4. Cut lengthwise slices $1/8$-inch thick to prepare the julienne stick cut. Use the ruler for a reference if needed.

5. Stack two or three of these slices and cut them lengthwise into $1/8$-inch thick sticks or juliennes.

Chef's Note: A julienne of potato is called an allumette, which means "matchstick" in French. A properly cut julienne is approximately the size of a matchstick.

6. Place approximately half of the juliennes on a small plate, label, and set aside. Reserve remaining juliennes for Part 3.

(Continued)

Name _____

Part 3: Preparing Brunoise

1. Turn the reserved juliennes perpendicular to the knife and cut across the sticks every $1/8$ inch to form cubes or dice. This cut is called *brunoise*.

2. Place the brunoise on a plate, label, and set aside.

Part 4: Preparing Paysanne

1. Peel and trim a carrot so it is flat on one side. This keeps the food steady while you are cutting and forms the first side of a rectangle.

2. Trim the other five sides of the carrot to create a rectangular box.

3. Cut carrot into manageable lengths.

4. Cut lengthwise slices ½-inch thick. Use the ruler for a reference if needed.

5. Stack two or three of these slices and cut them lengthwise into ½-inch thick sticks.

6. Turn the sticks perpendicular to the knife and cut across the sticks every ¼ inch to form paysanne.

7. Place the paysanne on a plate, label, and set aside.

Part 5: Preparing Rondelles

1. Peel and trim carrot. Shave it slightly on one side to prevent it from rolling during cutting.

2. Turn carrot perpendicular to the knife. Make ¼-inch cuts across the carrot creating small round disks or rondelles. Use the ruler for a reference if needed.

3. Place the rondelles on a plate, label, and set aside.

Performance Review

Ask your instructor to review your performance using the form on the next page.

Performance Review: **Basic Knife Cuts II**
Julienne, Brunoise, Rondelles, and Paysanne

Name _____ **Date**_____

Core knowledge/skills: setting up a workstation, knife skills; julienne, brunoise, rondelles, paysanne

Culinary Proficiency	Expectations	Instructor's Review
Professionalism: Demonstrate appropriate workplace hygiene and appearance.	Hair neat and restrained	
	Clean chef uniform and apron; nonslip, closed-toe shoes	
	No nail polish or jewelry	
Sanitation: Wash hands properly. Demonstrate safe food handling.	Display correct handwashing at beginning and throughout production	
	Clean, peel, and trim carrots	
	Clean and sanitize workstation before and after work	
Preparation: Set up workstation properly. Review lab.	Position cutting board at a comfortable height, secure so it does not slip during cutting	
	Needed equipment available and ready	
Knife Skills: Demonstrate correct cutting technique.	Select appropriate knife for each cut	
	Use a sharp knife	
	Use appropriate knife grip	
	Position guiding hand properly	
	Use correct cutting motion	
Product Evaluation: Demonstrate correct knife cuts.	Dimensions of knife cuts are accurate	
	Cuts are uniform and neat ____julienne ____brunoise ____rondelles ____paysanne	

Lab Activity 13-1: **Identifying Smallwares**

Name _____ **Date** _____ **Period** _____

Identify each smallware pictured and give a brief description of its use.

1.   Name _____

Uses _____

_____

2.   Name _____

Uses _____

_____

3.   Name _____

Uses _____

_____

4.   Name _____

Uses _____

_____

5.   Name _____

Uses _____

_____

(Continued)

6.

Name _____

Uses _____

_____

7.

Name _____

Uses _____

_____

8.

Name _____

Uses _____

_____

9.

Name _____

Uses _____

_____

10.

Name _____

Uses _____

_____

11.

Name _____

Uses _____

_____

(Continued)

Name _____

12.

Name _____

Uses _____

_____

13.

Name _____

Uses _____

_____

14.

Name _____

Uses _____

_____

15.

Name _____

Uses _____

_____

16.

Name _____

Uses _____

_____

17.

Name _____

Uses _____

_____

(Continued)

18.   Name _____

       Uses _____

       _____

19.   Name _____

       Uses _____

       _____

20.   Name _____

       Uses _____

       _____

21.   Name _____

       Uses _____

       _____

22.   Name _____

       Uses _____

       _____

23.      Name _____

       Uses _____

       _____

(Continued)

Name _____

24.

Name _____

Uses _____

_____

25.

Name _____

Uses _____

_____

26.

Name _____

Uses _____

_____

27.

Name _____

Uses _____

_____

28.

Name _____

Uses _____

_____

Additional Instructor's Comments

Lab Activity 14-1: **Identifying Large Equipment**

Name _____ **Date** _____ **Period** _____

Identify each piece of equipment pictured.

1.   Name _____

2.   Name _____

3.   Name _____

4.   Name _____

5.   Name _____

(Continued)

6. 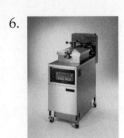 Name _____

7.  Name _____

8.  Name _____

9.  Name _____

10.  Name _____

11.  Name _____

(Continued)

Name _____

12.

Name _____

13.

Name _____

14.

Name _____

15.

Name _____

16.

Name _____

(Continued)

17.    Name _____

18.   Name _____

Lab Activity 14-2: Identifying Foodservice Equipment Symbols of Standards

Name _____ **Date** _____ **Period** _____

Foodservice equipment must be designed with safety and sanitation in mind. It is becoming increasingly important that the equipment is also energy efficient. A number of federal and international agencies develop and oversee standards for foodservice equipment. The agencies created symbols that are easily recognized. Foodservice equipment that complies with specific standards can display the symbol or mark of that agency.

Objectives

After completing this lab, you will be able to

- identify various agencies' symbols denoting foodservice equipment standards.
- summarize the standards represented by each symbol.

Lab Procedure

For each of the symbols that follow, research to learn the name of the agency each symbol represents. Write a brief explanation of the agency's standard(s). Then, examine equipment in your school or home kitchen to locate at least one piece of equipment for each symbol. Note the name of the equipment, where it was located, and if possible, take a photo. If you cannot find an example of a symbol, search online for a description and photo of foodservice equipment that bears the symbol. Attach a copy of the photo and description to this lab.

1. **NSF**

Agency name _____

Standards _____

_____

Equipment and location _____

2. **UL**

Agency name _____

Standards _____

_____

Equipment and location _____

(Continued)

3.

Agency name _____

Standards _____

_____

Equipment and location _____

4.

Agency name _____

Standards _____

_____

Equipment and location _____

Image Courtesy of ENERGY STAR

Lab Activity 15-1: **Converting Recipe Yields**

Name _____ **Date** _____ **Period** _____

Group Members _____

The majority of recipes that you use and produce will need to be adjusted at some time. Once you have mastered using the conversion factor, you can change any recipe safely, knowing that the finished product will be as delicious as the original recipe.

Objectives

After completing this lab, you will be able to

- implement a conversion factor to increase or decrease a recipe yield.
- execute measurement conversions.

Preparation

1. Read Lab Procedure and gather the following supplies:
   - calculator
   - Recipe Yield Conversion Worksheet (2 copies)
   - pencil
2. Review weight and volume conversion charts in text Chapter 15.
3. Review *Mix In Math: Converting Measures* and *Converting Fractions to Decimals* in text Chapter 15.
4. Review text *Appendix E—Common Fraction to Decimal Equivalents Used in Foodservice*.

Key Terms

Define the following terms used in this activity. Some may have been defined in previous chapters.

1. recipe _____

   _____

2. standardized recipe _____

   _____

3. yield _____

   _____

4. portion size _____

   _____

5. conversion factor _____

   _____

(Continued)

Lab Procedure

1. Use the Recipe Yield Conversion Worksheet to convert the following standardized recipe to yield four 8-fluid ounce portions.
2. Use the Recipe Yield Conversion Worksheet to convert the following standardized recipe to yield 100 8-fluid ounce portions.
3. Be sure to convert your new quantities to the largest possible measure. For example, if the new quantity for dried thyme is 9½ teaspoons, convert it to 3 tablespoons and ½ teaspoon.

Chef's Note: You may have noticed that some ingredients may be more difficult to increase or decrease. In a working kitchen, chefs may make decisions not to measure exactly. For example, a bay leaf can be difficult to divide precisely.

Additionally, some recipes may be easier to scale up and down using metric measures, which are based on units of 10, 100, and 1000. The US system of measurement, which is based on a unit of 16 ounces to a pound or 8 fluid ounces to a cup, can sometimes result in numbers that are difficult to work with.

Chicken Vegetable Soup

Yield: 1 gal. (3.8 L)
Portion size: 8 fl. oz. (240 mL)
Number of portions: 16

Ingredients

2 lb.	900 g	chicken pieces (breast, legs, thighs)
8 oz.	225 g	carrot, diced
1 lb.	450 g	onion, diced
8 oz.	225 g	celery, diced
8 oz.	225 g	parsnips (optional)
128 fl. oz.	3.8 L	water or chicken stock
Sachet:		sachet:
2 ea.		bay leaves
2 tsp.	10 mL	dried thyme leaf
1 tsp.	5 mL	black peppercorn
to taste		salt and white pepper

Method

1. Place all ingredients in a stockpot.
2. Bring to a boil over medium heat.
3. Skim to remove all scum. Simmer about 1 hour until the chicken is tender and reaches 165°F (74°C).
4. Remove the chicken and allow it to cool briefly until it can be handled easily.
5. Remove meat from the chicken bones and tear or cut into bite-size pieces. Place the chicken back in the pan and bring the soup back to a simmer.
6. Remove sachet and season with salt and pepper. Moments before serving, mix soup with minced parsley.

(Continued)

Name _____ **Date**_____ **Period** _____

Recipe Yield Conversion Worksheet

Recipe name _____

Original recipe yield _____ **New recipe yield** _____

Calculate conversion factor (new yield ÷ original yield = conversion factor):

_____ ÷ _____ = _____

Ingredient	Original quantity	multiply	Conversion factor	equals	New quantity
		×		=	
		×		=	
		×		=	
		×		=	
		×		=	
		×		=	
		×		=	
		×		=	
		×		=	
		×		=	
		×		=	
		×		=	
		×		=	
		×		=	
		×		=	
		×		=	
		×		=	
		×		=	
		×		=	

Additional Instructor's Comments

Lab Activity 16-1: **Basic Knife Cuts III**
Dicing Onion, Mincing Parsley, Chiffonade, and Concassé

Name _____ **Date**_____ **Period** _____

Group Members _____

Although julienne and brunoise are the most commonly known and practiced knife cuts in the culinary world, other equally important cuts need to be mastered as well. Dicing onion, mincing parsley, chiffonade, and concassé are key knife cuts that are used by chefs around the world. Each one requires a particular technique and method of cutting and are best mastered by practice and then more practice.

Objectives

After completing this lab, you will be able to

- organize a proper workstation.
- execute correct cutting technique.
- execute the following knife cuts: dicing onion, mincing parsley, chiffonade, and concassé.

Preparation

1. Read Lab Procedure and gather the following supplies:

   - chef knife
   - damp towel
   - paper towels
   - cutting board
   - small saucepan of boiling water
   - spider or tongs
   - small bowl of ice water
   - leaf lettuce
   - tomato
   - parsley
   - onion
   - 4 small plates

2. Review the sections *Peeling, Slicing, and Dicing an Onion, Mincing Parsley, Chiffonade,* and *Peeling, Seeding, and Dicing Tomatoes* in text Chapter 16.

3. Sharpen knife if needed.

Sanitation and Safety Reminders

1. Clean and sanitize workstation before beginning to work.

2. Wash hands properly and as often as needed.

3. Wash and trim produce.

(Continued)

Key Terms

Define the following terms used in this activity. Some may have been defined in previous chapters.

1. chiffonade _____

   _____

2. concassé _____

   _____

Lab Procedure

Part 1: Set Up the Workstation

1. Select a cleaned and sanitized cutting board.

2. Place a damp towel between the cutting board and worktable to keep the cutting board from shifting during knife work.

3. Assess the height of the worktable and cutting board. If the cutting board is too low, a series of sheet trays can be used to elevate the cutting board. Place the sheet trays right side up on the worktable and nest the cutting board inside the top sheet tray. If the cutting board is too high, it may be necessary to stand on a step stool. Some worktables have height-adjustable legs.

Chef's Note: Working at a station that is not at a comfortable height can be dangerous and cause excessive fatigue.

4. Select the appropriate knife and make sure the edge is sharp.

5. Stand facing the worktable. Feet should be shoulder-width apart with weight evenly distributed on both feet.

Part 2: Dicing an Onion

1. Cut the ends off the onion. Be careful to remove only a small amount of each end. If too much is cut off, the onion will fall apart and be difficult to cut properly.

2. Cut the onion in half lengthwise through the stem and root end of the onion.

3. Remove the peel from the onion using a paring knife.

4. Place the peeled onion half, cut side down, on the cutting board.

5. Place your guiding hand on top of the onion half. Be sure that the root end of the onion faces away from the knife.

6. Position the guiding hand as for slicing. Slice the onion lengthwise by drawing the knife backward instead of in the usual forward motion. The slice should begin just short of the root end of the onion so that the root end remains intact. Do not cut through the root end core of the onion either.

7. Continue slicing until the onion has been evenly sliced except for the small area on the root end of the onion.

8. Reposition the guiding hand so it is placed on top of the onion. Be sure that the fingertips are up and out of harm's way. With the knife blade parallel to the cutting board, draw the knife backward through the onion to cut slices. These slices begin at the stem end and stop before cutting through the root end.

(Continued)

Name _____

9. Reposition the guiding hand on the onion. Beginning at the stem end, slice the onion crosswise, perpendicular to the previous cuts to create a dice. As the onion becomes difficult to hold safely, lay it down on the cutting board. Cut this small piece of onion into a dice by slicing and then cutting across the slices.

10. Place the onion dice on a plate, label, and set aside.

Part 3: Mincing Parsley

1. Dry parsley between paper towels or in a salad spinner.

2. Separate the parsley leaves from the stems.

3. Roll the leaves into a tight ball. Cut finely with a chef knife.

4. Mince the cut parsley by placing the tip of the knife on the cutting board. Place the guiding hand on the back of the tip of the knife. Keep the fingers of the guiding hand away from the blade.

5. To mince a product, lower and raise the chef knife repeatedly while pivoting the knife on the rounded front section of the blade.

6. Place minced parsley on a plate, label, and set aside.

Part 4: Preparing Chiffonade

1. Pat lettuce leaves dry with paper towel.

Chef's Note: The chiffonade is most often performed on basil.

2. Stack five to six leaves on top of each other.

3. Tightly roll the stack and cut thin slices across the roll.

4. Unroll the cuts to reveal the chiffonade, place on plate, and label.

Part 5: Preparing Concassé

1. Remove the tomato's core using the tip of the paring knife. Cut an "X" through the skin of the opposite end of the tomato.

2. Plunge the tomatoes in boiling water for 30 seconds. Remove tomatoes using a spider or pair of tongs and shock them in ice water.

3. When the tomatoes are cold, remove them from the ice water. Using a paring knife, pull the skin from the tomato by grabbing the skin where the "X" was cut in the tomato.

4. Cut the tomato in half. Cut through the middle of the tomato not the core.

5. Squeeze the tomato gently to push out seeds and excess moisture.

6. Flatten the tomato half slightly with the palm of the hand.

7. Cut into strips and then a dice using a chef knife.

8. Place concassé on a plate, label, and set aside.

Performance Review

Ask your instructor to review your performance using the form on the next page.

Performance Review: **Basic Knife Cuts III**
Dicing Onion, Mincing Parsley, Chiffonade, and Concassé

Name _____ Date _____

Core knowledge/skills: setting up a workstation, knife skills; dicing onion, mincing parsley, chiffonade, concassé

Culinary Proficiency	Expectations	Instructor's Review
Professionalism: Demonstrate appropriate workplace hygiene and appearance.	Hair neat and restrained	
	Clean chef uniform and apron; nonslip, closed-toe shoes	
	No nail polish or jewelry	
Sanitation: Wash hands properly. Demonstrate safe food handling.	Display correct handwashing at beginning and throughout production	
	Clean and trim produce	
	Clean and sanitize workstation before and after work	
Preparation: Set up workstation properly. Review lab.	Position cutting board at a comfortable height, secure so it does not slip during cutting	
	Needed equipment available and ready	
Knife Skills: Demonstrate correct cutting technique.	Select appropriate knife for each cut	
	Use sharp knife	
	Use appropriate knife grip	
	Position guiding hand properly	
	Use correct cutting motion	
Product Evaluation: Demonstrate correct knife cuts.	Accurate knife cut dimensions	
	Uniform, neat cuts ____Onion is small to medium dice ____Minced parsley is roughly the size of ground pepper ____Chiffonade is approx. 1/8-inch thick ____Concassé is small dice and contains no seeds or skin	

Lab Activity 18-1: **Cooking Methods I**
Poaching

Name _____ **Date**_____ **Period** _____

Group Members _____

Poaching is the gentlest cooking method. Close monitoring and control of the cooking liquid temperature is required. When performed correctly, poaching produces a moist and delicate product. In this activity, you will also discover how the pH of a cooking solution affects the final product.

Objectives

After completing this lab, you will be able to

- execute correct poaching technique.
- recognize how acids affect protein.

Preparation

1. Read Lab Procedure and gather the following supplies:

   - 2 raw shell eggs
   - distilled white vinegar (approx. 2 fl. oz.)
   - medium saucepan
   - thermometer
   - 3 small dishes
   - slotted spoon

2. Review the sections *Proteins Coagulate* and *Poaching* in text Chapter 18.

3. Review the discussion about pH and *Science & Technology: pH Values* in text Chapter 7.

4. Check calibration on thermometer.

Sanitation and Safety Reminders

1. Clean and sanitize workstation before beginning to work.

2. Inspect eggs for cracks and discard.

3. Wash hands properly and as often as needed.

Key Terms

Define the following terms used in this activity. Some may have been defined in previous chapters.

1. cooking _____

_____

(Continued)

2. poaching _____

_____

3. coagulation _____

_____

4. pH _____

_____

Lab Procedure

1. Fill a medium saucepan with enough water to fully cover an egg and bring to a boil. Lower heat to poaching temperature, which is 160°F–180°F (71°C–82°C).

2. Crack an egg into a small bowl or cup. Lower the egg to the water and turn it out of the bowl.

3. Using a slotted spoon, gently turn or swirl the egg to form a round shape with the white enveloping the yolk.

Chef's Note: The egg white is made up of several types of protein. When you poach an egg, it is normal that some protein spreads out into a thin film; discard this for service.

4. Poach the egg for about 3 minutes. When properly cooked, the egg can be easily handled. Check doneness by removing the egg from the water with a slotted spoon and gently pressing on the egg with your finger. The egg should be soft to indicate that the yolk is still liquid.

5. After the poached egg is removed with a slotted spoon, shock it in ice water or pat dry on a clean towel for immediate service. Trim off any ragged edges of egg white for a neat presentation.

Chef's Note: In large production situations, eggs are often poached and then shocked in ice water. They are held submerged in water until ready to use. At service, they are reheated in water at poaching temperature.

6. Next, add 1 ounce vinegar for every quart of water (30 mL per liter) in the saucepan.

Chef's Note: If too much vinegar is used, it will cause the protein to spread and prevent it from forming a nice oval shape. This is called "spidering" and is not desired.

7. Repeat steps 1–5 with the second egg.

8. Place eggs in two remaining clean dishes. Label "With vinegar" and "Without vinegar" and present to instructor.

Observations/Questions

1. What is the approximate pH of vinegar? (*Hint: Read Science & Technology sidebar in text Chapter 7.*)

_____

2. If acid causes proteins to coagulate, why do you suppose many chefs add vinegar to the cooking water when poaching eggs?

_____

_____

3. What is the other factor acting to coagulate the proteins during poaching?

_____

_____

(Continued)

Name _____

4. Did you observe any differences during cooking or in the final products when poaching the eggs with and without vinegar? Explain.

_____

_____

Chef's Journal

Write an evaluation of your lab performance. Would your finished product and performance meet the standards of a professional kitchen? Describe how your recipe turned out and what techniques and procedures you need to improve.

_____

_____

_____

_____

_____

_____

Performance Review: **Cooking Methods I**
Poaching

Name _____ **Date**_____

Core knowledge/skills: effects of cooking, poaching, coagulation, pH, thermometer use

Culinary Proficiency	Expectations	Instructor's Review
Professionalism: Demonstrate appropriate workplace hygiene and appearance.	Hair neat and restrained	
	Clean chef uniform and apron; nonslip, closed-toe shoes	
	No nail polish or jewelry	
Sanitation: Wash hands properly. Demonstrate safe food handling.	Display correct handwashing throughout production	
	Discard any broken or cracked eggs	
	Clean and sanitize workstation before and after work	
Preparation: Set up workstation properly. Review lab recommended reading.	Needed equipment available and ready	
	Understands how vinegar impacts the pH of the cooking water	
Cooking Method: Demonstrate proper poaching technique.	Poaching liquid in correct temperature range	
	Correct amount of vinegar for volume of cooking water used	
Product Evaluation: Display finished products in small bowls. Taste finished product.	Egg is well-formed oval shape with no ragged edges or excessive "spidering"	
	Thin coat of white evenly covers the yolk	
	Texture is delicate and soft to the touch, not rubbery or overcooked	
	Yolk is still slightly runny	
	Egg well drained and dried, no excess cooking liquid or ice water in dish	

Lab Activity 18-2: **Cooking Methods II**
Sautéing

Name _____ **Date**_____ **Period** _____

Group Members _____

French toast is a delicious breakfast food that is prepared using the sautéing cooking method. The secret to success with this method is properly heating the sauté pan and fat before beginning to cook.

Objectives

After completing this lab, you will be able to

- execute correct sautéing technique.
- recognize changes in food due to caramelization.

Mise en Place

1. Carefully read through the recipe before starting production. Adjust the yield as needed. Review how to convert recipe yield in text Chapter 15.
2. Review the sections *Flavors Blend and Change* and *Sautéing* in text Chapter 18.
3. Gather all ingredients and equipment required.
4. Prepare clarified butter if necessary. Review the section *Clarified Butter* in text Chapter 16.

Sanitation and Safety Reminders

1. Clean and sanitize workstation before beginning to work.
2. Wash hands properly and as often as needed.
3. Inspect eggs and discard any broken or cracked eggs. Store egg mixture on ice during this activity.

Key Terms

Define the following terms used in this activity. Some may have been defined in previous chapters.

1. cooking _____

   _____

2. sautéing _____

   _____

3. carmelization _____

   _____

4. clarified butter _____

   _____

(Continued)

5. sauteuse _____

    _____

6. griddle _____

    _____

French Toast

Yield: 10 portions

Ingredients

4 ea.		eggs, beaten
16 fl. oz.	480 mL	milk
4 oz.	115 g	sugar
to taste		vanilla extract
10 sl.		white bread, preferably day-old
4 fl. oz.	120 mL	clarified butter

Method

1. Combine the eggs, milk, sugar, and vanilla extract and mix well.
2. Place the egg mixture in a shallow pan.
3. Dip the pieces of bread into the egg mixture and allow them to absorb some of the liquid.
4. Heat some of the clarified butter in a sauteuse or on a griddle.
5. Cook the slices of bread over moderate heat until golden brown. Turn and cook until the other side is evenly browned.

Chef's Note: If using a sauteuse, practice turning the French toast by dipping the front of the pan forward then flipping up and back, catching the toast on the return back down.

6. Serve immediately with syrup or dusted with powdered sugar.

Chef's Journal

Write an evaluation of your lab performance. Would your finished product and performance meet the standards of a professional kitchen? Describe how your recipe turned out and what techniques and procedures you need to improve.

_____

_____

_____

_____

_____

Performance Review: **Cooking Methods II**
Sautéing

Name _____ **Date**_____

Core knowledge/skills: effects of cooking, sautéing, caramelization

Culinary Proficiency	Expectations	Instructor's Review
Professionalism: Demonstrate appropriate workplace hygiene and appearance.	Hair neat and restrained	
	Clean chef uniform and apron; nonslip, closed-toe shoes	
	No nail polish or jewelry	
Sanitation: Wash hands properly. Demonstrate safe food handling.	Display correct handwashing at beginning and throughout production	
	Inspect eggs for cracks	
	Hold egg mixture on ice	
	Clean and sanitize workstation before and after work	
Mise en Place: Set up workstation properly. Review lab recommended reading. Organized recipe method and sequence of work.	Needed equipment available and ready	
	Clarified butter contains little if any milk solids or water	
	Understand how caramelization impacts the flavor and appearance of food	
Cooking Technique: Demonstrate proper sautéing technique.	Preheat pan and fat	
	Appropriate amount of fat was used, food was not greasy	
Product Evaluation: Display finished product on a plate. Taste finished product.	French toast has a golden-brown, caramelized sugar exterior giving a slightly crisp texture	
	Inside is soft and warm with a rich flavor	

Additional Instructor's Comments

Lab Activity 19-1: **Garden Salad**

Name _____ **Date** _____ **Period** _____

Group Members _____

Garden salad is also referred to as *chef's salad*. The name of this salad is vague and undefined for a reason—it gives the chef the flexibility with the choice of ingredients. The chef may choose ingredients that are in season or simply take the opportunity to use up product in the refrigerator. Garden salads are known for two things—an ingredient list that is flexible, and a fresh, crunchy, and crisp final product.

Objectives

After completing this lab, you will be able to

- execute the preparation of salad greens.
- implement procedures to ensure a sanitary, quality salad.
- produce a simple salad.

Mise en Place

1. Carefully read through the entire recipe before starting production. Adjust the yield as needed. Review how to convert recipe yields in text Chapter 15.

2. Review the section *Preparing Salad Greens* in text Chapter 19.

3. Gather all ingredients and equipment required.

4. Set up cutting board properly. Select appropriate knife and sharpen if needed.

Sanitation and Safety Reminders

1. Clean and sanitize workstation before beginning to work.

2. Wash hands properly and as often as needed.

3. Thoroughly wash, dry, and trim salad ingredients.

Key Terms

Define the following terms used in this activity. Some may have been defined in previous chapters.

1. simple salad _____

_____

2. julienne _____

_____

(Continued)

Garden Salad

Yield: 10–12 salads

Ingredients

1 hd.		iceberg lettuce
1 hd.		romaine lettuce
½ hd.		curly endive
2 oz.	60 g	carrots, julienne
2 oz.	60 g	red cabbage, shredded
4 ea.		tomatoes, wedged
1 ea.		cucumber, sliced

Method

1. Remove cores, trim and cut lettuces into bite-size pieces.
2. Wash and dry lettuces.
3. Combine lettuces with cabbage and carrots; toss gently until items are uniformly mixed.

Chef's Note: Red cabbage leaves tend to be slightly tougher than other greens, so cut it into very thin strips to make it easier to eat. Also, it has been known to stain other ingredients red, so cut it as close to preparation and service as possible.

4. Portion salad on chilled plates.
5. Garnish each plate with two tomato wedges and two cucumber slices. Present with the dressing of your choice.

Chef's Note: Salads may be tossed with a dressing before plating. This should be done immediately before serving, giving a very thin and light coat to each ingredient.

Chef's Journal

Write an evaluation of your lab performance. Would your finished product and performance meet the standards of a professional kitchen? Describe how your recipe turned out and what techniques and procedures you need to improve. _____

_____

_____

_____

_____

_____

Performance Review: **Garden Salad**

Name _____ **Date**_____

Core knowledge/skills: simple salad, julienne cuts, preparation of salad greens, knife skills

Culinary Proficiency	Expectations	Instructor's Review
Professionalism: Demonstrate appropriate workplace hygiene and appearance.	Hair neat and restrained	
	Clean chef uniform and apron; nonslip, closed-toe shoes	
	No nail polish or jewelry	
Sanitation: Wash hands properly. Demonstrate safe food handling.	Display correct handwashing throughout production, disposable gloves or utensils used as needed	
	Clean and trim produce to eliminate heavy stalks, damage, or infestation	
	Clean and sanitize workstation before and after work	
Mise en Place: Ingredients ready for assembly. Organized recipe method and sequence of work.	Use scale to measure ingredients correctly	
	Cut ingredients in bite-size pieces	
	Chill plate	
	Complete recipe in timely fashion and maintain organized work area	
Product Evaluation: Display finished product on a plate. Taste finished product.	Salad is colorful and bright	
	Texture is crunchy and crisp	
	Taste is even, no one ingredient overpowers another	
	Salad is dressed with a thin, light coating	
	Plates are consistent and complete according to the recipe	
	Plate coverage is pleasing	

Additional Instructor's Comments

Lab Activity 19-2: **Emulsified French Dressing**

Name _____ **Date** _____ **Period** _____

Group Members _____

In simple terms, an emulsion is tiny drops of one ingredient that are suspended in another ingredient. Vinaigrettes are temporary emulsions that soon separate. This classic French dressing uses emulsifiers such as egg yolks and mustard that help the oil and vinegar remain suspended. When correctly prepared, this dressing binds and holds all the ingredients in a uniform, smooth consistency that remains bound for several hours without separating.

Objectives

After completing this lab, you will be able to

- understand the various roles of ingredients in emulsified dressings.
- execute an emulsified dressing using the mayonnaise technique.

Mise en Place

1. Carefully read through the entire recipe before starting production. Adjust the yield as needed. Review how to convert recipe yields in text Chapter 15.

2. Review the section *Mayonnaise and Emulsified Dressings* in text Chapter 19.

3. Gather all ingredients and equipment required.

Sanitation and Safety Reminders

1. Clean and sanitize workstation before beginning to work.

2. Wash hands properly and as often as needed.

Key Terms

Define the following terms used in this activity. Some may have been defined in previous chapters.

1. emulsion _____

   _____

2. vinaigrette_____

   _____

3. mayonnaise_____

   _____

(Continued)

Emulsified French Dressing

Yield: 2 qt. (1.9 L), 64 portions

Ingredients

2 fl. oz.	60 mL	pasteurized egg yolks
2 fl. oz.	60 mL	water
2 Tbsp.	30 mL	sugar
1 tsp.	5 mL	dry mustard
1 tsp.	5 mL	paprika
4 fl. oz.	120 mL	ketchup
40 fl. oz.	1.2 L	salad oil
6 fl. oz.	180 mL	cider vinegar
to taste		salt
to taste		white pepper

Method

1. Combine egg yolks, water, sugar, and dry spices in a mixing bowl. Beat until thick and frothy.
2. While whipping, add oil in a thin stream. When thickened, add some vinegar. Alternate oil and vinegar until all has been used.
3. Add ketchup and seasonings. If too thick, thin with some water.
4. Refrigerate immediately at or below 41°F (5°C).

Chef's Note: If stored for a day or two in the refrigerator, shake or whisk briefly to re-emulsify.

Chef's Journal

Write an evaluation of your lab performance. Would your finished product and performance meet the standards of a professional kitchen? Describe how your recipe turned out and what techniques and procedures you need to improve.

_____

_____

_____

_____

_____

Performance Review: **Emulsified French Dressing**

Name _____ **Date**_____

Core knowledge/skills: emulsified dressing, measuring ingredients

Culinary Proficiency	Expectations	Instructor's Review
Professionalism: Demonstrate appropriate workplace hygiene and appearance.	Hair neat and restrained	
	Clean chef uniform and apron; nonslip, closed-toe shoes	
	No nail polish or jewelry	
Sanitation: Wash hands properly. Demonstrate safe food handling.	Display correct handwashing throughout production	
	Clean and sanitize workstation before and after work	
Mise en Place: Ingredients ready for assembly. Organized recipe method and sequence of work.	Measure ingredients correctly	
	Complete recipe in a timely fashion and maintain organized work area	
	Maintain clean work area throughout production	
Cooking Technique: Demonstrate correct mayonnaise/ emulsion technique.	Add ingredients in appropriate order	
	Alternate addition of vinegar and oil	
	Add oil in a thin stream	
Product Evaluation: Display finished product on a plate. Taste finished product.	No separation of oil and vinegar is observed	
	Texture is smooth and uniform in viscosity	
	Viscosity is appropriate (not too thick or thin)	
	Seasoning adjusted well	

Additional Instructor's Comments

Lab Activity 19-3: **Marinated Pasta Salad**

Name _____ **Date** _____ **Period** _____

Group Members _____

Foods are marinated by soaking or coating them in a seasoned liquid. Marinating is done to add flavor to foods and sometimes to tenderize a food prior to cooking. The recipe in this lab activity uses a light vinaigrette to marinate pasta and vegetables to produce a salad. Pastas can be combined with many different foods to create marinated salads—the possible combinations are limited only by your imagination.

Objectives

After completing this lab, you will be able to

- produce a vinaigrette.
- execute properly cooked pasta.
- execute a marinated salad.
- implement procedures to ensure a sanitary, quality salad.

Mise en Place

1. Carefully read through both recipes before starting production. Adjust the yields as needed. Review how to convert recipe yields in text Chapter 15.
2. Review section *Cooking Pasta* in text Chapter 29.
3. Gather all ingredients and equipment required.
4. Set up cutting board properly. Select appropriate knife and sharpen if needed.

Sanitation and Safety Reminders

1. Clean and sanitize workstation before beginning to work.
2. Wash hands properly and as often as needed.
3. Wash and trim produce.

Key Terms

Define the following terms used in this activity. Some may have been defined in previous chapters.

1. marinated salad _____

_____

2. vinaigrette_____

_____

3. chiffonade _____

_____

(Continued)

4. concassé _____

_____

5. small dice _____

_____

6. rondelles _____

_____

Chef's Journal

Write an evaluation of your lab performance. Would your finished product and performance meet the standards of a professional kitchen? Describe how your recipe turned out and what techniques and procedures you need to improve.

_____

_____

_____

_____

_____

_____

_____

_____

_____

_____

_____

_____

_____

_____

_____

_____

(Continued)

Marinated Pasta Salad

Yield: 12 portions

Ingredients

8 oz.	225 g	short pasta, uncooked
8 oz.	225 g	zucchini, rondelles
8 oz.	225 g	tomato concassé
4 oz.	115 g	red onion, small dice
4 oz.	115 g	ripe olives, sliced
2 oz.	60 g	Parmesan cheese, grated
¼ c.	60 mL	fresh basil, chiffonade
8 fl. oz.	240 mL	Italian-style vinaigrette (recipe follows)
to taste		salt

Method

1. Cook pasta. Rinse in cold water and drain.
2. Combine all ingredients.
3. Adjust seasoning.
4. Cool below 70°F (21°C) in two hours or less, and below 41°F (5°C) in less than a total of six hours.

Chef's Note: Penne, rotelle, mostaccioli, fusilli, or elbow macaroni could be used for the pasta.

Italian-Style Vinaigrette

Yield: 2½ c. (600 mL), 20 portions

Ingredients

1 Tbsp.	15 mL	garlic, minced
1 tsp.	5 mL	dried oregano
1 tsp.	5 mL	dried basil
4 fl. oz.	120 mL	red wine vinegar
8 fl. oz.	240 mL	olive oil, extra virgin
8 fl. oz.	240 mL	salad oil
to taste		salt
to taste		freshly ground black pepper

Method

1. Mix all ingredients well.
2. Adjust seasoning to taste.

Performance Review: **Marinated Pasta Salad**

Name _____ Date _____

Core knowledge/skills: marinated salad, boiling pasta, vinaigrette, knife skills, chiffonade, rondelles, small dice

Culinary Proficiency	Expectations	Instructor's Review
Professionalism: Demonstrate appropriate workplace hygiene and appearance.	Hair neat and restrained	
	Clean chef uniform and apron; nonslip, closed-toe shoes	
	No nail polish or jewelry	
Sanitation: Wash hands properly. Demonstrate safe food handling.	Display correct handwashing throughout production; disposable gloves or utensils used as needed	
	Wash, trim, and dry vegetables as appropriate	
	Clean and sanitize workstation before and after work	
Mise en Place: Set up workstation properly. Review lab recommended reading. Organized recipe method and sequence of work.	Use scale to measure ingredients correctly	
	Cut ingredients in bite-size pieces	
	Complete recipe in timely fashion and maintain organized work area	
Cooking Technique: Pasta cooked properly. Demonstrate correct knife cuts.	Cook pasta until tender, but not soft and mushy	
	Produce neat, uniform vegetable cuts	
	Blend vinaigrette well and adjust seasoning properly	
Product Evaluation: Display finished product on a plate. Taste finished product.	Flavors from vinaigrette blended evenly throughout salad	
	Pleasing variety and balance of colors and shapes from vegetables	
	Ingredients and plate are chilled	

Lab Activity 19-4: **Chicken Salad**

Name _____ **Date** _____ **Period** _____

Group Members _____

Bound salads are a versatile form of prepared salad that typically uses mayonnaise to bind the ingredients together. These salads are cost effective for many kitchens to produce. Chefs often create bound salads to use up ingredients that are available in the kitchen. Chicken salad is a classic example of a bound salad.

Objectives

After completing this lab, you will be able to

- select and execute the correct poaching technique for this lab preparation.
- produce a bound salad.

Mise en Place

1. Carefully read through the entire recipe before starting production. Adjust the yield as needed. Review how to convert recipe yields in text Chapter 15.
2. Review the section *Poaching* in text Chapter 18.
3. Gather all ingredients and equipment required.

Sanitation and Safety Reminders

1. Clean and sanitize workstation before beginning to work.
2. Wash hands properly and as often as needed.
3. Take appropriate steps to avoid cross-contamination between raw chicken and celery.
4. Make sure poached chicken is cooked to appropriate internal temperature and the poached chicken and chicken salad are cooled to appropriate temperatures within time guidelines. Review the sections *Cooking* and *Cooling* in text Chapter 8.

Key Terms

Define the following terms used in this activity. Some may have been defined in previous chapters.

1. bound salad _____

   _____

2. poaching _____

   _____

3. medium dice_____

   _____

(Continued)

4. large dice_____

_____

5. cross-contamination _____

_____

Chicken Salad

Yield: 1 qt. (0.95 L)

Ingredients

1 lb.	450 g	skinless, boneless chicken breasts, large dice
8 oz.	225 g	celery, medium dice
8 fl. oz.	240 mL	mayonnaise
to taste		salt and white pepper

Method

1. Poach chicken breast. Refrigerate at or below 41°F (5°C) to cool. Once chilled, dice and reserve until needed.
2. Thoroughly wash celery and dice. Reserve until required.
3. Gently mix all ingredients in a bowl, being careful not to crush the diced chicken.
4. Refrigerate at or below 41°F (5°C) until ready for service.

Chef's Note: For a more robust flavor, grill chicken and chill. When mixing, do so very gently so as not to color the mayonnaise too much.

Chef's Journal

Write an evaluation of your lab performance. Would your finished product and performance meet the standards of a professional kitchen? Describe how your recipe turned out and what techniques and procedures you need to improve.

_____

_____

_____

_____

_____

Performance Review: **Chicken Salad**

Name _____ **Date**_____

Core knowledge/skills: bound salad, poaching, measuring temperature, knife skills, dice cuts

Culinary Proficiency	Expectations	Instructor's Review
Professionalism: Demonstrate appropriate workplace hygiene and appearance.	Hair neat and restrained	
	Clean chef uniform and apron; nonslip, closed-toe shoes	
	No nail polish or jewelry	
Sanitation: Wash hands properly. Demonstrate safe food handling. Take precautions to avoid cross-contamination.	Display correct handwashing throughout production	
	Clean and sanitize workstation before and after work	
	Use separate cleaned, sanitized knives and cutting boards for chicken and celery	
	Place poached chicken and salad in refrigerator at or below 41°F (5°C)	
Mise en Place: Set up workstation properly. Review recommended reading. Organized recipe method and sequence of work.	Adjust recipe yield as needed	
	Maintain clean and organized work area throughout entire lab	
	Needed equipment available and ready	
	Measure ingredients correctly	
	Produce uniform, appropriate-size chicken and celery cuts per recipe	
	Maintain orderly, efficient workflow, follow recipe	
Cooking Technique: Demonstrate correct poaching technique.	Use deep-poaching method	
	Poached chicken is moist and soft with no color, cooked to minimum internal temperature of 165°F (73.9°C)	
	Practice appropriate knife grip and safety techniques.	
Product Evaluation: Display finished product on a plate. Taste finished product.	Color is a bright, clean white	
	Salad holds together without excessive use of mayonnaise	
	Final yield is correct	

Additional Instructor's Comments

Lab Activity 21-1: **Poached Pears**

Name _____ **Date**_____ **Period** _____

Group Members _____

Poaching is a versatile and gentle cooking method. Since pears are a delicate fruit and must be both handled and cooked with care, poaching is the ideal cooking method to use. The slightest bump or drop on the counter can result in an unappealing brown bruise. When cooking pears, they should be cooked only long enough for the inside to become tender and no more. Pears can become extremely soft very quickly, if overcooked.

Objectives

After completing this lab, you will be able to

- apply poaching technique to a fruit product.
- execute basic fruit preparation skills including washing, peeling, and coring fruit.

Mise en Place

1. Carefully read through the recipe before starting production. Adjust the yield as needed. Review how to convert recipe yields in text Chapter 15.

2. Review the section on *Poaching* in text Chapter 18, the section on *Pears* in text Chapter 20, and the sections *Basic Skills*, *Acidulating Fruits*, and *Cooking Fruits* in text Chapter 21.

3. Gather all ingredients and equipment required.

Sanitation and Safety Reminders

1. Clean and sanitize workstation before beginning to work.

2. Wash hands properly and as often as needed.

3. Wash fruit.

Key Terms

Define the following terms used in this activity. Some may have been defined in previous chapters.

1. poaching _____

   _____

2. oxidation _____

   _____

3. acidulation _____

   _____

(Continued)

Poached Pears

Yield: 10 portions

Ingredients

10 ea.		pears
2 qt.	1.9 L	water
1 lb.	450 g	sugar
2 ea.		lemons, cut in half, juice and rind
1 tsp.	5 mL	whole black peppercorns
1 piece		fresh ginger (1 in.), peeled
1 ea.		cinnamon stick

Method

1. Peel and core pears. Cut in even halves.

Chef's Note: If peeled pears are not going to be used immediately, they should be dipped in acidulated water to prevent oxidation.

2. Combine the remaining ingredients in a pot and bring to a boil to make syrup.
3. Reduce liquid to poaching temperature, 160°F–180°F (71°C–82°C). Add pears and cook until tender.

Chef's Note: Carefully insert a paring knife into the pear to test doneness. The knife should just pull out of the pear without lifting the pear up.

4. Allow pears to cool in the syrup.
5. Drain pears and serve.

Chef's Journal

Write an evaluation of your lab performance. Would your finished product and performance meet the standards of a professional kitchen? Describe how your recipe turned out and what techniques and procedures you need to improve.

_____

_____

_____

_____

_____

_____

Performance Review: **Poached Pears**

Name _____ **Date** _____

Core knowledge/skills: knife skills, moist-heat cooking method, poaching, peeling, coring, acidulation, oxidation

Culinary Proficiency	Expectations	Instructor's Review
Professionalism: Demonstrate appropriate workplace hygiene and appearance.	Hair neat and restrained	
	Clean chef uniform and apron; nonslip, closed-toe shoes	
	No nail polish or jewelry	
Sanitation: Wash hands properly. Demonstrate safe food handling.	Display correct handwashing throughout production	
	Wash fruit thoroughly	
	Clean and sanitize workstation before and after work	
Mise en Place: Set up workstation properly. Review recommended reading. Organized recipe method and sequence of work.	Measure ingredients correctly	
	Select fruit that is clean and free from scarring and soft spots with firm texture	
	Select appropriate method for peeling pear	
	Practice appropriate knife safety and holding techniques	
Cooking Technique: Demonstrate proper poaching technique.	Maintain poaching liquid in the correct temperature range	
	Peel and trim pears neatly	
Product Evaluation: Display finished product on a plate. Taste finished product.	Pears were not brown or discolored from bruising or oxidation	
	Texture of pear is slightly firm, but not extremely soft	
	Taste is sweeter than original pear; color is a softer, more uniform pale	

Additional Instructor's Comments

Lab Activity 21-2: **Tropical Fruit Salad**

Name _____ **Date** _____ **Period** _____

Group Members _____

Tropical fruit salad sounds very exotic and conjures up images of banana trees gently moving in the cool ocean breeze on soft golden sands. Once you master several key techniques, you will be able to prepare a salad guaranteed to bring the flavors of the tropics to the table.

Chef's Note: Some fruits may not be available due to seasonal changes, so simply buy what is readily available and create your own recipe.

Objectives

After completing this lab, you will be able to

- execute fruit preparation skills including washing, coring, peeling, seeding, zesting, and suprêmes.
- apply a cooking method to coconut to produce caramelization.

Mise en Place

1. Carefully read through the recipe before starting production. Adjust the yield as needed. Review how to convert recipe yields in text Chapter 15.
2. Review the section *Flavors Blend and Change* in text Chapter 18 and the section *Basic Skills* in text Chapter 21.
3. Gather and prepare all ingredients and equipment required.

Sanitation and Safety Reminders

1. Clean and sanitize workstation before beginning to work.
2. Wash hands properly and as often as needed.
3. Wash fruit.

Key Terms

Define the following terms used in this activity. Some may have been defined in previous chapters.

1. zest _____

_____

2. suprêmes _____

_____

3. caramelization _____

_____

4. acidulation _____

_____

(Continued)

5. oxidation _____

_____

6. salamander _____

_____

Tropical Fruit Salad

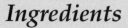

Yield: 10 portions

Ingredients

6 fl. oz.	180 mL	lime juice
1 oz.	30 g	sugar
1 tsp.	5 mL	grated lime zest
½ ea.		pineapple, peeled and cored, large chunks
2 ea.		bananas, peeled and sliced
1 ea.		papaya, peeled, seeded, medium chunks
3 ea.		kiwifruit, peeled, medium chunks
4 ea.		oranges, cut in suprêmes
20 ea.		pineapple leaves
¼ c.	60 mL	toasted coconut

Method

1. Combine the lime juice, sugar, and zest in a saucepan and bring to a simmer to dissolve the sugar. Remove from the heat and cool.
2. Combine the fruits in a mixing bowl and pour the cooled lime syrup over the fruit. Mix well.

Chef's Note: If peeled fruits are not going to be used immediately, bananas should be dipped in acidulated water to prevent oxidation.

3. Using a slotted spoon, divide the fruit evenly on 10 chilled plates.
4. Garnish each plate with two pineapple leaves and sprinkle with the toasted coconut.

Chef's Note: Coconut can be toasted in a dry sauté pan, under a salamander, or baked in the oven. The natural sugars in the coconut caramelize quickly, so watch it closely to avoid burned coconut.

Chef's Journal

Write an evaluation of your lab performance. Would your finished product and performance meet the standards of a professional kitchen? Describe how your recipe turned out and what techniques and procedures you need to improve.

_____

_____

_____

Performance Review: **Tropical Fruit Salad**

Name _____ **Date** _____

Core knowledge/skills: caramelization, washing fruits, zesting, peeling, coring, seeding, suprêmes

Culinary Proficiency	Expectations	Instructor's Review
Professionalism: Demonstrate appropriate workplace hygiene and appearance.	Hair neat and restrained	
	Clean chef uniform and apron; nonslip, closed-toe shoes	
	No nail polish or jewelry	
Sanitation: Wash hands properly. Demonstrate safe food handling.	Display correct handwashing throughout production	
	Wash fruit thoroughly	
	Clean and sanitize workstation before and after work	
Mise en Place: Set up workstation properly. Review lab recommended reading. Organized recipe method and sequence of work.	Measured ingredients correctly	
	Select and use appropriate tools and methods to produce various fruit preparations	
	Apply fruit preparation techniques well—no pith in zest, no eyes or fibrous core on pineapple, no skin on kiwifruit, no seeds in papaya, no membrane on suprêmes	
	Practice appropriate knife safety and holding techniques	
Product Evaluation: Display finished product on a plate. Taste finished product.	Uniform knife cuts for various fruits. Cuts were appropriate size for ease of serving and eating.	
	Flavors balanced, coconut did not overpower fruit	
	Pineapple leaves used creatively for artistic display	

Additional Instructor's Comments

Lab Activity 22-1: **Club Sandwich**

Name _____ **Date**_____ **Period** _____

Group Members _____

The club sandwich is one of the all-time classic triple-decker sandwiches. It supplies a complete meal—starch, vegetable, and protein—in a convenient portable sandwich. It is simultaneously crispy and soft, dry and moist, and packed with flavor. This sandwich keeps your taste buds busy!

Objectives

After completing this lab, you will be able to

- produce a closed, multidecker sandwich.
- implement cooking technique for bacon.

Mise en Place

1. Carefully read through recipe before starting production. Adjust the yield as needed. Review how to convert recipe yields in text Chapter 15.
2. Review the section *Breakfast Meats* in text Chapter 38.
3. Set up cutting board properly. Select appropriate knife and sharpen if needed.
4. Locate all ingredients and equipment needed. Prepare ingredients as required for assembly.

Sanitation and Safety Reminders

1. Clean and sanitize workstation before beginning to work.
2. Wash hands properly and as often as needed.
3. Wash and trim produce ingredients before preparing.
4. Wear disposable gloves when handling ready-to-eat ingredients.
5. Use frilled toothpicks when assembling sandwich.

Key Terms

Define the following terms used in this activity. Some may have been defined in previous chapters.

1. sandwich_____

   _____

2. Pullman loaf _____

   _____

(Continued)

Club Sandwich

Yield: 10 sandwiches

Ingredients

30 slices		white or whole wheat Pullman bread, toasted
40 slices		cooked bacon
2 lb. 3 oz.	1 kg	cooked turkey, thinly sliced
40 ea.		tomato slices
20 ea.		lettuce leaves
5 fl. oz.	150 mL	mayonnaise

Method

1. Cook bacon, remove from pan once crisp, and drain off the fat.
2. To assemble sandwiches, spread a thin layer of mayonnaise on 10 pieces of toast.
3. Place a piece of lettuce on top of each mayonnaise-covered piece of toast.
4. Place 2 slices of tomato on top of the lettuce.
5. Neatly arrange 1½ oz. (40 g) of sliced turkey on top of the tomato slices.
6. Top the turkey with 2 slices of bacon.
7. Place a slice of toast on top of each sandwich. Repeat steps 2–6 so as to create a triple-decker sandwich.
8. Finish the sandwich by placing the remaining slice of toast on top of the sandwich.
9. Use 4 extra-long toothpicks with frills to hold each sandwich together. (Use frilled toothpicks so the customer sees the toothpicks and does not bite into them.) Cut the sandwich into 4 pieces. Lay each piece down on the plate and serve.

Chef's Note: The toothpicks used to hold the sandwich together have bright frilly tops for safety and are known as "club sticks."

Chef's Journal

Write an evaluation of your lab performance. Would your finished product and performance meet the standards of a professional kitchen? Describe how your recipe turned out and what techniques and procedures you need to improve.

_____

_____

_____

_____

_____

Performance Review: **Club Sandwich**

Name _____ **Date**_____

Core knowledge/skills: ingredient portioning, baking/panfrying, breakfast meat cookery, slicing, sandwich assembly

Culinary Proficiency	Expectations	Instructor's Review
Professionalism: Demonstrate appropriate workplace hygiene and appearance.	Hair neat and restrained	
	Clean chef uniform and apron; nonslip, closed-toe shoes	
	No nail polish or jewelry	
Sanitation: Wash hands properly. Demonstrate safe food handling.	Display correct handwashing throughout production	
	Wash and trim produce before use	
	Use disposable gloves to handle ready-to-eat foods, change as needed	
	Clean and sanitize workstation before and after work	
Mise en Place: Set up workstation properly. Review lab recommended reading. Organized recipe method and sequence of work.	Prepare ingredients for assembly	
	Produce neat, consistent tomato slices, select clean, crisp lettuce leaves	
	Hold toast uncovered in warmer	
Cooking Technique: Demonstrate correct preparation of bacon.	Select appropriate cooking method (oven or sauté pan) for bacon based on amount being cooked	
	Produce crisp, well-drained bacon	
Product Evaluation: Display finished product on a plate. Taste finished product.	Finished product presents attributes of a successful sandwich	
	Sandwich is arranged attractively on plate using frilled toothpicks	
	Sandwich is neatly assembled so it is easy to eat	
	Textures of various ingredients are appropriate (toast is dry and crisp; lettuce is clean and crisp; mayonnaise, meat, and tomato are moist; bacon is crisp, etc.)	

Additional Instructor's Comments

Lab Activity 22-2: **Hummus Canapé**

Name _____ **Date**_____ **Period** _____

Group Members _____

Hummus originated in the Middle East and North Africa and is becoming increasingly popular in the United States. It is a versatile, healthy bean spread made by puréeing garbanzo beans and tahini (sesame paste) with olive oil. In this lab activity, the hummus is spread over wedges of a Middle Eastern bread called *pita*. This bite-size, open-faced sandwich with a colorful garnish can be served as a canapé.

Objectives

After completing this lab, you will be able to

- produce a canapé.
- implement a food processor to purée food.

Mise en Place

1. Carefully read through recipe before starting production. Adjust the yield as needed. Review how to convert recipe yields in text Chapter 15.
2. Review the sections *Peeling and Mincing Garlic*; *Mincing Parsley*; and *Peeling, Seeding, and Dicing Tomatoes* in text Chapter 16.
3. Locate all ingredients and equipment needed. Prepare ingredients as required for assembly.

Sanitation and Safety Reminders

1. Clean and sanitize workstation before beginning to work.
2. Wash hands properly and as often as needed.
3. Wash and trim produce ingredients before preparing.
4. Wear disposable gloves when handling ready-to-eat ingredients.

Key Terms

Define the following terms used in this activity. Some may have been defined in previous chapters.

1. canapé _____

   _____

2. sandwich _____

   _____

Hummus Canapés

Yield: 16 canapés

Ingredients

30 oz.	850 g	garbanzo beans, cooked or canned
2 tsp.	10 mL	garlic, minced
¾ tsp.	4 mL	cumin, ground
8 fl. oz.	240 mL	tahini (sesame paste)
3 ea.		lemons, juice of
2 fl. oz.	60 mL	extra virgin olive oil
to taste		salt
to taste		white pepper
2 ea.		pita bread
2 Tbsp.	30 mL	black olive slices
2 oz.	60 g	tomato, diced
1 Tbsp.	15 mL	parsley, chopped

Method

1. Drain garbanzo beans, reserving the cooking or can liquid.
2. Place garbanzo beans, garlic, cumin, tahini, lemon juice, and olive oil in a food processor. Purée until a smooth, thick paste is obtained. If the mixture is too dry, add a small amount of reserved cooking liquid.
3. Add salt and white pepper as needed.
4. Toast pita in a 400°F (204°C) oven until lightly toasted (about 10 minutes).
5. Cut each pita into 8 small wedges.
6. Spoon a dollop of hummus on each wedge. (The hummus could also be applied using a pastry bag.)
7. Garnish each wedge with black olives and a sprinkle of both tomato and parsley.
8. Wrap and refrigerate at or below 41°F (5°C) until service.

Chef's Journal

Write an evaluation of your lab performance. Would your finished product and performance meet the standards of a professional kitchen? Describe how your recipe turned out and what techniques and procedures you need to improve. _____

_____

_____

_____

_____

Performance Review: **Hummus Canapé**

Name _____ **Date**_____

Core knowledge/skills: ingredient portioning, puréeing, mincing, knife skills, sandwich assembly, use of food processor

Culinary Proficiency	Expectations	Instructor's Review
Professionalism: Demonstrate appropriate workplace hygiene and appearance.	Hair neat and restrained	
	Clean chef uniform and apron; nonslip, closed-toe shoes	
	No nail polish or jewelry	
Sanitation: Wash hands properly. Demonstrate safe food handling.	Display correct handwashing throughout production	
	Wash and trim produce before use	
	Use disposable gloves to handle ready-to-eat foods, change as needed	
	Clean and sanitize workstation before and after work	
Mise en Place: Set up workstation properly. Review recommended reading. Organized recipe method and sequence of work.	Prepare ingredients for assembly	
	Produce neat, uniform minced and diced ingredients, no evidence of green germ in garlic	
	Complete recipe in timely fashion and maintain organized work area	
Cooking Technique: Demonstrate correct blending technique and toasting of pita bread.	Use food processor and ingredient ratios correctly to achieve desired taste and texture	
	Produce crisp pita wedges, but not overcooked and excessively dry	
Product Evaluation: Display finished product on a plate. Taste finished product.	Canapés are attractively arranged on a plate	
	Canapés are neat, uniform, and bite-size	
	Garnish is attractive without overpowering the taste of the hummus	
	Hummus is smooth and even with a very slight texture	

Additional Instructor's Comments

Lab Activity 22-3: **Spicy Chicken Wrap**

Name _____ **Date** _____ **Period** _____

Group Members _____

Wraps are compact, portable meals that are becoming increasingly popular in the United States. Chefs can create many variations of wraps, limited only by the selection of ingredients in their kitchens and their imaginations. Wraps are quick, easy, and offer a complete meal in a neat package.

Objectives

After completing this lab, you will be able to

- produce a wrap.
- apply the grilling cooking method.

Mise en Place

1. Carefully read through recipe before starting production. Adjust the yield as needed. Review how to convert recipe yields in text Chapter 15.

2. Review the sections *Chiffonade* and *Peeling, Seeding, and Dicing Tomatoes* in text Chapter 16. Review section *Basic Knife Cuts* in text Chapter 12. Review the sections on *Grilling* in text Chapter 18 and *Grilling and Broiling* in text Chapter 32.

3. Locate all ingredients and equipment needed. Prepare ingredients as required for assembly.

Sanitation and Safety Reminders

1. Clean and sanitize workstation before beginning to work.

2. Wash hands properly and as often as needed.

3. Take appropriate steps to avoid cross-contamination of other ingredients by raw chicken.

4. Make sure grilled chicken is cooked and cooled to appropriate internal temperatures according to local health code. Review the sections *Cooking* and *Cooling* in text Chapter 8.

5. Wear disposable gloves when handling jalapeño peppers.

Key Terms

Define the following terms used in this activity. Some may have been defined in previous chapters.

1. cross-contamination _____

   _____

2. sandwich _____

   _____

3. wrap _____

   _____

4. grilling _____

   _____

(Continued)

Spicy Chicken Wrap

Yield: 10 wraps

Ingredients

10 ea.		large flour tortillas, 14 in. (36 cm) diam.
2½ lb.	1.12 kg	black beans, canned or cooked
2 lb.	900 g	grilled chicken breast, sliced ¼ in. (6 mm) thick
1¼ qt.	1.2 L	lettuce, chiffonade
3 ea.		avocado
as needed		lemon juice
1 lb.	450 g	Monterey Jack cheese, grated

Pico de gallo:

8 ea.		large tomatoes, seeded and diced
½ c.	120 mL	red onion, finely chopped
2 ea.		jalapeño peppers, minced
2 fl. oz.	60 mL	lime juice
to taste		salt and pepper

Method

1. Combine ingredients for pico de gallo and mix well. Reserve.
2. Drain black beans and reserve the liquid. Purée black beans to a paste in a blender or food processor. (If the beans are too dry, add a small amount of the reserved liquid.) Season with salt and pepper if necessary.
3. Lay tortillas on the work surface and spread with a ¼ in. (6 mm) layer of beans leaving a 1 in. (2.5 cm) wide ring around the outside of the tortilla.
4. Cut the avocado in half and remove pit. Using a large spoon, scoop the flesh from the skin, keeping the avocado in one piece. Slice each avocado half lengthwise into 5 segments. Sprinkle with lemon juice to prevent the slices from darkening.
5. Arrange sliced chicken and avocado on top of the black bean paste. Sprinkle with lettuce and cheese. Spoon pico de gallo on each tortilla.
6. Roll up the tortilla and secure with a frilled toothpick.
7. Wrap and refrigerate at or below 41°F (5°C) until service.

Chef's Journal

Write an evaluation of your lab performance. Would your finished product and performance meet the standards of a professional kitchen? Describe how your recipe turned out and what techniques and procedures you need to improve.

Performance Review: **Spicy Chicken Wrap**

Name _____ **Date**_____

Core knowledge/skills: measuring temperature, puréeing, chiffonade, grilling, mincing, dicing, knife skills, sandwich assembly, use of food processor

Culinary Proficiency	Expectations	Instructor's Review
Professionalism: Demonstrate appropriate workplace hygiene and appearance.	Hair neat and restrained	
	Clean chef uniform and apron; nonslip, closed-toe shoes	
	No nail polish or jewelry	
Sanitation: Wash hands properly. Take precautions to avoid cross-contamination. Demonstrate safe food handling.	Display correct handwashing throughout production	
	Disposable gloves used to handle ready-to-eat foods, changed as needed	
	Wash and trim produce before use	
	Use separate cleaned, sanitized knives and cutting boards for chicken and other ingredients	
	Clean and sanitize workstation before and after work	
Mise en Place: Set up workstation properly. Review recommended reading. Organized recipe method and sequence of work.	Prepare ingredients for assembly	
	Needed equipment available and ready	
	Adjust recipe yield as needed	
	Preserve avocado slices' appealing color, not turning brown	
	Maintain orderly, efficient workflow orderly and follow recipe	
Cooking Technique: Demonstrate correct wrap preparation. Demonstrate correct grilling technique.	Perform cutting techniques (chiffonade, dice, mince, chop) correctly	
	Purée black beans to spreadable consistency	
	Cook chicken to minimum internal temperature of 165°F (73.9°C) with appealing grill marks	
Product Evaluation: Display finished product on a plate. Taste finished product.	Sandwich is arranged attractively on plate	
	Chicken is moist and tender with good flavor	
	Wrap should be tightly rolled, showing no air gaps or loose food hanging out and secured with a frilled toothpick	
	Wrap is moist but not soggy	

Additional Instructor's Comments

Lab Activity 22-4: Vietnamese Spring Roll Appetizer

Name _____ **Date**_____ **Period** _____

Group Members _____

Spring rolls have become popular appetizers in many restaurants. They are deceptively easy to make and can be varied to fit a range of flavor preferences. To make them truly customized, place the individual ingredients on the table and allow each guest to place his or her own favorite ingredients into the roll.

Objectives

After completing this lab, you will be able to

- produce an appetizer.
- assemble a wrap, or rolled sandwich.

Mise en Place

1. Carefully read through recipe before starting production. Adjust the yield as needed. Review how to convert recipe yields in text Chapter 15.
2. Review the sections *Peeling and Mincing Garlic* in text Chapter 16 and *Preparing Salad Greens* in text Chapter 19.
3. Locate all ingredients and equipment needed. Prepare ingredients as required for assembly.

Sanitation and Safety Reminders

1. Clean and sanitize workstation before beginning to work.
2. Wash hands properly and as often as needed.
3. Wash and trim produce ingredients before preparing.
4. Wear disposable gloves when handling ready-to-eat ingredients.

Key Terms

Define the following terms used in this activity. Some may have been defined in previous chapters.

1. julienne _____

_____

2. wrap _____

_____

3. sandwich _____

_____

4. rehydrate _____

_____

(Continued)

Vietnamese Spring Roll Appetizer

Yield: 16 rolls

Ingredients

Spring roll:

16 oz.	450 g	pork tenderloin, cooked
12 oz.	340 g	shrimp, cooked, peeled and deveined, 21-25 ct.
6 oz.	170 g	rice vermicelli (noodles)
16 ea.		round rice wrappers
3 Tbsp.	45 mL	fresh basil, chopped
6 Tbsp.	90 mL	fresh cilantro, chopped
6 Tbsp.	90 mL	fresh mint leaves, chopped
6 Tbsp.	90 mL	Boston lettuce, chopped

Dipping sauce:

¼ c.	60 mL	fish sauce
¼ c.	60 mL	water
2 Tbsp.	30 mL	lime juice
1 clove		garlic, minced
1 tsp.	5 mL	fresh ginger, minced
2½ Tbsp.	35 mL	granulated sugar
½ tsp.	5 mL	sriracha hot sauce

Method

1. Mix basil, cilantro, mint, and lettuce together and set aside.
2. Cut chilled pork tenderloin into juliennes.
3. Lay shrimp on cutting board and cut the shrimp in half to yield two flat pieces (knife will be parallel to cutting board when cutting).

Chef's note: Use caution when cutting shrimp---place palm of hand on top of shrimp with fingers up and out of the way of the knife blade.

4. Bring salted water to a boil, turn off heat, and stir in rice vermicelli. Allow to soak for 4 minutes or until al dente. Drain and rinse with cold running water.
5. Rehydrate a sheet of rice wrapper in warm water until it is pliable (1 to 2 seconds). Remove from water and place on cutting board.
6. Arrange 2 pieces of shrimp and 1 oz. of julienned pork in a line running across the center of the wrapper stopping about 1½ inches from either end. Top with about $1^{1}/_{3}$ Tbsp. of herb and lettuce mixture and ¼ c. of rice vermicelli.

Chef's note: Many other ingredients can be used in the roll such as pressed tofu, Serrano chiles, and Daikon radish or cucumber juliennes.

7. Begin by folding the 1½ inch excess wrapper over the ends of the filling. Then fold one side of wrapper over the top of the filling and roll tightly.
8. Combine dipping sauce ingredients.
9. Serve rolls immediately with dipping sauce or cover and refrigerate at or below 41°F (5°C) until service.

Chef's Journal

Write an evaluation of your lab performance. Would your finished product and performance meet the standards of a professional kitchen? Describe how your recipe turned out and what techniques and procedures you need to improve.

_____

_____

_____

_____

_____

_____

_____

_____

_____

_____

_____

_____

_____

_____

_____

_____

_____

Performance Review: **Vietnamese Spring Roll Appetizer**

Name _____ **Date**_____

Core knowledge/skills: ingredient portioning, mincing, knife skills, sandwich assembly, starch cookery

Culinary Proficiency	Expectations	Instructor's Review
Professionalism: Demonstrate appropriate workplace hygiene and appearance.	Hair neat and restrained	
	Clean chef uniform and apron; nonslip, closed-toe shoes	
	No nail polish or jewelry	
Sanitation: Wash hands properly. Demonstrate safe food handling.	Display correct handwashing throughout production	
	Wash and trim produce before use	
	Use disposable gloves to handle ready-to-eat foods, change as needed	
	Clean and sanitize workstation before and after work	
Mise en Place: Set up workstation properly. Review recommended reading. Organized recipe method and sequence of work.	Prepare ingredients for assembly	
	Produce neat, uniform julienned and chopped ingredients, no evidence of green germ in garlic	
	Complete recipe in timely fashion and maintain organized work area	
Cooking Technique: Demonstrate correct rehydration and cooking of rice products.	Rice wrappers are not torn or soggy	
	Rice vermicelli is al dente, not mushy or crunchy	
Product Evaluation: Display finished product on a plate. Taste finished product.	Spring rolls are uniform in size and shape	
	Rolls are tightly wrapped with no tears, air pockets, or food hanging out	
	Ingredients are evenly distributed throughout roll so each bite delivers all flavors	

Lab Activity 23-1: **White Chicken Stock**

Name _____ **Date** _____ **Period** _____

Group Members _____

White chicken stock is perhaps the most widely used stock in the kitchen. When properly prepared, it has wonderful color, clarity, flavor, and body. This stock contributes a deep, rich, flavorful liquid to soups, mother sauces, and small sauces. It is used for deglazing when preparing pan sauces. White stock is very versatile and, therefore, most professional kitchens prepare it in large batches. When handled properly, it can be held under refrigeration for several days.

Objectives

After completing this lab, you will be able to

- produce a white mirepoix.
- produce a sachet.
- execute white chicken stock production.

Mise en Place

1. Carefully read through the recipe before starting production. Adjust the yield as needed. Review how to convert recipe yields in text Chapter 15.

2. Review the sections *Mirepoix* and *Washing and Cutting Leeks* in text Chapter 16. Review the sections *Aromatic Ingredients* and *White Stock* in text Chapter 23.

3. Locate all ingredients and equipment needed. Prepare ingredients as required for assembly.

Sanitation and Safety Reminders

1. Clean and sanitize workstation before beginning to work.

2. Wash hands properly and as often as needed.

3. Take appropriate steps to avoid cross-contamination of other ingredients by raw bones.

4. Cool stock according to local health code. Review the section *Cooling* in Chapter 8.

Key Terms

Define the following terms used in this activity. Some may have been defined in previous chapters.

1. stock _____

   _____

2. white stock _____

   _____

(Continued)

3. white mirepoix _____

_____

4. sachet _____

_____

5. cross-contamination _____

_____

6. bouquet garni _____

_____

7. reduce _____

_____

8. china cap _____

_____

9. chinois _____

_____

10. mouthfeel _____

_____

(Continued)

White Chicken Stock

Yield: 5 qt. (4.75 L)

Ingredients

10 lb.	4.54 kg	chicken bones (necks and gizzards can also be added)
5 qt.	4.75 L	cold water (or enough to cover bones)
8 oz.	225 g	onion, medium dice
4 oz.	115 g	celery, medium dice
4 oz.	115 g	white part of leek, medium dice
Sachet:		
20 ea.		black peppercorns
2 tsp.	10 mL	dried thyme leaf
1 ea.		dried bay leaf
6 ea.		parsley stems

Method

1. Place bones in a small stockpot. Cover bones with cold water.
2. Over medium heat, bring water to a simmer.
3. Skim stock using a ladle to remove all scum and grease.
4. Tie peppercorns, thyme leaf, bay leaf, and parsley stems into a sachet.
5. Add sachet and white mirepoix to the stock.

Chef's Note: A bouquet garni can be used for this stock. To use a bouquet garni, tie 3 sprigs of fresh thyme and a fresh or dried bay leaf to a 3 inch piece of celery. The peppercorns would still be placed in a small sachet.

6. Continue simmering for 3 hours. If the water level reduces below the bones, add additional cold water to cover. Skim the stock periodically.
7. Strain the stock using a china cap or chinois. Cool below 70°F (21°C) in two hours or less, and below 41°F (5°C) in less than a total of six hours.

Chef's Journal

Write an evaluation of your lab performance. Would your finished product and performance meet the standards of a professional kitchen? Describe how your recipe turned out and what techniques and procedures you need to improve.

_____

_____

_____

_____

_____

_____

Performance Review: **White Chicken Stock**

Name _____ **Date**_____

Core knowledge/skills: white stock, white mirepoix, knife skills, deglazing, sachet, gelatin, simmer

Culinary Proficiency	Expectations	Instructor's Review
Professionalism: Demonstrate appropriate workplace hygiene and appearance.	Hair neat and restrained	
	Clean chef uniform and apron; nonslip, closed-toe shoes	
	No nail polish or jewelry	
Sanitation: Wash hands properly. Take precautions to avoid cross-contamination. Demonstrate safe food handling.	Display correct handwashing at beginning and throughout production	
	Hold raw bones at or below 41°F (5°C) until ready to use	
	Clean and sanitize workstation before and after work	
Mise en Place: Set up workstation properly. Review recommended reading. Organized recipe method and sequence of work.	Prepare ingredients for assembly	
	Adjust recipe yield as needed	
	Wash bones to remove blood	
	Needed equipment available and ready	
Cooking Technique: Demonstrate correct white stock preparation.	Cut white mirepoix to appropriate size for type of stock	
	Use proper amount of cold water	
	Skim stock properly and maintain at a simmer, do not allow to boil	
	Note any changes that should be made to improve the stock for next production	
Product Evaluation: Present in a plain, white bowl for ease of observation. Taste finished product.	Stock has clarity and golden hue	
	Texture is smooth with a good level of gelatin giving it a rich, full-bodied mouthfeel	
	Taste is clear with intense flavor	

Lab Activity 23-2: **Brown Stock**

Name _____ **Date**_____ **Period** _____

Group Members _____

All chefs agree that a rich, deep, mouth-coating brown stock doubles the flavor of any dish in which it is used. This elegant, gelatinized stock coats your lips and taste buds with a satisfying, deep range of aromatic flavor. In this lab, you will practice the important techniques that are key to producing a quality stock.

Chef's Note: Veal bones are the preferred bone for stock making. Veal is a calf—typically male—that is fed a special diet to control the color of the meat. This method results in very tender cuts of beef with a pale pink color. Since veal is a young animal, its bones contain more collagen and produce a stock with higher levels of gelatin.

Objectives

After completing this lab, you will be able to

- execute brown stock production.
- produce a mirepoix.
- produce a sachet.
- apply the deglazing technique.

Mise en Place

1. Carefully read through the recipe before starting production. Adjust the yield as needed. Review how to convert recipe yields in text Chapter 15.
2. Review the section *Mirepoix* in text Chapter 16. Review the sections *Aromatic Ingredients* and *Brown Stock* in text Chapter 23.
3. Locate all ingredients and equipment needed. Prepare ingredients as required for assembly.

Sanitation and Safety Reminders

1. Clean and sanitize workstation before beginning to work.
2. Wash hands properly and as often as needed.
3. Take appropriate steps to avoid cross-contamination of other ingredients by raw bones.
4. Cool stock according to local health code. Review the section *Cooling* in text Chapter 8.

Key Terms

Define the following terms used in this activity. Some may have been defined in previous chapters.

1. stock_____

   _____

2. brown stock _____

   _____

(Continued)

3. collagen _____

_____

4. gelatin _____

_____

5. mirepoix _____

_____

6. sachet _____

_____

7. deglazing _____

_____

8. cross-contamination _____

_____

9. reduce _____

_____

10. china cap _____

_____

11. chinois _____

_____

12. mouthfeel _____

_____

Chef's Journal

Write an evaluation of your lab performance. Would your finished product and performance meet the standards of a professional kitchen? Describe how your recipe turned out and what techniques and procedures you need to improve.

_____

_____

_____

_____

_____

_____

_____

_____

_____

(Continued)

Brown Stock

Yield: 5 qt. (4.75 L)

Ingredients

10 lb.	4.54 kg	veal or beef bones, cut into 2–3 inch pieces
5 qt.	4.75 L	cold water (or enough to cover bones)
1 lb.	450 g	mirepoix, cut into 1 in. (2.54 cm) pieces
3 Tbsp.	45 mL	vegetable oil
3 Tbsp.	45 mL	tomato paste
Sachet:		
20 ea.		black peppercorns
2 tsp.	10 mL	dried thyme leaf
1 ea.		bay leaf
6 ea.		parsley stems

Method

1. Place bones in a lightly oiled roasting pan. Roast in a 350°F (177°C) oven until bones are well browned (about 1 hour), stirring occasionally.

2. Place bones in a stockpot and discard any grease left in roasting pan.

3. Place the pan over a medium heat and cover bottom of pan with ½ inch of water to deglaze. Bring the water to a boil while scraping the bottom of the pan with a wooden spoon. When all the browned bits on the pan have been loosened, pour the contents into the stockpot with the bones. (Taste the deglazing water before adding to the bones. If it is bitter, do not use it.)

4. Sauté mirepoix in 3 Tbsp. oil over medium heat until softened and lightly browned.

5. Add tomato paste to mirepoix and cook for 5 more minutes or until the tomato paste has turned a dark red. Stir often to prevent burning.

Chef's Note: In addition to flavor and color, the acidic tomato paste helps pull out and dissolve the gelatin from the bones.

6. Cover bones with cold water and bring to a simmer over medium heat.

7. Skim stock using a ladle to remove all scum and grease.

8. Tie peppercorns, thyme, bay leaf, and parsley into a sachet. Add sachet along with mirepoix to the stock.

9. Simmer for 9–12 hours. As the water level reduces below the bones, add more cold water to cover bones again. Skim the stock periodically.

10. Strain the stock using a china cap or chinois. Cool below 70°F (21°C) in two hours or less, and below 41°F (5°C) in less than a total of six hours.

Performance Review: **Brown Stock**

Name _____ **Date** _____

Core knowledge/skills: roasting, brown stock, mirepoix, knife skills, deglazing, sachet, gelatin, simmer

Culinary Proficiency	Expectations	Instructor's Review
Professionalism: Demonstrate appropriate workplace hygiene and appearance.	Hair neat and restrained	
	Clean chef uniform and apron; nonslip, closed-toe shoes	
	No nail polish or jewelry	
Sanitation: Wash hands properly. Take precautions to avoid cross-contamination. Demonstrate safe food handling.	Display correct handwashing at beginning and throughout production	
	Hold raw bones on ice until used	
	Use separate cleaned, sanitized knives and cutting boards for raw bones and other ingredients	
	Clean and sanitize workstation before and after work	
Mise en Place: Set up workstation properly. Review recommended reading. Organized recipe method and sequence of work.	Needed equipment available and ready	
	Prepare ingredients for assembly	
	Adjust recipe yield as needed	
Cooking Technique: Demonstrate correct brown stock preparation.	Roast bones to rich brown color Deglaze roasting pan, no bitter flavor Cook tomato paste to dark red color Cut mirepoix to appropriate size for type of stock Use proper amount of cold water Skim stock properly and maintain at a simmer, do not allow to boil Note any changes that should be made to improve the stock for next production	
Product Evaluation: Present in a plain, white bowl for ease of observation. Taste finished product.	Stock is rich, dark brown in color and unclouded	
	Texture is smooth and coats the back of a spoon, gelatin coats your mouth	
	Taste is deep, rich, and lasts several minutes	

Lab Activity 23-3: **White Vegetable Stock**

Name _____ **Date** _____ **Period** _____

Group Members _____

White vegetable stock is often misunderstood and incorrectly made. When properly prepared, it is one of the cornerstones in the culinary arts. This stock lacks gelatin because no bones are used in its preparation. Due to the absence of natural gelatin, the mouthfeel is lighter. However, the stock's flavors developed from the varied vegetables used are outstandingly complex.

Objectives

After completing this lab, you will be able to

- produce a sachet.
- implement various knife cuts.
- execute white vegetable stock production.

Mise en Place

1. Carefully read through the recipe before starting production. Adjust the yield as needed. Review how to convert recipe yields in text Chapter 15.
2. Review the section *Washing and Cutting Leeks* in text Chapter 16. Review the sections *White Stock* and *Vegetable Stock* in text Chapter 23.
3. Locate all ingredients and equipment needed. Prepare ingredients as required for assembly.

Sanitation and Safety Reminders

1. Clean and sanitize workstation before beginning to work.
2. Wash hands properly and as often as needed.
3. Cool stock according to local health code. Review the section *Cooling* in text Chapter 8.

Key Terms

Define the following terms used in this activity. Some may have been defined in previous chapters.

1. stock_____

_____

2. white stock _____

_____

3. gelatin _____

_____

4. mouthfeel _____

_____

(Continued)

5. sweating _____

_____

6. sachet _____

_____

7. bouquet garni _____

_____

Chef's Journal

Write an evaluation of your lab performance. Would your finished product and performance meet the standards of a professional kitchen? Describe how your recipe turned out and what techniques and procedures you need to improve.

_____

_____

_____

_____

_____

_____

_____

_____

_____

_____

(Continued)

White Vegetable Stock

Yield: 1 gal. (3.8 L)

Ingredients

5 qt.	4.75 L	cold water (or enough to cover)
3 Tbsp.	45 mL	extra virgin olive oil
4 oz.	115 g	onion, cut into ½ in. (13 mm) pieces
6 oz.	170 g	celery, cut into ½ in. (13 mm) pieces
4 oz.	115 g	carrot, cut into ½ in. (13 mm) pieces
4 oz.	115 g	leek, cut into ½ in. (13 mm) pieces
4 oz.	115 g	fennel bulb, cut into ½ in. (13 mm) pieces
2 oz.	60 g	parsnip, cut into ½ in. (13 mm) pieces (optional)
8 ea.		garlic cloves, peeled and coarsely chopped
4 oz.	115 g	button mushrooms, washed and coarsely chopped
3 ea.		ripe tomatoes, seeded and cut into a large dice

Sachet:

20 ea.		black peppercorns
2 tsp.	10 mL	dried thyme leaves
5 ea.		parsley stems
1 ea.		bay leaf

Method

1. Over medium heat, sweat all vegetables except tomatoes in olive oil until softened. Do not allow the vegetables to brown.
2. Place sweated vegetables and tomatoes in a small stockpot. Cover with water.
3. Over medium heat, bring water to a simmer. Skim broth using a ladle to remove any scum and grease.
4. Tie peppercorns, thyme leaf, parsley, and bay leaf into a sachet. Add to the stock.

Chef's Note: A bouquet garni can be used for this stock. To use a bouquet garni, tie 3 sprigs of fresh thyme and a fresh or dried bay leaf to a 3-inch piece of celery. The peppercorns would still be placed in a small sachet.

5. Continue simmering for 1 hour. Skim the stock periodically.
6. Strain the stock and cool below 70°F (21°C) in two hours or less, and below 41°F (5°C) in less than a total of six hours.

Performance Review: **White Vegetable Stock**

Name _____ **Date** _____

Core knowledge/skills: white stock, knife skills, sachet, sweating

Culinary Proficiency	Expectations	Instructor's Review
Professionalism: Demonstrate appropriate workplace hygiene and appearance.	Hair neat and restrained	
	Clean chef uniform and apron; nonslip, closed-toe shoes	
	No nail polish or jewelry	
Sanitation: Wash hands properly. Demonstrate safe food handling.	Display correct handwashing at beginning and throughout production	
	Clean and trim produce	
	Clean and sanitize workstation before and after work	
Mise en Place: Set up workstation properly. Review recommended reading. Organized recipe method and sequence of work.	Prepare ingredients for assembly	
	Needed equipment available and ready	
	Adjust recipe yield as needed	
	Sweat vegetables without browning	
	Skim scum from top of stock	
Cooking Technique: Demonstrate correct white stock preparation.	Practice appropriate knife safety and holding techniques	
	Demonstrate correct measuring of liquid and ingredients	
	Sweat all vegetables to correct color and doneness	
	Note any changes that should be made to improve the stock for next production	
Product Evaluation: Present in a plain, white bowl for ease of observation. Taste finished product.	Stock has clarity and golden hue	
	Flavor is complex with light mouthfeel	

Lab Activity 24-1: **White Sauce (Béchamel)**

Name _____ **Date**_____ **Period** _____

Group Members _____

White sauce preparation is a fundamental technique that all chefs must master. The ingredients are quite basic, but the production technique must be followed precisely to obtain a rich, silky-smooth sauce. This mother sauce is often used to make derivative sauces, also called *compound* or *small sauces*.

Objectives

After completing this lab, you will be able to

- produce a white roux and incorporate it into a liquid.
- implement an onion piqué.
- execute a white sauce preparation.

Mise en Place

1. Carefully read through the recipe before starting production. Adjust the yield as needed. Review how to convert recipe yields in text Chapter 15.
2. Review the sections *Roux* and *White Sauce* in text Chapter 24.
3. Locate all ingredients and equipment needed. Prepare ingredients as required for assembly.
4. Prepare clarified butter if necessary. Review the section *Clarified Butter* in text Chapter 16.

Sanitation and Safety Reminders

1. Clean and sanitize workstation before beginning to work.
2. Wash hands properly and as often as needed.
3. Cool sauce according to local health code. Review the section *Cooling* in text Chapter 8.

Key Terms

Define the following terms used in this activity. Some may have been defined in previous chapters.

1. sauce _____

   _____

2. mother sauce _____

   _____

3. derivative sauce _____

   _____

4. roux _____

   _____

(Continued)

5. onion piqué _____

_____

6. white stock _____

_____

7. clarified butter _____

_____

8. sachet _____

_____

9. chinois _____

_____

(Continued)

White Sauce (Béchamel)

Yield: 1 gal. (3.8 L)

Ingredients

8 fl. oz.	240 mL	clarified butter
8 oz.	225 g	all-purpose flour
1 gal.	3.8 L	milk
1 ea.		small onion, peeled
2 ea.		whole cloves
1 ea.		bay leaf
pinch		nutmeg, grated

Method

1. Prepare a white roux:
   a. Melt clarified butter in a small pan.
   b. Add flour and cook over low heat for 5 minutes or until the raw flour taste is cooked out of the roux. Stir the roux so the color does not deepen.
   c. Remove roux from pan and let cool.

Chef's Note: Roux can be made in advance, labeled and dated, and stored in the refrigerator for future use.

2. Prepare an onion piqué by spearing the bay leaf to the onion with the 2 cloves.
3. Add onion piqué to milk and bring to a boil.
4. Remove onion piqué and reserve.
5. Add the cool roux to the milk and stir with whisk to dissolve the roux.
6. Add the onion piqué back to the sauce.
7. Bring sauce back to a boil, reduce heat to very low and simmer for 20–30 minutes. Stir often so that sauce does not stick to the bottom of the pan and burn. (A heavy bottomed pot will lessen the chance that the sauce will burn.)

Chef's Note: Avoid using an aluminum saucepan. The frequent whisking and scraping of the sides of the aluminum saucepan during preparation can yield a dull, gray sauce instead of a white sauce.

8. Remove onion piqué and strain sauce through a chinois. Season with nutmeg. If the sauce is not being turned into a derivative sauce, add salt and white pepper to taste.
9. Cover the surface of the sauce with plastic wrap to prevent a skin from forming. Cool below 70°F (21°C) in two hours or less, and below 41°F (5°C) in less than a total of six hours.

Chef's Journal

Write an evaluation of your lab performance. Would your finished product and performance meet the standards of a professional kitchen? Describe how your recipe turned out and what techniques and procedures you need to improve.

_____

_____

Performance Review: **White Sauce (Béchamel)**

Name _____   **Date**_____

Core knowledge/skills: mother sauce, derivative sauce, onion piqué, clarified butter, roux, sachet, nappé

Culinary Proficiency	Expectations	Instructor's Review
Professionalism: Demonstrate appropriate workplace hygiene and appearance.	Hair neat and restrained	
	Clean chef uniform and apron; nonslip, closed-toe shoes	
	No nail polish or jewelry	
Sanitation: Wash hands properly. Demonstrate safe food handling.	Display correct handwashing at beginning and throughout production	
	Clean and sanitize workstation before and after work	
Mise en Place: Set up workstation properly. Review recommended reading. Organized recipe method and sequence of work.	Prepare ingredients for assembly	
	Adjust recipe yield as needed	
	Needed equipment available and ready	
	Produce clarified butter that is reasonably free of milk solids	
	Assemble onion piqué properly	
Cooking Technique: Demonstrate correct white roux preparation and incorporation. Demonstrate correct white sauce preparation. Demonstrate correct simmering technique.	Cook roux until there is no taste of raw flour and it has not darkened	
	Skim skin off milk as it is brought to boil	
	Blend roux into liquid well with few or no lumps, achieve correct consistency	
	Do not allow sauce to scorch or burn	
	Strain sauce through chinois	
Product Evaluation: Present in a plain, white bowl for observation. Taste finished product.	Sauce has a smooth, white sheen, not dull gray or brown	
	Texture is smooth, nappé consistency, not grainy or lumpy	
	No raw flour taste is detected	
	Onion and seasonings can be tasted, but do not overpower the sauce	

Lab Activity 24-2: **Velouté**

Name _____ Date_____ Period _____

Group Members _____

Velouté is a mother sauce to which other ingredients can be added to make derivative sauces. Since white stock is the main ingredient, it is essential that a good quality stock be used. *Velouté* means "velvety" in French and clearly sets the expectation for the final product.

Objectives

After completing this lab, you will be able to

- produce a blond roux and incorporate it into a liquid.
- execute a velouté sauce.

Mise en Place

1. Carefully read through the recipe before starting production. Adjust the yield as needed. Review how to convert recipe yields in text Chapter 15.
2. Review the sections *Roux* and *Velouté* in text Chapter 24.
3. Locate all ingredients and equipment needed. Prepare ingredients as required for assembly.
4. Prepare clarified butter if necessary. Review the section *Clarified Butter* in text Chapter 16.

Sanitation and Safety Reminders

1. Clean and sanitize workstation before beginning to work.
2. Wash hands properly and as often as needed.
3. Cool sauce according to local health code. Review the section *Cooling* in text Chapter 8.

Key Terms

Define the following terms used in this activity. Some may have been defined in previous chapters.

1. sauce _____

_____

2. mother sauce _____

_____

3. derivative sauce _____

_____

4. roux _____

_____

(Continued)

5. white stock _____

_____

6. clarified butter _____

_____

Chef's Journal

Write an evaluation of your lab performance. Would your finished product and performance meet the standards of a professional kitchen? Describe how your recipe turned out and what techniques and procedures you need to improve.

_____

_____

_____

_____

_____

_____

_____

_____

(Continued)

Velouté

Yield: 1 gal. (3.8 L)

Ingredients

8 fl. oz.	240 mL	clarified butter
8 oz.	225 g	flour
1 gal.	3.8 L	white stock (chicken, veal, etc.)
to taste		salt and white pepper

Method

1. Prepare a blond roux:
   a. Melt clarified butter in a small pan.
   b. Add flour and cook over low heat for 10–20 minutes or until it has a straw color. The finished roux should not have a raw flour taste. Stir the roux from time to time to be sure that the roux does not color unevenly.
   c. Remove roux from pan and let cool.

Chef's Note: Roux is made in one of three colors—white, blond, or brown. The same ingredients are used, but simply cooked longer to achieve the darker color. As the roux gets darker, a nutty aroma is generated and the thickening power decreases.

2. Bring the stock to a boil.

3. Add the cool roux to the stock and stir well with a whisk to be sure that all the roux is well dissolved.

Chef's Note: When adding a roux to a liquid, one ingredient should be cold and the other hot. Never mix cold with cold or hot with hot—the risk of lumps or the roux turning into a solid mass is very high.

4. Once the sauce comes back to a boil, reduce heat to very low and let simmer for 45–60 minutes. Stir periodically to be sure that the sauce does not stick to the bottom of the pan and burn. (A heavy bottomed pot will reduce the chance that the sauce will burn.) Skim any scum that rises to the surface during cooking.

5. Strain through a chinois. If the sauce is to be used as is and not turned into a derivative sauce, add salt and white pepper to taste.

6. Cover the surface of the sauce with plastic wrap to prevent a skin from forming. Hold above 135°F (57.2°C) or cool below 70°F (21°C) in two hours or less, and below 41°F (5°C) in less than a total of six hours.

Performance Review: **Velouté**

Name _____ **Date**_____

Core knowledge/skills: mother sauce, derivative sauce, clarified butter, roux, sachet, nappé

Culinary Proficiency	Expectations	Instructor's Review
Professionalism: Demonstrate appropriate workplace hygiene and appearance.	Hair neat and restrained	
	Clean chef uniform and apron; nonslip, closed-toe shoes	
	No nail polish or jewelry	
Sanitation: Wash hands properly. Demonstrate safe food handling.	Display correct handwashing at beginning and throughout production	
	Clean and sanitize workstation before and after work	
Mise en Place: Set up workstation properly. Review recommended reading. Organized recipe method and sequence of work.	Prepare ingredients for assembly	
	Adjust recipe yield as needed	
	Needed equipment available and ready	
	Produce clarified butter that is reasonably free of milk solids and water	
Cooking Technique: Demonstrate correct blond roux preparation and incorporation. Demonstrate correct white sauce preparation. Demonstrate correct simmering technique.	Cook roux until there is no taste of raw flour, and roux is light, golden-brown or straw colored	
	Blend roux into liquid well with few or no lumps, correct consistency achieved	
	Do not allow sauce to scorch or burn	
	Strain sauce through chinois	
Product Evaluation: Present in a plain, white bowl for observation. Taste finished product.	Sauce has a smooth, beige sheen	
	Texture is smooth, nappé consistency not grainy or lumpy	
	No raw flour taste is detected, flavor should be the dominant flavor of the original stock	

Lab Activity 24-3: **Tomato Sauce**

Name _____ **Date**_____ **Period** _____

Group Members _____

A key ingredient in many Italian and Hispanic cuisines, tomato sauce has become an increasingly more common sight on the cooktop in professional kitchens. It is a versatile mother sauce that is used in many different dishes and styles. Typically, this sauce is reduced then puréed, rather than thickened with a roux.

Objectives

After completing this lab, you will be able to

- execute tomato sauce production.
- apply sweating technique to vegetable ingredients.

Mise en Place

1. Carefully read through the recipe before starting production. Adjust the yield as needed. Review how to convert recipe yields in text Chapter 15.

2. Review the section *Peeling, Seeding, and Dicing Tomatoes* in text Chapter 16. Review the discussion about sweating in the section *Sautéing* in text Chapter 18. Review the section *Tomato Sauce* in text Chapter 24.

3. Locate all ingredients and equipment needed. Prepare ingredients as required for assembly.

Sanitation and Safety Reminders

1. Clean and sanitize workstation before beginning to work.

2. Wash hands properly and as often as needed.

3. Wash vegetables before preparation.

4. Cool sauce according to local health code. Review the section *Cooling* in text Chapter 8.

Key Terms

Define the following terms used in this activity. Some may have been defined in previous chapters.

1. sauce _____

   _____

2. mother sauce _____

   _____

3. roux _____

   _____

(Continued)

4. sweating _____

_____

5. white stock _____

_____

6. sachet_____

_____

7. bouquet garni_____

_____

8. nappé_____

_____

Chef's Journal

Write an evaluation of your lab performance. Would your finished product and performance meet the standards of a professional kitchen? Describe how your recipe turned out and what techniques and procedures you need to improve.

_____

_____

_____

_____

_____

_____

_____

_____

_____

_____

_____

_____

_____

_____

_____

(Continued)

Tomato Sauce

Yield: 1 gal. (3.8 L)

Ingredients

2⅔ fl. oz.	80 mL	extra virgin olive oil
4 oz.	115 g	carrot, diced
4 oz.	115 g	onion, diced
8 oz.	225 g	celery, diced
2 Tbsp.	30 mL	garlic, minced
2 ea.		bay leaves
1 Tbsp.	15 mL	dried thyme
1½ gal.	5.7 L	tomatoes (fresh or canned), seeded and diced
1 qt.	0.95 L	white stock (optional)
1 lb.	450 g	pork neck bone (optional)
to taste		salt and white pepper
to taste		sugar

Method

1. In a saucepot, sweat carrot, celery, and onion in olive oil.
2. Add garlic and cook 2 more minutes.
3. Make a sachet with the dried herbs or bouquet garni with fresh herbs.
4. Add tomatoes, stock, and neck bone. Bring to a boil then reduce to a simmer.
5. Simmer until the sauce begins to thicken. This may take well over 1 hour. Stir often to be sure that it does not burn.
6. Remove sachet or bouquet garni and pork bone.
7. Purée sauce in a blender or food processor, or pass through a food mill.
8. If the sauce is still too thin, put back on the heat and reduce to the proper consistency. Stir often to be sure that it does not burn.
9. Season with sugar, salt, and white pepper.
10. Cool below 70°F (21°C) in two hours or less, and below 41°F (5°C) in less than a total of six hours.

Performance Review: **Tomato Sauce**

Name _____ **Date**_____

Core knowledge/skills: sweating, mother sauce, knife skills, reducing, sachet, puréeing, nappé

Culinary Proficiency	Expectations	Instructor's Review
Professionalism: Demonstrate appropriate workplace hygiene and appearance.	Hair neat and restrained	
	Clean chef uniform and apron; nonslip, closed-toe shoes	
	No nail polish or jewelry	
Sanitation: Wash hands properly. Demonstrate safe food handling.	Display correct handwashing at beginning and throughout production	
	Wash vegetables before preparation	
	Clean and sanitize workstation before and after work	
Mise en Place: Set up workstation properly. Review recommended reading. Organized recipe method and sequence of work.	Prepare ingredients for assembly	
	Adjust recipe yield as needed	
	Needed equipment available and ready	
	Practice appropriate knife safety and holding techniques	
Cooking Technique: Demonstrate correct tomato sauce preparation. Demonstrate correct simmering technique.	Sweat vegetables until soft without browning	
	Remove tomato seeds and skin	
	Skim scum from top of sauce during early cooking	
	Do not allow sauce to scorch or burn	
	Note any changes that should be made to improve the stock for next production	
Product Evaluation: Present in a plain, white bowl for observation. Taste finished product.	Sauce is deep red color	
	Texture is smooth, nappé consistency with no lumps	
	Flavor is rich with no scorched taste	
	Balance between acid and sweet is achieved	

Lab Activity 25-1: **Beef and Barley Soup**

Name _____ **Date** _____ **Period** _____

Group Members _____

Beef and barley soup is as healthy and satisfying as food gets. This recipe is packed full of culinary techniques and even better taste and flavor. The beef and barley must be prepared in advance, therefore your mise en place may begin the day before soup production is scheduled.

Objectives

After completing this lab, you will be able to

- implement mincing, dicing, and concassé knife skills.
- apply sauté and starch cookery techniques.
- execute broth soup production.

Mise en Place

1. Carefully read through the recipe before starting production. Adjust the yield as needed. Review how to convert recipe yields in text Chapter 15.

2. Review the section *Broth Soups* in text Chapter 25. Review the section *Grains* in text Chapter 29.

3. Locate all ingredients and equipment needed. Prepare ingredients as required for assembly.

Sanitation and Safety Reminders

1. Clean and sanitize workstation before beginning to work.

2. Wash hands properly and as often as needed.

3. Thoroughly wash vegetable ingredients prior to cutting.

4. Cool, hold, and reheat barley and cooked beef according to local health code until needed for soup production. Review the section *Time and Temperature Principle* in text Chapter 8.

Key Terms

Define the following terms used in this activity. Some may have been defined in previous chapters.

1. mise en place _____

   _____

2. mincing _____

   _____

3. concassé_____

   _____

4. sautéing_____

   _____

(Continued)

Beef and Barley Soup

Yield: 1 gal. (3.8 L)

Ingredients

2 Tbsp.	30 mL	vegetable oil
8 oz.	225 g	carrot, small dice
8 oz.	225 g	celery, small dice
12 oz.	340 g	mushrooms, sliced
12 oz.	340 g	onions, small dice
½ tsp.	3 mL	garlic, minced
1 gal.	3.8 L	beef broth or stock
8 oz.	225 g	tomatoes, concassé
1 ea.		bay leaf
8 oz.	225 g	frozen peas
1 lb.	450 g	cooked beef, diced
1 lb.	450 g	cooked barley
to taste		salt and black pepper

Method

1. Brown the celery, carrot, mushrooms, and onions in oil over high heat in a large saucepan. Stir often.
2. When the vegetables are browned and softened, add the garlic. Cook for 1 more minute.
3. Add the tomatoes, broth or stock, and bay leaf. Bring to a boil. Reduce heat to a simmer and cook for 45 minutes.

Chef's Note: If beef broth is used, watch the salt content. A brown stock would produce a superior soup product.

4. Remove bay leaf. Add peas, cooked beef, and barley. Continue simmering until the soup reaches 165°F (74°C) and barley is tender.
5. Season soup with salt and black pepper. Serve when hot.

Chef's Journal

Write an evaluation of your lab performance. Would your finished product and performance meet the standards of a professional kitchen? Describe how your recipe turned out and what techniques and procedures you need to improve.

_____

_____

_____

_____

Performance Review: **Beef and Barley Soup**

Name _____ **Date** _____

Core knowledge/skills: knife skills, mincing, dicing, concassé, broth soup, mise en place, sauté

Culinary Proficiency	Expectations	Instructor's Review
Professionalism: Demonstrate appropriate workplace hygiene and appearance.	Hair neat and restrained	
	Clean chef uniform and apron; nonslip, closed-toe shoes	
	No nail polish or jewelry	
Sanitation: Wash hands properly. Demonstrate safe food handling.	Display correct handwashing at beginning and throughout production	
	Clean and sanitize workstation before and after work	
Mise en Place: Set up workstation properly. Review recommended reading. Organized recipe method and sequence of work.	Prepare ingredients for assembly	
	Needed equipment available and ready	
	Cook barley and beef to appropriate doneness	
	Adjust recipe yield as needed	
Cooking Technique: Demonstrate sauté and grain cookery techniques. Demonstrate correct broth soup technique.	Sauté vegetables to light caramelized color	
	Cook barley to correct doneness, not crunchy	
	Select appropriate cooking method for beef according to cut of meat, not chewy or tough	
	Simmer soup without scorching, do not allow to boil	
Product Evaluation: Present in a plain, white bowl for observation. Taste finished product.	Soup is a rich, dark brown and slightly opaque	
	Vegetables are tender, not overcooked and mushy	
	Flavor is rich and full-bodied	
	Seasoning adjusted, not too salty	

Additional Instructor's Comments

Lab Activity 25-2: **Chicken Vegetable Soup**

Name _____ **Date**_____ **Period** _____

Group Members _____

The ingredients and procedure for chicken vegetable soup are relatively simple and humble. However, the preparation requires close attention when dicing the vegetables. The vegetables should be cut to approximately the same size to ensure even cooking.

Chef's Note: The starch of your choosing—perhaps pasta or potatoes—would make a great addition to this soup. However, to avoid mushy pasta or potatoes, cook them separately and add just before serving.

Objectives

After completing this lab, you will be able to

- execute dice cuts.
- prepare a sachet.
- execute a broth soup.

Mise en Place

1. Carefully read through the recipe before starting production. Adjust the yield as needed. Review how to convert recipe yields in text Chapter 15.
2. Review the section *Broth Soups* in text Chapter 25.
3. Locate all ingredients and equipment needed. Prepare ingredients as required for assembly.

Sanitation and Safety Reminders

1. Clean and sanitize workstation before beginning to work.
2. Wash hands properly and as often as needed.
3. Thoroughly wash vegetable ingredients prior to cutting.
4. Take appropriate steps to avoid cross-contamination of other ingredients by raw chicken.

Key Terms

Define the following terms used in this activity. Some may have been defined in previous chapters.

1. sachet_____

   _____

2. cross-contamination _____

   _____

(Continued)

Chicken Vegetable Soup

Yield: 1 gal. (3.8 L)

Ingredients

2 lb.	900 g	chicken pieces (breast, legs, thighs)
8 oz.	225 g	carrot, diced
1 lb.	450 g	onion, diced
8 oz.	225 g	celery, diced
8 oz.	225 g	parsnips (optional)
1 gal.	3.8 L	water or chicken stock
Sachet:		
2 ea.		bay leaves
2 tsp.	10 mL	dried thyme leaf
1 tsp.	5 mL	black peppercorn
to taste		salt and white pepper

Method

1. Sweat onions in a small amount of oil. Place all ingredients in a stockpot.

Chef's Note: For best flavor, start with vegetable or chicken stock rather than water. Additional vegetables can be added if available or preferred.

2. Bring to a boil over medium heat.

3. Skim to remove all scum. Simmer about 1 hour until the chicken is tender and reaches 165°F (74°C).

4. Remove the chicken and allow it to cool briefly until it can be handled easily.

5. Remove meat from the chicken bones and tear or cut into bite-size pieces. Place the chicken back in the pan and bring the soup back to a simmer.

6. Remove sachet and season with salt and pepper. Moments before serving, mix soup with minced parsley.

Chef's Journal

Write an evaluation of your lab performance. Would your finished product and performance meet the standards of a professional kitchen? Describe how your recipe turned out and what techniques and procedures you need to improve.

_____

_____

_____

_____

_____

Performance Review: **Chicken Vegetable Soup**

Name _____ **Date**_____

Core knowledge/skills: knife skills, mincing, dicing, mise en place, sachet, sweating

Culinary Proficiency	Expectations	Instructor's Review
Professionalism: Demonstrate appropriate workplace hygiene and appearance.	Hair neat and restrained	
	Clean chef uniform and apron; nonslip, closed-toe shoes	
	No nail polish or jewelry	
Sanitation: Wash hands properly. Demonstrate safe food handling.	Display correct handwashing at beginning and throughout production	
	Clean and sanitize workstation before and after work	
	Use separate cleaned, sanitized knives and cutting boards for chicken and other ingredients	
Mise en Place: Set up workstation properly. Review recommended reading. Organized recipe method and sequence of work.	Prepare ingredients for assembly	
	Needed equipment available and ready	
	Produce uniform vegetable dice cuts	
	Adjust recipe yield as needed	
Cooking Technique: Demonstrate correct broth soup technique.	Cook chicken to minimum internal temperature of 165°F (73.9°C), but not tough or overcooked	
	Cook vegetables until slightly crunchy and not mushy	
	Sweat onions to correct color and doneness	
Product Evaluation: Present in a plain, white bowl for observation. Taste finished product.	No excessive scum or cloudiness should be visible to indicate the soup has been boiled rather than simmered	
	Vegetables are tender, not mushy	
	Chicken is tender, not tough	

Additional Instructor's Comments

Lab Activity 25-3: **Gazpacho**

Name _____ **Date**_____ **Period** _____

Group Members _____

Eating cold soup may sound like a strange idea, but you could compare it to having sweet tea on a hot day. This concept of a cold, refreshing, full-flavored tomato soup on a hot day makes perfect sense.

Chef's Note: Try making a half batch of gazpacho using red tomato and red pepper, and then make a half batch using green tomato and green pepper in the recipe. Once you have made both red and green soups, pour the red gazpacho in one side of a dish and the green gazpacho in the other side for an interesting presentation.

Objectives

After completing this lab, you will be able to

- apply purée technique to soup.
- implement garnishes.
- execute cold soup production.

Mise en Place

1. Carefully read through the recipe before starting production. Adjust the yield as needed. Review how to convert recipe yields in text Chapter 15.

2. Review the section *Cold Soups* in text Chapter 25.

3. Locate all ingredients and equipment needed. Prepare ingredients as required for assembly.

Sanitation and Safety Reminders

1. Clean and sanitize workstation before beginning to work.

2. Wash hands properly and as often as needed.

3. Review *Safety Savvy: Blender Safety* in text Chapter 25.

4. Thoroughly wash vegetable ingredients prior to cutting.

5. Wear disposable gloves when handling ready-to-eat ingredients.

Key Terms

Define the following terms used in this activity. Some may have been defined in previous chapters.

1. puréeing _____

   _____

2. Parisienne scoop _____

   _____

3. brunoise_____

   _____

(Continued)

4. garnish_____

_____

Gazpacho

Yield: 3 qt. (2.85 L)

Ingredients

2 ea.		cucumber, peeled and seeded
3 lb.	1.36 kg	ripe tomato, seeded
4 Tbsp.	60 mL	onion, diced
4 ea.		red peppers, seeded
1 tsp.	5 mL	garlic, minced
4 fl. oz.	120 mL	extra virgin olive oil
4 oz.	115 g	bread crumbs
8 fl. oz.	240 mL	tomato juice
2 fl. oz.	60 mL	sherry vinegar or red wine vinegar
as needed		water
to taste		salt and white pepper
as needed		garnishes*

Method

1. Grind all ingredients in a blender or food processor. Do not allow the ingredients to become completely smooth.

Chef's Note: The success of this recipe is dependent on the quality of the ingredients, especially the tomatoes.

2. Taste for seasoning and cool to 41°F (5°C) or less within four hours.

3. Serve the garnishes on top of individual cups of soup or serve them separately on the side of the soup. (*Appropriate garnishes for gazpacho might include diced or Parisienne scoop cucumber, brunoise red pepper, croutons sautéed in butter, diced tomato, and minced parsley.)

Chef's Journal

Write an evaluation of your lab performance. Would your finished product and performance meet the standards of a professional kitchen? Describe how your recipe turned out and what techniques and procedures you need to improve.

_____

_____

_____

_____

Performance Review: **Gazpacho**

Name _____ **Date**_____

Core knowledge/skills: puréeing, blender, cold soup, garnish

Culinary Proficiency	Expectations	Instructor's Review
Professionalism: Demonstrate appropriate workplace hygiene and appearance.	Hair neat and restrained	
	Clean chef uniform and apron; nonslip, closed-toe shoes	
	No nail polish or jewelry	
Sanitation: Wash hands properly. Demonstrate safe food handling.	Display correct handwashing at beginning and throughout production	
	Workstation cleaned and sanitized before and after work.	
	Wash and trim vegetables	
Mise en Place: Set up workstation properly. Review recommended reading. Organized recipe method and sequence of work.	Prepare ingredients for assembly	
	Adjust recipe yield as needed	
	Needed equipment available and ready	
	Use vegetables that are free of any discoloration, damage, or infestation	
Product Evaluation: Present in a plain, white bowl for observation. Taste finished product.	Soup is garnished to create a visually appealing presentation	
	Soup is puréed just long enough so that it has a little texture	
	Seasoning is corrected	

Additional Instructor's Comments

Lab Activity 27-1: **Green Beans Amandine**

Name _____ **Date**_____ **Period** _____

Group Members _____

Green beans amandine is a tasty dish with an attractive presentation. In addition, this recipe can be prepared using a variety of different vegetables to complement the meal you are preparing. The recipe employs several demanding techniques that are fundamental in the kitchen. Once you learn the techniques, be creative with the ingredients.

Chef's Note: The term amandine means "with almonds." It comes from amande, the French word for "almond."

Objectives

After completing this lab, you will be able to

- execute parcooking of vegetables.
- execute sautéing finishing technique.

Mise en Place

1. Carefully read through the recipe before starting production. Adjust the yield as needed. Review how to convert recipe yield in text Chapter 15.
2. Review the sections *Parcooking Vegetables* and *Finishing Techniques for Blanched Vegetables* in text Chapter 27.
3. Gather all ingredients and equipment required.

Sanitation and Safety Reminders

1. Clean and sanitize workstation before beginning to work.
2. Wash hands properly and as often as needed.
3. Wash and trim beans prior to preparation.

Key Terms

Define the following terms used in this activity. Some may have been defined in previous chapters.

1. sautéing _____

_____

2. blanching _____

_____

3. shocking _____

_____

4. al dente _____

_____

(Continued)

Green Beans Amandine

Yield: 2 lb. (900 g)

Ingredients

2 lb.	900 g	green beans, fresh
3 qt.	2.85 L	water
2 Tbsp.	30 mL	salt
3 oz.	85 g	butter
1 oz.	30 g	almonds, sliced
to taste		salt and white pepper

Method

Parcooking:

1. Trim the green beans, removing the stem and tips with a paring knife.
2. Bring the water and salt to a boil.
3. Add the green beans to the boiling water and return to a boil. Cook beans uncovered at a rapid boil, until they are tender. Doneness will vary with the size and maturity of the beans. Test doneness by removing a bean from the pot to check its texture.
4. When beans are done, remove them from the water and shock in ice water. Drain beans and hold at or below 41°F (5°C) until service.

Finishing:

5. Bring a pot of water large enough to hold a strainer to a boil.
6. Melt the butter in a sauteuse large enough to hold the beans.
7. Place the green beans in the strainer and lower into the boiling water to reheat. Beans should be cooked al dente.
8. Add the almonds to the butter and cook over moderate heat until the almonds are lightly browned.
9. Drain the green beans and toss with almonds and butter. Season with salt and white pepper.

Chef's Journal

Write an evaluation of your lab performance. Would your finished product and performance meet the standards of a professional kitchen? Describe how your recipe turned out and what techniques and procedures you need to improve.

_____

_____

_____

_____

Performance Review: **Green Beans Amandine**

Name _____ **Date**_____

Core knowledge/skills: vegetable preparation and cookery, blanching, shocking, finishing techniques, al dente

Culinary Proficiency	Expectations	Instructor's Review
Professionalism: Demonstrate appropriate workplace hygiene and appearance.	Hair neat and restrained	
	Clean chef uniform and apron; nonslip, closed-toe shoes	
	No nail polish or jewelry	
Sanitation: Wash hands properly. Demonstrate safe food handling.	Display correct handwashing at beginning and throughout production	
	Wash and trim beans	
	Clean and sanitize workstation before and after work	
Mise en Place: Set up workstation properly. Review lab recommended reading. Organized recipe method and sequence of work.	Prepare ingredients for assembly	
	Needed equipment available and ready	
	Set up blanching/shocking station before work began	
	Parcook beans to al dente maintaining attractive green color	
Cooking Technique: Demonstrate correct sautéing finishing technique of the beans.	Sauté almonds until light brown, not overly dark	
	Reheat beans just until hot and drain well	
	Sauté beans just long enough to coat with butter	
Product Evaluation: Present on a plain, white plate for observation. Taste finished product.	Beans are bright, fresh green and not gray	
	Almonds are light brown	
	Beans are cooked al dente, well drained, and coated with butter	
	Beans are well seasoned and almonds are not bitter	

Additional Instructor's Comments

Lab Activity 27-2: **Honey-Glazed Carrots**

Name _____ **Date** _____ **Period** _____

Group Members _____

This recipe requires the use of knife skills, and blanching and shocking techniques. Carrots can be cut in a variety of cuts such as rondelle or batonnet. The cuts must be uniform to ensure even cooking to al dente doneness. To finish, the carrots are reheated and then glazed with butter and honey. Other forms of sugar can be used to replace or change flavor profiles.

Objectives

After completing this lab, you will be able to

- implement rondelle and batonnet cuts.
- execute parcooking of vegetables.

Mise en Place

1. Carefully read through the recipe before starting production. Adjust the yield as needed. Review how to convert recipe yield in text Chapter 15.
2. Review the section *Basic Knife Cuts* in text Chapter 12. Review the sections *Parcooking Vegetables* and *Finishing Techniques for Blanched Vegetables* in text Chapter 27.
3. Gather all ingredients and equipment required.
4. Set up cutting board properly. Select appropriate knife and sharpen if needed.

Sanitation and Safety Reminders

1. Clean and sanitize workstation before beginning to work.
2. Wash hands properly and as often as needed.
3. Wash, peel, and trim carrots prior to preparation.

Key Terms

Define the following terms used in this activity. Some may have been defined in previous chapters.

1. blanching _____

_____

2. shocking _____

_____

3. rondelle _____

_____

4. batonnet _____

_____

(Continued)

5. al dente _____

_____

Honey-Glazed Carrots

Yield: 2 lb. (0.9 kg)

Ingredients

2 lb.	0.9 kg	carrots, peeled and trimmed
2 qt.	1.9 L	water
1 Tbsp.	15 mL	salt
2 oz.	60 g	butter
2 oz.	60 g	honey
to taste		salt and white pepper

Method

Parcooking:

1. Cut carrots into desired shape such as rondelles or batonnets.

Chef's Note: A variety of vegetables can be used for this recipe following the same techniques.

2. In a large pot, bring the water and salt to a boil.

3. Add the carrots to the pot and cook covered at a rapid boil until the carrots are tender. Test by piercing a piece of carrot with a paring knife.

4. Shock the carrots in ice water. Drain and hold at or below 41°F (5°C) until service.

Finishing:

5. Bring a pot of water large enough to hold a strainer to a boil.

6. Place the carrots in the strainer and lower into the boiling water to reheat.

7. Melt the butter and honey in a large sauteuse.

8. Drain the carrots and toss them with the butter and honey. Season with salt and pepper.

Chef's Note: Other sweet ingredients can be substituted for the honey such as maple syrup, brown sugar, or orange juice concentrate.

Chef's Journal

Write an evaluation of your lab performance. Would your finished product and performance meet the standards of a professional kitchen? Describe how your recipe turned out and what techniques and procedures you need to improve.

_____

_____

_____

Performance Review: **Honey-Glazed Carrots**

Name _____ **Date**_____

Core knowledge/skills: vegetable preparation and cookery, rondelle, batonnet, blanching, shocking, finishing techniques, al dente

Culinary Proficiency	Expectations	Instructor's Review
Professionalism: Demonstrate appropriate workplace hygiene and appearance.	Hair neat and restrained	
	Clean chef uniform and apron; nonslip, closed-toe shoes	
	No nail polish or jewelry	
Sanitation: Wash hands properly. Demonstrate safe food handling.	Display correct handwashing throughout production	
	Wash, peel, and trim carrots	
	Clean and sanitize workstation before and after work	
Mise en Place: Set up workstation properly. Review lab recommended reading. Organized recipe method and sequence of work.	Prepare ingredients for assembly	
	Needed equipment available and ready	
	Set up blanching/shocking station before work began	
	Cut carrots to consistent size and parcook to al dente	
Cooking Technique: Demonstrate correct sauté finishing technique of the carrots.	Heat honey and butter mixture properly so it does not darken too much	
	Reheat carrots just until hot and drain well	
	Sauté carrots just long enough to coat with butter and honey	
Product Evaluation: Present on a plain, white plate for observation. Taste finished product.	Carrots have bright orange color	
	Texture of carrots should be slightly crisp	
	Carrots are well seasoned	

Additional Instructor's Comments

Lab Activity 27-3: **Deep-Fried Vegetable Medley**

Name _____ **Date**_____ **Period** _____

Group Members _____

When properly prepared, deep-fried vegetables provide your senses with a pleasing contrast as you bite through the crunchy crisp breading and into the tender, moist vegetable inside. The standard breading method used to prepare vegetables for deep frying helps to seal in the moisture and prevent the vegetables from becoming greasy. The seasoning in the breading mix can be adjusted if a stronger taste is desired. Since deep-fried vegetables are rather rich, they are often paired with a protein that is prepared with a light cooking method.

Objectives

After completing this lab, you will be able to

- execute parcooking of vegetables.
- implement the standard breading method.
- execute correct deep-frying technique.

Mise en Place

1. Carefully read through the recipe before starting production. Adjust the yield as needed. Review how to convert recipe yield in text Chapter 15.

2. Review the sections *Parcooking Vegetables* and *Deep Frying* in text Chapter 27. Review the section *Deep Frying* in text Chapter 18.

3. Gather all ingredients and equipment required.

Sanitation and Safety Reminders

1. Clean and sanitize workstation before beginning to work.

2. Wash hands properly and as often as needed.

3. Store egg mixture on ice during this activity.

4. Wash and trim all vegetables prior to preparation.

Key Terms

Define the following terms used in this activity. Some may have been defined in previous chapters.

1. deep frying _____

   _____

2. rondelles _____

   _____

3. blanching _____

   _____

(Continued)

4. shocking _____

_____

5. al dente _____

_____

Deep-Fried Vegetable Medley

Yield: 3.75 lb. (1.7 kg)

Ingredients

20 ea.		cauliflower florets
20 ea.		zucchini rondelles, ¼ in. (0.5 cm) thick
20 ea.		mushroom caps
1 lb.	450 g	flour
2 Tbsp.	30 mL	salt
¼ tsp.	1 mL	ground white pepper
10 ea.		eggs, large
½ lb.	225 g	bread crumbs
as needed		oil for deep frying

Method

1. Add a small amount of lemon juice or vinegar to cooking water to make acidic. Blanch the cauliflower florets, shock, and pat dry.
2. Mix the flour, salt, and pepper, and place it in a shallow pan. Beat the eggs. Place the bread crumbs in a shallow pan.

Chef's Note: The seasoning for the breading mix should not contain too much salt because it reacts with the hot oil causing it to "spit."

3. Coat the vegetables first in flour, then in beaten eggs, and finally the bread crumbs.
4. Cook the vegetables in batches in a deep-fat fryer at 350°F (176.7°C) for 2–3 minutes. Drain well and serve.

Chef's Journal

Write an evaluation of your lab performance. Would your finished product and performance meet the standards of a professional kitchen? Describe how your recipe turned out and what techniques and procedures you need to improve. _____

_____

_____

_____

Performance Review: Deep-Fried Vegetable Medley

Name _____ **Date**_____

Core knowledge/skills: breading, blanching, shocking, deep frying, rondelles

Culinary Proficiency	Expectations	Instructor's Review
Professionalism: Demonstrate appropriate workplace hygiene and appearance.	Hair neat and restrained	
	Clean chef uniform and apron; nonslip, closed-toe shoes	
	No nail polish or jewelry	
Sanitation: Wash hands properly. Demonstrate safe food handling.	Display correct handwashing throughout production	
	Inspect eggs and discard if cracked or broken	
	Hold beaten eggs on ice	
	Wash and trim vegetables	
	Clean and sanitize workstation before and after work	
Mise en Place: Set up workstation properly. Review lab recommended reading. Organized recipe method and sequence of work.	Prepare ingredients for assembly	
	Needed equipment available and ready	
	Set up blanching/shocking and breading stations before beginning work	
	Parcook vegetables appropriately, maintain cauliflower's attractive white color	
Cooking Technique: Demonstrate correct deep-frying technique.	Use sufficient amount of fat in the fryer to maintain temperature during cooking	
	Ensure fat is correct temperature for deep frying	
	Do not overload fryer with product	
Product Evaluation: Present on a plain, white plate for observation. Taste finished product.	Coat vegetables evenly with breading, cooked to golden brown color	
	Breading is crisp, not greasy	
	Vegetables are al dente and moist, colors are bright	
	Flavors are balanced, no off flavor from cooking oil	
	Product is well seasoned	

Additional Instructor's Comments

Lab Activity 29-1: **Rice Pilaf**

Name _____ **Date**_____ **Period** _____

Group Members _____

The pilaf method requires several key techniques such as sweating onions, simmering stock, and baking. When properly performed, this method produces a highly seasoned, moist rice dish. Pilaf method requires precise measuring of the liquid and rice to ensure even cooking with perfect doneness—neither too dry nor moist.

Objectives

After completing this lab, you will be able to

- apply sweating technique.
- execute pilaf method to prepare rice.

Mise en Place

1. Carefully read through the recipe before starting production. Adjust the yield as needed. Review how to convert recipe yield in text Chapter 15.

2. Review the section *Pilaf Method* in text Chapter 29. Review the section *Baking* in text Chapter 18.

3. Gather all ingredients and equipment required.

Sanitation and Safety Reminders

1. Clean and sanitize workstation before beginning to work.

2. Wash hands properly and as often as needed.

3. Wash and trim vegetables before preparation.

Key Terms

Define the following terms used in this activity. Some may have been defined in previous chapters.

1. sweating _____

_____

2. baking _____

_____

3. small dice _____

_____

4. white rice_____

_____

(Continued)

Rice Pilaf

Yield: 1½ qt. (1.44 L)

Ingredients

2 oz.	60 g	butter
2 oz.	60 g	onion, small dice
1 pt.	480 mL	long grain white rice
1 qt.	0.95 L	chicken stock
1 ea.		dried bay leaf
1 ea.		parsley sprig
to taste		salt and white pepper

Method

1. Sweat the onion in the butter.
2. Add rice and stir to coat with the butter.
3. Add the stock, bay leaf, and parsley sprig. Season to taste.
4. Bring the ingredients to a simmer. Cover tightly and place in a 350°F (177°C) oven for 18–20 minutes or until all the liquid is absorbed.
5. Remove from the oven, fluff with a fork, and serve or hold at 135°F (57.2°C) or above.

Chef's Journal

Write an evaluation of your lab performance. Would your finished product and performance meet the standards of a professional kitchen? Describe how your recipe turned out and what techniques and procedures you need to improve.

_____

_____

_____

_____

_____

_____

_____

_____

Performance Review: Rice Pilaf

Name _____ **Date**_____

Core knowledge/skills: starch cookery, pilaf method, baking, sweating, dicing

Culinary Proficiency	Expectations	Instructor's Review
Professionalism: Demonstrate appropriate workplace hygiene and appearance.	Hair neat and restrained	
	Clean chef uniform and apron; nonslip, closed-toe shoes	
	No nail polish or jewelry	
Sanitation: Wash hands properly. Demonstrate safe food handling.	Display correct handwashing throughout production	
	Clean and sanitize workstation before and after work	
Mise en Place: Set up workstation properly. Review lab recommended reading. Organized recipe method and sequence of work.	Prepare ingredients for assembly	
	Measure ingredients accurately	
	Needed equipment available and ready	
Cooking Technique: Demonstrate correct pilaf technique.	Sweat onions to correct color and doneness	
	Cook rice until all liquid is absorbed	
Product Evaluation: Present on a plain, white plate for observation. Taste finished product.	Appealing pale golden color	
	Rice is fluffy and tender, onions are soft and proper size	
	Dish is well seasoned and moist	

Additional Instructor's Comments

Lab Activity 29-2: **Basic Fried Rice**

Name _____ **Date** _____ **Period** _____

Group Members _____

Once the rice is cooked, fried rice is very quick to finish. Ideally, this recipe is prepared using a wok. Woks made with heavier gauge metals are better for even heat distribution. Since wok recipes are cooked over very high heat, using a lighter weight wok may result in scorched food due to uneven heating.

Objectives

After completing this lab, you will be able to

- select an appropriate cooking method for rice.
- execute sautéing cooking method.

Mise en Place

1. Carefully read through the recipe before starting production. Adjust the yield as needed. Review how to convert recipe yield in text Chapter 15.
2. Review the section *Grains* in text Chapter 29. Review the section *Sautéing* in text Chapter 18.
3. Gather all ingredients and equipment required.

Sanitation and Safety Reminders

1. Clean and sanitize workstation before beginning to work.
2. Wash hands properly and as often as needed.
3. Inspect eggs and discard any that are broken or cracked.
4. Wash and trim vegetables before preparation.

Key Terms

Define the following terms used in this activity. Some may have been defined in previous chapters.

1. sautéing _____

   _____

2. white rice _____

   _____

3. mincing _____

   _____

4. small dice _____

   _____

(Continued)

5. sweating _____

Basic Fried Rice
Yield: 2½ qt. (2.4 L)

Ingredients

5½ c.	1.3 L	white rice, cooked long grain
4 ea.		eggs
6 oz.	170 g	onion, small dice
4 tsp.	20 mL	garlic, minced
4 Tbsp.	60 mL	peanut oil
1 Tbsp.	15 mL	sesame oil
8 oz.	225 g	bean sprouts
4 oz.	115 g	green peas, IQF
to taste		soy sauce
to taste		green onion, thin sliced

Method

1. Heat one tablespoon of peanut oil in a wok or large skillet and cook eggs until firm and broken into small pieces. Remove and set aside.

Chef's Note: Peanut oil has a high smoke point, which means it can be heated to very high temperatures. However, many people are allergic to peanut products, so customers should be informed of its use.

2. Add another tablespoon of oil to the skillet or wok and sweat onions until soft but not brown. Add garlic and stir for thirty seconds.
3. Add remaining oil to pan and add rice. Stir until rice is hot.
4. Add egg, onion, sesame oil, bean sprouts, peas, and soy sauce. Stir until everything is well mixed and reaches 155°F (68.3°C).

Chef's Note: Sesame oil burns more easily and quickly loses its flavor. Always add it to a dish toward the end of cooking to avoid flavor loss.

5. Serve as a side dish garnished with green onion.

Chef's Journal

Write an evaluation of your lab performance. Would your finished product and performance meet the standards of a professional kitchen? Describe how your recipe turned out and what techniques and procedures you need to improve.

_____

_____

Performance Review: **Basic Fried Rice**

Name _____ **Date**_____

Core knowledge/skills: starch cookery, sautéing, dicing, mincing

Culinary Proficiency	Expectations	Instructor's Review
Professionalism: Demonstrate appropriate workplace hygiene and appearance.	Hair neat and restrained	
	Clean chef uniform and apron; nonslip, closed-toe shoes	
	No nail polish or jewelry	
Sanitation: Wash hands properly. Demonstrate safe food handling.	Display correct handwashing throughout production	
	Discard cracked or broken eggs	
	Clean and sanitize workstation before and after work	
Mise en Place: Set up workstation properly. Review lab recommended reading. Organized recipe method and sequence of work.	Prepare ingredients for assembly	
	Select appropriate rice cookery method, cook rice to proper doneness	
	Needed equipment available and ready	
Cooking Technique: Demonstrate correct sauté technique.	Cook eggs just through, still moist not dry and hard	
	Heat oil to appropriate temperature without smoking	
	Add ingredients in correct progression and timing to avoid overcooking items	
Product Evaluation: Present on a plain, white plate for observation. Taste finished product.	Rice is dark brown from soy sauce; peas are an appealing green, not overcooked; plate is attractively garnished	
	Overall texture should be light and fluffy; eggs are still soft; rice is tender, neither crunchy nor mushy and clumping	
	Taste is not dominated by one product, soy sauce does not have a burnt aroma and taste	

Additional Instructor's Comments

Lab Activity 29-3: **Basic Pasta Dough**

Name _____ **Date** _____ **Period** _____

Group Members _____

Freshly made pasta cooks quickly, is soft and delicate, and tastes superior to dry pasta. Many pasta recipes use both semolina and all-purpose flours. For centuries, the ratios of these two flours used in successful pasta recipes have been kept closely guarded secrets. Very few chefs will tell you exactly how their pasta dough is made.

Objectives

After completing this lab, you will be able to

- produce pasta dough.
- apply kneading technique or use an electric mixer to mix dough.

Mise en Place

1. Carefully read through the recipe before starting production. Adjust the yield as needed. Review how to convert recipe yield in text Chapter 15.

2. Review the section *Pasta Dough* in text Chapter 29. Review the section *Mixers* in text Chapter 38 and *Mixing and Kneading Dough* in text Chapter 43.

3. Gather all ingredients and equipment required.

Sanitation and Safety Reminders

1. Clean and sanitize workstation before beginning to work.

2. Wash hands properly and as often as needed.

3. Review *Safety Savvy: Mixer Safety* in text Chapter 38.

4. Inspect eggs and discard any that are broken or cracked.

Key Term

Define the following term used in this activity. It may have been defined in previous chapters.

1. semolina _____

_____

(Continued)

Basic Pasta Dough

Yield: 1½ lb. (680 g)

Ingredients

4 oz.	115 g	semolina flour
12 oz.	340 g	all-purpose flour
4 ea.		large eggs
2 ea.		egg yolks
½ tsp.	2 mL	salt

Method

1. Combine the semolina and all-purpose flours.
2. Place the eggs, egg yolks, and salt in the bowl of a large mixer fitted with a paddle. Smaller quantities of dough can be mixed by hand.
3. Turn the mixer on low and break up egg yolks.
4. Turn off mixer, add ¹/₃ of the flour and mix until flour is incorporated.
5. Remove paddle; clean off any dough stuck to paddle and attach dough hook.
6. With mixer on low speed, slowly add remaining flour until incorporated.
7. Turn off the mixer; remove dough from dough hook and mixer bowl.
8. Roll dough in a ball, cover with plastic wrap and refrigerate at or below 41°F (5°C) for at least 30 minutes to allow dough to rest before rolling and cutting into desired shape. Reserve for use in Lab Activity 29-4: *Shaping and Cooking Pasta.*

Chef's Journal

Write an evaluation of your lab performance. Would your finished product and performance meet the standards of a professional kitchen? Describe how your recipe turned out and what techniques and procedures you need to improve.

_____

_____

_____

_____

_____

_____

_____

_____

Performance Review: **Basic Pasta Dough**

Name _____ **Date** _____

Core knowledge/skills: starch cookery, semolina, kneading, electric mixer

Culinary Proficiency	Expectations	Instructor's Review
Professionalism: Demonstrate appropriate workplace hygiene and appearance.	Hair neat and restrained	
	Clean chef uniform and apron; nonslip, closed-toe shoes	
	No nail polish or jewelry	
Sanitation: Wash hands properly. Demonstrate safe food handling.	Display correct handwashing throughout production	
	Inspect eggs and discard if cracked or broken	
	Cover prepared dough and store at 41°F (5°C) until ready to roll out	
	Clean and sanitize workstation before and after work	
Mise en Place: Set up workstation properly. Review lab recommended reading. Organized recipe method and sequence of work.	Prepare ingredients for assembly	
	Needed equipment available and ready	
Cooking Technique: Demonstrate correct technique for making pasta dough.	Form trough in flour to contain eggs if mixing by hand, dust work surface with flour to prevent sticking	
	Knead or mix dough until smooth consistency without lumps or dry spots	
Product Evaluation: Once rested for 30 minutes or more, observe the texture of the dough.	Dough is soft to the touch, indentation remains when a finger is pushed into the dough	
	Dough is slightly damp, not dry and crumbly nor too sticky	
	Texture of the dough should be smooth, without lumps or particles of unmixed flour or egg	
	Uniform color throughout the dough	

Additional Instructor's Comments

Lab Activity 29-4: **Shaping and Cooking Pasta**

Name _____ **Date**_____ **Period** _____

Group Members _____

Use the pasta dough from Lab Activity 29-3: *Basic Pasta Dough* to complete this activity.

Objectives

After completing this lab, you will be able to

- execute rolling and cutting pasta either by hand or machine.
- produce fresh pasta cooked al dente.

Mise en Place

1. Carefully read through the recipe before starting production. Adjust the yield as needed. Review how to convert recipe yield in text Chapter 15.

2. Review the sections *Shaping Fresh Pasta* and *Cooking Pasta* in text Chapter 29.

3. Gather all ingredients and equipment required.

Sanitation and Safety Reminders

1. Clean and sanitize workstation before beginning to work.

2. Wash hands properly and as often as needed.

Key Terms

Define the following terms used in this activity. Some may have been defined in previous chapters.

1. al dente _____

_____

2. shocking _____

_____

Lab Procedure

Part 1: Cutting Noodles

Cut the pasta dough into noodles using one of the following techniques as assigned by your instructor.

By Hand

1. Start with a manageable amount of pasta dough.

2. Dust a work surface with flour and flatten the dough with the heel of your hand.

3. Roll out the dough with a rolling pin making sure to sprinkle with flour to prevent the dough from sticking to the pin or work surface.

(Continued)

4. Continue to roll the dough into a thin rectangular sheet approximately $1/8$-inch thick.

5. Beginning at one end of the rectangle, loosely roll the dough up.

6. Use a sharp knife to make ¼- to ½-inch thick slices in the roll, forming individual spirals.

7. Unwind spirals to form noodles and place on a sheet pan.

8. Proceed to *Part 2: Boiling Pasta.*

With a Manual Pasta Machine

1. Start with a manageable amount of pasta dough.

2. Open the rollers of the pasta machine to the widest possible setting.

3. Flatten the dough with the heel of your hand so that it fits between the rollers of the pasta machine. Dust the dough and the rollers lightly with flour.

4. Run the dough through the pasta machine holding one end of the dough with one hand while holding up the dough as it comes out of the machine.

5. Fold the dough into thirds so that the sheet of dough is in three layers.

6. Run the dough through the machine three or four more times to knead the dough until it is smooth.

7. When the dough is smooth, move the rollers together one or two notches and pass the dough through without folding.

8. Continue moving the rollers together and passing the dough through the machine until the dough is at the desired thickness—usually $1/8$ inch.

9. Cut the sheet with the cutting attachment to create the width of pasta ribbons desired.

10. Proceed to *Part 2: Boiling Pasta.*

Part 2: Boiling Pasta

1. Bring one gallon (3.8 L) of slightly salted water (2 to 3 Tbsp. salt) per pound of pasta to a boil.

2. Add pasta and stir to separate the pieces.

3. Cook pasta at a rolling boil until al dente.

4. Drain pasta immediately and serve. Pasta can be shocked in ice water to stop cooking, coated with a little olive oil, and reheated for later service.

Chef's Journal

Write an evaluation of your lab performance. Would your finished product and performance meet the standards of a professional kitchen? Describe how your recipe turned out and what techniques and procedures you need to improve.

_____

_____

_____

_____

Performance Review: **Shaping and Cooking Pasta**

Name _____ **Date**_____

Core knowledge/skills: starch cookery, rolling pasta, cutting pasta, al dente

Culinary Proficiency	Expectations	Instructor's Review
Professionalism: Demonstrate appropriate workplace hygiene and appearance.	Hair neat and restrained	
	Clean chef uniform and apron; nonslip, closed-toe shoes	
	No nail polish or jewelry	
Sanitation: Wash hands properly. Demonstrate safe food handling.	Display correct handwashing throughout production	
	Clean and sanitize workstation before and after work	
Mise en Place: Set up workstation properly. Review lab recommended reading. Organized recipe method and sequence of work.	Prepare ingredients for assembly	
	Cut uniform noodles that separate readily, unwind spirals if cutting by hand	
	Boil appropriate amount of properly salted water for cooking noodles	
	Needed equipment available and ready	
Cooking Technique: Demonstrate correct boiling technique to cook pasta.	Bring water to a full boil when pasta is added	
	Stir pasta to separate pieces when added to water	
	Cook noodles al dente, verified by tasting a piece of pasta	
	Drain and shock pasta if appropriate	
Product Evaluation: Present on a plain, white plate for observation. Taste finished product.	Color is consistent throughout pasta	
	Pasta is well drained, not sitting in a pool of water	
	Pasta is cooked al dente (tender, but not soft or mushy)	

Additional Instructor's Comments

Lab Activity 29-5: **Lyonnaise Potatoes**

Name _____ **Date** _____ **Period** _____

Group Members _____

This dish is named for the town in the south of France from which it originates—Lyon. This simple recipe that was created in the kitchens of peasants, has survived the centuries to be served in fine restaurants.

Objectives

After completing this lab, you will be able to

- execute julienne onions.
- execute sautéing cooking method to finish parcooked potatoes.
- recognize caramelization of starch.

Mise en Place

1. Carefully read through the recipe before starting production. Adjust the yield as needed. Review how to convert recipe yield in text Chapter 15.

2. Review the section *Preparing Julienne Onions* in text Chapter 16 and the sections *Flavors Blend and Change* and *Sautéing* in text Chapter 18.

3. Gather all ingredients and equipment required.

4. Prepare clarified butter if necessary. Review the section *Clarified Butter* in text Chapter 16.

Sanitation and Safety Reminders

1. Clean and sanitize workstation before beginning to work.

2. Wash hands properly and as often as needed.

3. Wash and trim vegetables as needed before preparation.

Key Terms

Define the following terms used in this activity. Some may have been defined in previous chapters.

1. julienne _____

   _____

2. sautéing _____

   _____

3. caramelization _____

   _____

4. clarified butter _____

   _____

(Continued)

5. mealy potatoes _____

_____

Lyonnaise Potatoes
Yield: 2½ lb. (1.1 kg)

Ingredients

3 lb.	1.36 kg	mealy potatoes
10 oz.	280 g	onion, julienne
6 fl. oz.	180 mL	clarified butter
to taste		salt and white pepper

Method

1. Parcook the potatoes in their skins by boiling in water 20 minutes.
2. Allow the potatoes to cool and peel them.
3. Cut potatoes into ¼ in. slices.
4. Sauté the onions in 3 fl. oz. of clarified butter until just beginning to brown. Remove from pan and set aside.
5. Add the remaining butter to the reheated pan. Sauté potatoes on both sides until browned.
6. Return onion to pan with potatoes and sauté until well mixed.
7. Season to taste with salt and pepper and toss. Hold at or above 135°F (57.2°C) until service.

Chef's Journal

Write an evaluation of your lab performance. Would your finished product and performance meet the standards of a professional kitchen? Describe how your recipe turned out and what techniques and procedures you need to improve.

_____

_____

_____

_____

_____

_____

_____

_____

_____

Performance Review: **Lyonnaise Potatoes**

Name _____ **Date**_____

Core knowledge/skills: starch cookery, sautéing, knife skills, julienne, clarified butter, caramelization

Culinary Proficiency	Expectations	Instructor's Review
Professionalism: Demonstrate appropriate workplace hygiene and appearance.	Hair neat and restrained	
	Clean chef uniform and apron; nonslip, closed-toe shoes	
	No nail polish or jewelry	
Sanitation: Wash hands properly. Demonstrate safe food handling.	Display correct handwashing throughout production	
	Wash potatoes before parcooking	
	Clean and sanitize workstation before and after work	
Mise en Place: Set up workstation properly. Review lab recommended reading. Organized recipe method and sequence of work.	Prepare ingredients for assembly	
	Needed equipment available and ready	
	Set up blanching/shocking and breading stations before beginning work	
	Julienne onions neatly	
Cooking Technique: Demonstrate correct sauté technique.	Parcook potatoes properly, peel potatoes and uniformly slice	
	Cook onions and potatoes separately to correct doneness and both are caramelized	
	Cook potato until tender, not overcooked and falling apart nor hard and crunchy	
Product Evaluation: Present on a plain, white plate for observation. Taste finished product.	Onions and potatoes should be a rich caramelized brown color	
	Onions are soft, potatoes hold together but are not hard	
	Seasoning does not overpower the sweet taste from the onion, but balances and complements	

Additional Instructor's Comments

Lab Activity 32-1: **Sautéed Chicken Breasts with Tomatoes and Scallions**

Name _____ **Date**_____ **Period** _____

Group Members _____

This recipe is sautéed and finished in the same pan. Once the chicken is caramelized to golden brown on both sides, it is removed from the pan leaving behind a treasure of flavors. These highly condensed flavors are captured in the sauce by deglazing the pan. No flavor in the sauté pan is thrown away, rinsed out, or discarded. This technique is perhaps the most important and commonly used in all professional kitchens.

Objectives

After completing this lab, you will be able to

- execute sautéing method for poultry.
- implement mincing and concassé knife skills.
- execute a pan sauce by deglazing and reducing.

Mise en Place

1. Carefully read through the recipe before starting production. Adjust the yield as needed. Review how to convert recipe yields in text Chapter 15.

2. Review the section *Peeling, Seeding, and Dicing Tomatoes* in text Chapter 16, the discussion about reducing in text Chapter 23, and *Sautéing* in text Chapter 32.

3. Locate all ingredients and equipment needed. Prepare ingredients as required for assembly.

Sanitation and Safety Reminders

1. Clean and sanitize workstation before beginning to work.

2. Wash hands properly and as often as needed.

3. Thoroughly wash and trim vegetable ingredients prior to cutting.

4. Take appropriate steps to avoid cross-contamination of other ingredients by raw chicken.

Key Terms

Define the following terms used in this activity. Some may have been defined in previous chapters.

1. sauté _____

_____

2. deglazing _____

_____

3. dredging _____

_____

(Continued)

4. cross-contamination _____

_____

5. concassé _____

_____

Sautéed Chicken Breasts with Tomatoes and Scallions

Yield: 10 portions

Ingredients

10 ea.		chicken breasts, boneless, 6 oz. (170 g)
as needed		flour
to taste		salt and white pepper
2 fl. oz.	60 mL	olive oil
1 Tbsp.	15 mL	garlic, minced
8 oz.	225 g	tomato concassé
1 pt.	480 mL	chicken stock
¾ c.	180 mL	scallions, chopped
1 oz.	30 g	butter (optional)

Method

1. Dredge the chicken breasts in flour and season with salt and pepper.
2. Heat the oil in a sauté pan until it is sizzling hot.
3. Place the chicken breasts in the pan in a single layer (cook in two batches if necessary) and cook until they become an even brown color.
4. Turn the breasts and brown on the other side. Remove from the pan and finish cooking to 165°F (73.9°C) in the oven if necessary.
5. Add the garlic to the pan and sweat. Add tomatoes and chicken stock, and simmer. Reduce to evaporate excess liquid.
6. Add the scallions and butter, and simmer 2 minutes. Adjust seasoning with salt and pepper.
7. Serve chicken breasts coated with the sauce.

Chef's Journal

Write an evaluation of your lab performance. Would your finished product and performance meet the standards of a professional kitchen? Describe how your recipe turned out and what techniques and procedures you need to improve.

_____

_____

Performance Review: **Sautéed Chicken Breasts with Tomatoes and Scallions**

Name _____ Date_____

Core knowledge/skills: knife skills, concassé, dry-heat cooking method, sautéing, mincing, reducing, deglazing, pan sauce, dredging

Culinary Proficiency	Expectations	Instructor's Review
Professionalism: Demonstrate appropriate workplace hygiene and appearance.	Hair neat and restrained	
	Clean chef uniform and apron; nonslip, closed-toe shoes	
	No nail polish or jewelry	
Sanitation: Wash hands properly. Demonstrate safe food handling.	Display correct handwashing at beginning and throughout production	
	Clean and sanitize workstation before and after work	
	Use separate cleaned and sanitized knives and cutting boards for chicken and other ingredients	
Mise en Place: Set up workstation properly. Review recommended reading. Organized recipe method and sequence of work.	Prepare ingredients for assembly, adjust recipe yield as needed	
	Needed equipment available and ready	
	Cut vegetables neatly to uniform size	
	Season dredging flour well, shake excess flour from chicken	
Cooking Technique: Demonstrate correct sautéing technique. Demonstrate correct pan sauce technique.	Preheat pan and fat before adding chicken, do not overload pan with chicken	
	Brown chicken properly on both sides and cook to minimum internal temperature of 165°F (73.9°C), do not overcook	
	Reduce pan sauce to nappé consistency	
Product Evaluation: Present on a plain, white plate for observation. Taste finished product.	Chicken is appealing brown, sauce is nappé with interesting bits of tomatoes and scallions	
	Chicken is moist and easy to cut	

Additional Instructor's Comments

Lab Activity 32-2: **Grilled Beef Sirloin, Maître d'Hôtel**

Name _____ **Date** _____ **Period** _____

Group Members _____

Picture a perfectly grilled sirloin, hot off the grill with seasoned butter dripping down the sides. The key to achieving this dish is good grilling technique. The grill must be hot and the steak seasoned before it is placed on the grill.

Chef's Note: "Maître d'hôtel" refers to a butter that has been mixed with lemon juice and chopped parsley. It has been used for centuries as a quick, tasty sauce that coats many foods such as steak, asparagus, or pasta. Butter that has flavorings added to it is called a "compound butter." A compound butter is used as a sauce or as an addition to a sauce.

Objective

After completing this lab, you will be able to

* execute grilling method for meat.

Mise en Place

1. Carefully read through the recipe before starting production. Adjust the yield as needed. Review how to convert recipe yields in text Chapter 15.

2. Review the section *Grilling and Broiling* in text Chapter 32.

3. Locate all ingredients and equipment needed. Prepare ingredients as required.

Sanitation and Safety Reminders

1. Clean and sanitize workstation before beginning to work.

2. Wash hands properly and as often as needed.

3. Thoroughly wash parsley prior to chopping.

Key Term

Define the following term used in this activity. It may have been defined in previous chapters.

1. grilling _____

_____

(Continued)

Grilled Beef Sirloin, Maître d'Hôtel

Yield: 3½ lb. (1.6 kg)

Ingredients

1 lb.	450 g	butter, soft
2 Tbsp.	30 mL	parsley, chopped
2 Tbsp.	30 mL	lemon juice
to taste		salt and white pepper
3½ lb.	1.6 kg	beef sirloin, tri-tip
to taste		salt and black pepper
2 Tbsp.	30 mL	vegetable oil

Method

1. Combine the butter, parsley, lemon juice, salt, and white pepper, and mix well.
2. Form the butter into a log by rolling it in plastic wrap or waxed paper. Chill until butter is firm.
3. Season the sirloin with salt and black pepper and brush with oil.
4. Grill, searing well on all sides. Finish to desired doneness.
5. Slice the sirloin across the grain and serve each portion topped with a slice of the compound butter. Serve immediately.

Chef's Journal

Write an evaluation of your lab performance. Would your finished product and performance meet the standards of a professional kitchen? Describe how your recipe turned out and what techniques and procedures you need to improve.

_____
_____
_____
_____
_____
_____
_____
_____
_____
_____
_____

Performance Review: **Grilled Beef Sirloin, Maître d'Hôtel**

Name _____ **Date**_____

Core knowledge/skills: dry-heat cooking method, grilling, compound butter

Culinary Proficiency	Expectations	Instructor's Review
Professionalism: Demonstrate appropriate workplace hygiene and appearance.	Hair neat and restrained	
	Clean chef uniform and apron; nonslip, closed-toe shoes	
	No nail polish or jewelry	
Sanitation: Wash hands properly. Demonstrate safe food handling.	Display correct handwashing at beginning and throughout production	
	Clean and sanitize workstation before and after work	
	Clean grill with wire brush	
	Use separate cleaned and sanitized knives and cutting boards for beef and other ingredients	
Mise en Place: Set up workstation properly. Review recommended reading. Organized recipe method and sequence of work.	Prepare ingredients for assembly, adjust recipe yield as needed	
	Neatly chop parsley and mixed well with softened butter and lemon juice	
	Preheat grill, brush meat with oil or clarified butter	
	Needed equipment available and ready	
Cooking Technique: Demonstrate correct grilling technique.	Place meat on hot grill and allow grill marks to form before turning meat 90 degrees	
	Cook meat to desired doneness specified by instructor	
Product Evaluation: Present on a plain, white plate for observation. Taste finished product.	Steak is caramelized with crossed grill marks, butter is melting on top	
	Cut meat open to check for correct doneness as specified by instructor (well done, medium, or rare)	
	Butter flavor complements steak, does not overpower	

Additional Instructor's Comments

Lab Activity 32-3: Roast Cornish Hens with Pan Gravy

Name _____ **Date** _____ **Period** _____

Group Members _____

Cornish hens are small birds with a slight "wild game" flavor, but milder flavor than pheasant or duck. Cornish hens are typically roasted whole and the drippings used to make pan gravy. This recipe can be used for many types of poultry.

Objectives

After completing this lab, you will be able to

- execute roasting method for poultry.
- execute a pan gravy.

Mise en Place

1. Carefully read through the recipe before starting production. Adjust the yield as needed. Review how to convert recipe yields in text Chapter 15.

2. Review the sections *Mirepoix* in text Chapter 16, *Roux* in text Chapter 24, *Trussing* in text Chapter 31, and *Roasting* in text Chapter 32.

3. Locate all ingredients and equipment needed. Prepare ingredients as required for assembly.

Sanitation and Safety Reminders

1. Clean and sanitize workstation before beginning to work.

2. Wash hands properly and as often as needed.

3. Thoroughly wash vegetable ingredients prior to cutting.

4. Take appropriate steps to avoid cross-contamination of other ingredients by raw chicken.

Key Terms

Define the following terms used in this activity. Some may have been defined in previous chapters.

1. roasting _____

_____

2. gravy _____

_____

3. roux _____

_____

4. cross-contamination _____

_____

5. mirepoix _____

_____

(Continued)

6. giblets _____

_____

7. trussing _____

_____

Roast Cornish Hens with Pan Gravy

Yield: 10 portions

Ingredients

10 ea.		Cornish hens
to taste		salt and white pepper
as needed		clarified or melted butter
8 oz.	225 g	mirepoix, medium dice
3 oz.	85 g	blond roux
1 qt.	0.95 L	chicken stock

Method

1. Remove the giblets from the hens and reserve the necks. Season cavities with salt and pepper.
2. Truss the hens (optional), brush them with butter, and season the outsides.
3. Place the mirepoix and necks in the roasting pan, and place the hens on top.
4. Place the roasting pan in a preheated 375°F (190°C) oven. Roast for about 45 minutes or to 165°F (73.9°C). Test doneness by piercing the thickest part of the thigh. If juices run clear, the birds are done.
5. Remove the hens from the pan and hold at 135°F (57.2°C) or above.
6. Pour or skim any excessive grease from the roasting pan.
7. Add the stock to the pan to deglaze. Place the pan over a medium heat and simmer to dissolve the drippings.
8. Transfer liquid from the roasting pan to a saucepot. Stir in the roux and simmer for 15–20 minutes to extract flavor from the mirepoix and thicken the gravy.
9. Strain the gravy and adjust the seasoning.

Chef's Journal

Write an evaluation of your lab performance. Would your finished product and performance meet the standards of a professional kitchen? Describe how your recipe turned out and what techniques and procedures you need to improve.

_____

_____

_____

Performance Review: **Roast Cornish Hens with Pan Gravy**

Name _____ **Date**_____

Core knowledge/skills: knife skills, mirepoix, dry-heat cooking method, roasting, trussing, blond roux, deglazing, pan gravy

Culinary Proficiency	Expectations	Instructor's Review
Professionalism: Demonstrate appropriate workplace hygiene and appearance.	Hair neat and restrained	
	Clean chef uniform and apron; nonslip, closed-toe shoes	
	No nail polish or jewelry	
Sanitation: Wash hands properly. Demonstrate safe food handling.	Display correct handwashing at beginning and throughout production	
	Clean and sanitize workstation before and after work	
	Use separate cleaned and sanitized knives and cutting boards for chicken and other ingredients	
Mise en Place: Set up workstation properly. Review recommended reading. Organized recipe method and sequence of work.	Prepare ingredients for assembly, adjust recipe yield as needed	
	Needed equipment available and ready	
	Cut mirepoix vegetables to uniform size and in proper ratios	
	Truss bird properly (optional)	
Cooking Technique: Demonstrate correct roasting technique. Demonstrated correct pan gravy technique.	Preheat oven properly	
	Cook bird to minimum internal temperature of 165°F (73.9°C)and juices run clear	
	Cook roux until straw colored	
	Strain pan gravy, thicken with roux to nappé consistency	
Product Evaluation: Present on a plain, white plate for observation. Taste finished product.	Hen is golden brown color, sauce is smooth with even texture	
	Hen is moist and easy to cut, sauce nappés the bird	
	Sauce is smooth and well seasoned with no raw flour taste	

Additional Instructor's Comments

Lab Activity 33-1: **Chicken and Dumplings**

Name _____ **Date** _____ **Period** _____

Group Members _____

This dish is a classic example of moist-heat cooking method. The dumpling is an ancient food that has been a part of the cuisine of many different cultures. Possibly the original purpose of dumplings was to serve as a thrifty way to extend a recipe. Over the centuries chefs have created their own more complex versions of this classic.

Objectives

After completing this lab, you will be able to

- execute a mirepoix.
- produce a sachet.
- execute simmering method for poultry.

Mise en Place

1. Carefully read through the recipe before starting production. Adjust the yield as needed. Review how to convert recipe yields in text Chapter 15.

2. Review the sections *Poultry Fabrication* in text Chapter 31, *Simmering* in text Chapter 33, *Mirepoix* in text Chapter 16, and *Herbs and Spices* in text Chapter 23.

3. Locate all ingredients and equipment needed. Prepare ingredients as required for assembly.

4. Set up cutting board properly. Select appropriate knife, sharpen as needed.

Sanitation and Safety Reminders

1. Clean and sanitize workstation before beginning to work.

2. Wash hands properly and as often as needed.

3. Thoroughly wash and trim vegetable ingredients prior to cutting.

4. Take appropriate steps to avoid cross-contamination of other ingredients by raw chicken.

Key Terms

Define the following terms used in this activity. Some may have been defined in previous chapters.

1. simmering _____

   _____

2. mirepoix _____

   _____

3. sachet _____

   _____

(Continued)

4. cross-contamination _____

_____

5. medium dice _____

_____

6. fork-tender _____

_____

7. fabrication _____

_____

Chef's Journal

Write an evaluation of your lab performance. Would your finished product and performance meet the standards of a professional kitchen? Describe how your recipe turned out and what techniques and procedures you need to improve.

_____

_____

_____

_____

_____

_____

_____

_____

_____

_____

_____

_____

_____

_____

_____

Chicken and Dumplings

Yield: 8 portions

Ingredients

1 ea.		stewing hen or fowl, 8-cut
as needed		cold water
2 Tbsp.	30 mL	salt
4 oz.	115 g	carrots, medium dice
4 oz.	115 g	celery, medium dice
8 oz.	225 g	onion, medium dice

Sachet:

2 ea.		bay leaves
2 tsp.	10 mL	dried thyme leaf
1 tsp.	5 mL	black peppercorn
to taste		salt
to taste		white pepper

Dumplings:

8 oz.	225 g	flour
2 tsp.	10 mL	baking powder
½ tsp.	2 mL	salt
8 fl. oz.	240 mL	milk
1 Tbsp.	15 mL	parsley, chopped

Method

1. Place the cut chicken in a large pot and cover with cold water and salt. Bring to a boil and skim any scum.
2. Add the carrots, celery, onions, and sachet. Lower heat and simmer until thighs are fork-tender and chicken reaches 165°F (73.9°C) or more.
3. Remove chicken from broth and hold at or above 135°F (57.2°C).
4. Remove sachet.
5. Adjust seasoning of broth with salt and white pepper.
6. Combine dry ingredients for the dumplings. Mix in milk to create a thick batter.

Chef's Note: *Dumplings can be seasoned to complement the dish. For example, additions to dumpling dough might include various cheeses, ham, bacon, or any of a number of different herbs.*

7. Drop spoonfuls of the dumpling batter into the simmering broth. Cover pot and simmer 15 minutes.
8. To serve, place portions of chicken in soup plates, garnish with dumplings, and ladle broth and vegetables over them.

Performance Review: **Chicken and Dumplings**

Name _____ **Date**_____

Core knowledge/skills: poultry fabrication, disjointed (eight-cut), moist-heat cooking method, simmering, fork-tender, sachet, mirepoix, knife skills, medium dice

Culinary Proficiency	Expectations	Instructor's Review
Professionalism: Demonstrate appropriate workplace hygiene and appearance.	Hair neat and restrained	
	Clean chef uniform and apron; nonslip, closed-toe shoes	
	No nail polish or jewelry	
Sanitation: Wash hands properly. Demonstrate safe food handling.	Display correct handwashing at beginning and throughout production	
	Clean and sanitize workstation before and after work	
	Use separate cleaned and sanitized knives and cutting boards for chicken and other ingredients	
Mise en Place: Set up workstation properly. Review recommended reading. Organized recipe method and sequence of work.	Prepare ingredients for assembly, adjust recipe yield as needed	
	Needed equipment available and ready	
	Produce neat, uniform vegetable cuts, prepare sachet	
	Disjoint (eight-cut) chicken properly	
Cooking Technique: Demonstrate correct simmering technique. Demonstrate proper method for determining doneness of chicken.	Cook chicken to a minimum internal temperature of 165°F (73.9°C) and until fork-tender	
	Cook dumplings through (for a minute or so after they rise to the top of the pot), but not falling apart	
Product Evaluation: Present on a plain, white soup plate for observation. Taste finished product.	Broth is golden brown and not excessively thick or cloudy	
	Chicken is fork-tender, dumplings are not raw in center nor chewy in texture	
	Correct balance of vegetables in broth for garnish	
	Dish is well seasoned	

Lab Activity 33-2: **Chicken Cacciatore**

Name _____ **Date** _____ **Period** _____

Group Members _____

Chicken Cacciatore is an example of a combination cooking method. This dish is believed to date back to the 1500s. Cacciatore means "hunter style" in Italian. One story behind this name describes a hunter returning home empty-handed. As a result, the hunter's wife must resort to preparing one of her chickens for dinner.

Objectives

After completing this lab, you will be able to

- implement dredging and searing.
- execute braising method for poultry.

Mise en Place

1. Carefully read through the recipe before starting production. Adjust the yield as needed. Review how to convert recipe yields in text Chapter 15.

2. Review the sections *Poultry Fabrication* in text Chapter 31 and *Braising* in text Chapter 33.

3. Locate all ingredients and equipment needed. Prepare ingredients as required for assembly.

4. Set up cutting board properly. Select appropriate knife, sharpen as needed.

Sanitation and Safety Reminders

1. Clean and sanitize workstation before beginning to work.

2. Wash hands properly and as often as needed.

3. Thoroughly wash and trim vegetable ingredients prior to cutting.

4. Take appropriate steps to avoid cross-contamination of other ingredients by raw chicken.

Key Terms

Define the following terms used in this activity. Some may have been defined in previous chapters.

1. braising _____

_____

2. simmering _____

_____

3. sweating _____

_____

4. fabrication _____

_____

(Continued)

5. medium dice _____

_____

6. dredging _____

_____

7. searing _____

_____

8. fork-tender _____

_____

9. mincing _____

_____

Chef's Journal

Write an evaluation of your lab performance. Would your finished product and performance meet the standards of a professional kitchen? Describe how your recipe turned out and what techniques and procedures you need to improve.

_____

_____

_____

_____

_____

_____

_____

_____

_____

_____

_____

_____

_____

_____

_____

Chicken Cacciatore

Yield: 8 portions

Ingredients

2 ea.		chickens (2½–3 lb. fryers), 8-cut
3 oz.	85 g	flour
to taste		salt and white pepper
2 fl. oz.	60 mL	olive oil
3 oz.	85 g	onion, medium dice
3 oz.	85 g	green peppers, medium dice
2 oz.	60 g	mushrooms, sliced
2 Tbsp.	30 mL	garlic, minced
1 qt.	0.95 L	tomato sauce
1 pt.	480 mL	chicken stock
½ tsp.	2 mL	oregano
½ tsp.	2 mL	thyme
2 Tbsp.	30 mL	parsley, chopped

Method

1. Preheat an oven to 350°F (176.7°C).
2. Season chicken pieces with salt and pepper. Dredge in flour.
3. Heat olive oil in a large pan or braiser. Brown the chicken pieces in batches searing on all sides.
4. Remove chicken pieces from the pan and hold at or above 135°F (57.2°C). Add onions, green peppers, and mushrooms to the pan and sweat them.
5. Add garlic and cook one minute more.
6. Deglaze with tomato sauce and stock. Add oregano and thyme.

Chef's Note: Fresh herbs should be introduced at the end of cooking because they quickly lose flavor and become bitter. Dry herbs can be added early in the cooking.

7. Return chicken to pan and bring to a simmer.
8. Cover pan and place in the oven. Braise in the oven for 1 hour until chicken is fork-tender. Chicken should reach 165°F (73.9°C) or higher.
9. Remove from oven and skim off any excess grease. Adjust seasoning, finish with chopped parsley, and serve.

Performance Review: **Chicken Cacciatore**

Name _____ Date_____

Core knowledge/skills: poultry fabrication, disjointed (eight-cut), combination cooking method, simmering, fork-tender, braising, dredging, knife skills, medium dice, searing

Culinary Proficiency	Expectations	Instructor's Review
Professionalism: Demonstrate appropriate workplace hygiene and appearance.	Hair neat and restrained	
	Clean chef uniform and apron; nonslip, closed-toe shoes	
	No nail polish or jewelry	
Sanitation: Wash hands properly. Demonstrate safe food handling.	Display correct handwashing at beginning and throughout production	
	Clean and sanitize workstation before and after work	
	Use separate cleaned and sanitized knives and cutting boards for chicken and other ingredients	
Mise en Place: Set up workstation properly. Review recommended reading. Organized recipe method and sequence of work.	Prepare ingredients for assembly	
	Needed equipment available and ready	
	Produce neat, uniform vegetable cuts	
	Disjoint (eight-cut) chicken properly, dredge lightly in flour	
	Adjust recipe yield as needed	
Cooking Technique: Demonstrate correct braising technique. Demonstrate proper method for determining doneness of chicken.	Brown chicken in small batches before braising, cook to fork-tender	
	Sweat green pepper, onion, and mushrooms; caramelize tomato sauce; add herbs at proper time	
	Skim excess grease sauce; reduce sauce as needed	
Product Evaluation: Present on a plain, white soup plate for observation. Taste finished product.	Color should be golden brown with rich caramelized colors, dish garnished with parsley	
	Cacciatore sauce is thick enough to bind together ingredients, without being too thick or lumpy	
	Chicken is fork-tender, vegetables are tender but not mushy	

Lab Activity 33-3: **Beef Stew**

Name _____ **Date** _____ **Period** _____

Group Members _____

This recipe demonstrates a combination cooking method because the beef is first sautéed (dry heat) and then simmered (moist heat). After a few hours of stewing, a slightly tougher cut of meat becomes perfectly tender as its flavors intensify and are captured in the liquid in which it simmers.

Objectives

After completing this lab, you will be able to

- produce a sachet.
- execute stewing method for meat.

Mise en Place

1. Carefully read through the recipe before starting production. Adjust the yield as needed. Review how to convert recipe yields in text Chapter 15.
2. Review the sections *Combination Methods* in text Chapter 18, *Stewing* in text Chapter 33, and *Herbs and Spices* in text Chapter 23.
3. Locate all ingredients and equipment needed. Prepare ingredients as required for assembly.

Sanitation and Safety Reminders

1. Clean and sanitize workstation before beginning to work.
2. Wash hands properly and as often as needed.
3. Thoroughly wash and trim vegetable ingredients prior to cutting.
4. Take appropriate steps to avoid cross-contamination of other ingredients by raw beef.

Key Terms

Define the following terms used in this activity. Some may have been defined in previous chapters.

1. sautéing _____

_____

2. simmering _____

_____

3. stewing _____

_____

4. deglazing _____

_____

(Continued)

5. sachet _____

_____

6. small dice _____

_____

7. medium dice _____

_____

8. large dice _____

_____

9. fork-tender _____

_____

Chef's Journal

Write an evaluation of your lab performance. Would your finished product and performance meet the standards of a professional kitchen? Describe how your recipe turned out and what techniques and procedures you need to improve.

_____

_____

_____

_____

_____

_____

_____

_____

_____

_____

_____

_____

_____

_____

_____

(Continued)

Beef Stew

Yield: 10 portions

Ingredients

4 lb.	1.8 kg	beef chuck, cut into 1 in. cubes
to taste		salt and pepper
2 fl. oz.	60 mL	vegetable oil
2 oz.	60 g	tomato purée
2 oz.	60 g	flour
1 qt.	0.95 L	brown beef stock
Sachet		
2 ea.		bay leaves
2 tsp.	10 mL	dried thyme leaf
1 tsp.	5 mL	black peppercorn
8 oz.	225 g	carrots, large dice
4 oz.	115 g	celery, ½ in. bias cut
4 oz.	115 g	onions, medium dice
1 lb.	450 g	potatoes, large dice
4 oz.	115 g	peas, frozen

Method

1. Season the beef with salt and pepper.
2. Heat the oil in a large pot and brown the beef in small batches, searing well on all sides.
3. Stir in the tomato purée and flour and cook for 2 minutes over a low heat to create a roux.
4. Deglaze with the brown stock. Add the sachet and bring to a simmer.
5. Simmer beef for 1½ hours or until fork-tender. Beef must reach an internal temperature of 145°F (62.8°C) or higher. Add liquid as needed to compensate for evaporation.
6. Add the carrots, onions, and celery and simmer for 20 minutes. Add the potatoes and simmer until the potatoes are tender.
7. Remove sachet.
8. Add the peas and return to a simmer. Add salt and pepper to taste.
9. Hold at or above 135°F (57.2°C) until service.

Performance Review: **Beef Stew**

Name _____ **Date**_____

Core knowledge/skills: combination cooking method, stewing, small dice, medium dice, large dice, sachet, deglazing, simmering, fork-tender, sautéing

Culinary Proficiency	Expectations	Instructor's Review
Professionalism: Demonstrate appropriate workplace hygiene and appearance.	Hair neat and restrained	
	Clean chef uniform and apron; nonslip, closed-toe shoes	
	No nail polish or jewelry	
Sanitation: Wash hands properly. Demonstrate safe food handling.	Display correct handwashing at beginning and throughout production	
	Clean and sanitize workstation before and after work	
	Use separate cleaned and sanitized knives and cutting boards for beef and other ingredients	
Mise en Place: Set up workstation properly. Review recommended reading. Organized recipe method and sequence of work.	Prepare ingredients for assembly	
	Needed equipment available and ready	
	Produce neat, uniform vegetable cuts, prepare sachet	
	Adjust recipe yield as needed	
Cooking Technique: Demonstrate correct stewing technique. Demonstrate proper method for determining doneness of beef.	Sauté beef to caramelize	
	Simmer beef at appropriate temperature to avoid burning or scorching until fork-tender	
	Add vegetables at appropriate intervals to avoid over- or undercooking	
Product Evaluation: Present on a plain, white soup plate for observation. Taste finished product.	Color should be deep rich brown	
	Meat should be fork-tender, neither tough nor falling apart; vegetables are tender but not mushy	
	Sauce is just thick enough to nappé the back of a spoon, complements all flavors and binds the stew together	

Lab Activity 33-4: **Veal Blanquette**

Name _____ **Date** _____ **Period** _____

Group Members _____

This recipe is a benchmark of great flavors and culinary techniques. *Veal Blanquette* is often served over a puff pastry or rice to complete the meal. To achieve the trademark white color of this dish, the veal is first blanched and drained. Next, the meat is simmered and then finished with cream.

Objectives

After completing this lab, you will be able to

- apply blanching technique to meat.
- execute the simmering method.
- implement a white roux for thickening.

Mise en Place

1. Carefully read through the recipe before starting production. Adjust the yield as needed. Review how to convert recipe yields in text Chapter 15.

2. Review the discussion about blanching in text Chapter 23, and the sections *Simmering* in text Chapter 33 and *Roux* in text Chapter 24.

3. Locate all ingredients and equipment needed. Prepare ingredients as required for assembly.

Sanitation and Safety Reminders

1. Clean and sanitize workstation before beginning to work.

2. Wash hands properly and as often as needed.

3. Take appropriate steps to avoid cross-contamination of other ingredients by raw veal.

Key Terms

Define the following terms used in this activity. Some may have been defined in previous chapters.

1. blanching _____

_____

2. simmering _____

_____

3. onion piqué _____

_____

4. roux _____

_____

(Continued)

5. bouquet garni _____

_____

6. fork-tender _____

_____

Veal Blanquette

Yield: 10 portions

Ingredients

4½ lb.	2 kg	veal breast or shoulder, cut in 1 in. cubes
as needed		cold water
1 qt.	0.95 L	white stock (veal or chicken)
1 ea.		onion piqué
1 ea.		bouquet garni
3 oz.	85 g	white roux
8 fl. oz.	240 mL	cream
1 Tbsp.	15 mL	lemon juice
to taste		salt and white pepper

Method

1. Place the veal in a large pot and cover with cold water. Bring to a boil, drain, and rinse the meat.
2. Place the meat in a large pot with the white stock, onion piqué, and bouquet garni.
3. Simmer veal for 1½ hours.
4. Stir in roux and simmer for 20–30 minutes.
5. Finish by adding cream and lemon juice. Adjust seasoning with salt and pepper. Serve.

Chef's Note: Veal Blanquette is often garnished with pearl onions and mushrooms. If desired, add 12 oz. (340 g) sautéed quartered mushrooms and 6 oz. (170 g) blanched pearl onions.

Chef's Journal

Write an evaluation of your lab performance. Would your finished product and performance meet the standards of a professional kitchen? Describe how your recipe turned out and what techniques and procedures you need to improve.

_____

_____

_____

_____

Performance Review: **Veal Blanquette**

Name _____ **Date**_____

Core knowledge/skills: blanching, moist-heat cooking method, simmering, onion piqué, bouquet garni, white roux, knife skills

Culinary Proficiency	Expectations	Instructor's Review
Professionalism: Demonstrate appropriate workplace hygiene and appearance.	Hair neat and restrained	
	Clean chef uniform and apron; nonslip, closed-toe shoes	
	No nail polish or jewelry	
Sanitation: Wash hands properly. Demonstrate safe food handling.	Display correct handwashing at beginning and throughout production	
	Clean and sanitize workstation before and after work	
Mise en Place: Set up workstation properly. Review recommended reading. Organized recipe method and sequence of work.	Prepare ingredients for assembly	
	Adjust recipe yield as needed	
	Needed equipment available and ready	
	Prepare onion piqué correctly	
Cooking Technique: Demonstrate correct simmering technique. Demonstrate correct doneness of veal.	Blanch veal correctly, simmered until fork-tender	
	Prepare white roux correctly and work into the liquid without lumps; correct consistency of sauce as needed	
Product Evaluation: Present on a plain, white plate for observation. Taste finished product.	Color is creamy white, onion piqué is removed	
	Sauce is nappé consistency and smooth	
	Veal is moist and easy to cut, not overcooked and tough	

Additional Instructor's Comments

Lab Activity 35-1: **Grilled Mahi Mahi Fillet with Pineapple Relish**

Name _____ **Date** _____ **Period** _____

Group Members _____

Grilling fish well takes practice. Fish is more delicate than meat and will burn and fall apart more easily. The grill should be hot before you begin to cook. Always place the presentation side of the fish down first. The presentation side is the side that will be facing up when it is presented to the customer. This applies to cuts of meat as well—sear the best side first.

Objective

After completing this lab, you will be able to

- execute grilling method for fish.

Mise en Place

1. Carefully read through the recipe before starting production. Adjust the yield as needed. Review how to convert recipe yields in text Chapter 15.

2. Review the sections *Grilling* and *Determining Doneness* in text Chapter 35.

3. Locate all ingredients and equipment needed. Prepare ingredients as required for assembly.

Sanitation and Safety Reminders

1. Clean and sanitize workstation before beginning to work.

2. Wash hands properly and as often as needed.

3. Thoroughly wash and trim fresh fruit and vegetable ingredients prior to cutting.

4. Take appropriate steps to avoid cross-contamination of other ingredients by raw fish.

Key Terms

Define the following terms used in this activity. Some may have been defined in previous chapters.

1. grill _____

_____

2. grilling _____

_____

3. brunoise _____

_____

4. relish _____

_____

(Continued)

Grilled Mahi Mahi Fillet with Pineapple Relish

Yield: 10 portions

Ingredients

3 c.	720 mL	pineapple, diced
3 oz.	85 g	red onion, brunoise
2 fl. oz.	60 mL	lime juice
2 Tbsp.	30 mL	parsley, chopped
to taste		salt and white pepper
10 ea.		mahi mahi fillets, 5–6 oz. (140–170 g) each
2 fl. oz.	60 mL	vegetable oil
to taste		salt and white pepper

Method

1. Mix the pineapple, onion, lime juice, parsley, salt, and pepper; and allow it to marinate 30 minutes.
2. Preheat a grill.
3. Brush the mahi mahi fillets with oil and season with salt and pepper.
4. Grill the fillets first over high heat to create grill marks. Continue cooking over moderate heat until an internal temperature of 145°F (63°C) is reached. Flesh should flake and no longer be translucent.

Chef's Note: The key to grilling is not to move the food item too soon after it is placed on the grill. Allow the proteins to start to coagulate and the natural sugars to begin to caramelize. After a few minutes on the grill, it will be easier to turn.

5. Plate the fillets and serve accompanied by the relish.

Chef's Journal

Write an evaluation of your lab performance. Would your finished product and performance meet the standards of a professional kitchen? Describe how your recipe turned out and what techniques and procedures you need to improve.

_____

_____

_____

_____

_____

Performance Review: **Grilled Mahi Mahi Fillet with Pineapple Relish**

Name _____ **Date**_____

Core knowledge/skills: dry-heat cooking method, grilling, brunoise

Culinary Proficiency	Expectations	Instructor's Review
Professionalism: Demonstrate appropriate workplace hygiene and appearance.	Hair neat and restrained	
	Clean chef uniform and apron; nonslip, closed-toe shoes	
	No nail polish or jewelry	
Sanitation: Wash hands properly. Demonstrate safe food handling.	Display correct handwashing at beginning and throughout production	
	Clean and sanitize workstation before and after work	
	Use separate cleaned and sanitized knives and cutting boards for fish and other ingredients	
Mise en Place: Set up workstation properly. Review recommended reading. Organized recipe method and sequence of work.	Prepare ingredients for assembly	
	Adjust recipe yield as needed	
	Needed equipment available and ready	
	Produce neat, uniform fruit and vegetable cuts yielding an attractive relish	
Cooking Technique: Demonstrate correct grilling technique and doneness of fish.	Grill fish until opaque and flaky with attractive grill marks	
	Prevent fish from sticking to the grill or falling apart during grilling	
Product Evaluation: Present on a plain, white plate for observation. Taste finished product.	Fish has golden-brown grill marks and is still intact	
	Mahi is moist and easy to cut, relish is well marinated with uniform cuts	

Additional Instructor's Comments

Lab Activity 35-2: **Baked Cod Florentine**

Name _____ **Date** _____ **Period** _____

Group Members _____

The term *florentine* means "in the style of Florence, Italy." This term is used to describe recipes that are served with spinach. *Baked Cod Florentine* is a cod fillet nestled on a bed of sautéed spinach, coated with Mornay sauce, and then baked.

Objectives

After completing this lab, you will be able to

- execute a derivative sauce (Mornay).
- execute baking method for fish.

Mise en Place

1. Carefully read through the recipe before starting production. Adjust the yield as needed. Review how to convert recipe yields in text Chapter 15.

2. Review the sections *Basic Knife Cuts* in text Chapter 12, *Preparing Salad Greens* in text Chapter 19, *White Sauce* in text Chapter 24, and *Determining Doneness* in text Chapter 35.

3. Locate all ingredients and equipment needed. Prepare ingredients as required for assembly.

Sanitation and Safety Reminders

1. Clean and sanitize workstation before beginning to work.

2. Wash hands properly and as often as needed.

3. Thoroughly wash and trim fresh vegetable ingredients prior to cutting.

4. Take appropriate steps to avoid cross-contamination of other ingredients by raw fish.

Key Terms

Define the following terms used in this activity. Some may have been defined in previous chapters.

1. baking _____

   _____

2. derivative sauce _____

   _____

3. brunoise _____

   _____

4. sautéing _____

   _____

(Continued)

5. sweating _____

_____

6. salamander _____

_____

Baked Cod Florentine

Yield: 10 portions

Ingredients

2 lb.	900 g	spinach, fresh or frozen
2 oz.	60 g	shallots, brunoise
4 oz.	115 g	butter
to taste		salt and white pepper
pinch		nutmeg
10 ea.		cod fillet, 5 oz. (140 g)
24 fl. oz.	720 mL	Mornay sauce (recipe 21.2)
¼ c.	60 mL	bread crumbs

Method

1. If you are using fresh spinach, remove the stems. Blanch and shock the spinach leaves and squeeze out the excess moisture. If you are using frozen spinach, defrost it and squeeze out the excess moisture.
2. Heat the butter in a large sauteuse. Sweat the shallots. Add the spinach and sauté. Cook until excess moisture is evaporated. Season with salt, pepper, and nutmeg.
3. Place the spinach in an even layer on the bottom of a hotel pan or baking dish.
4. Place the cod fillets on top of the spinach. Season with salt and white pepper.
5. Coat each fillet with ¼ c. (60 mL) Mornay sauce. Sprinkle pan with bread crumbs.
6. Place in a 350°F (176.7°C) oven and bake for about 20 minutes or until fish reaches an internal temperature of 145°F (63°C). The fish should be flaky and no longer translucent.
7. Brown under broiler or salamander if desired and serve.

Chef's Journal

Write an evaluation of your lab performance. Would your finished product and performance meet the standards of a professional kitchen? Describe how your recipe turned out and what techniques and procedures you need to improve.

_____

_____

Performance Review: **Baked Cod Florentine**

Name _____ **Date**_____

Core knowledge/skills: knife skills, derivative sauce, dry-heat cooking method, baking, sweating, sautéing, blanching, shocking

Culinary Proficiency	Expectations	Instructor's Review
Professionalism: Demonstrate appropriate workplace hygiene and appearance.	Hair neat and restrained	
	Clean chef uniform and apron; nonslip, closed-toe shoes	
	No nail polish or jewelry	
Sanitation: Wash hands properly. Demonstrate safe food handling.	Display correct handwashing at beginning and throughout production	
	Clean and sanitize workstation before and after work	
	Use separate cleaned and sanitized knives and cutting boards for fish and other ingredients	
Mise en Place: Set up workstation properly. Review recommended reading. Organized recipe method and sequence of work.	Prepare ingredients for assembly	
	Adjust recipe yield as needed	
	Needed equipment available and ready	
Cooking Technique: Demonstrate correct baking technique for fish. Demonstrate correct doneness of fish.	Sauté spinach lightly , not overcooked	
	Produce smooth Mornay sauce with nappé consistency	
	Cook fish until opaque and flaky	
Product Evaluation: Present on a plain, white plate for observation. Taste finished product.	Mornay sauce is very light golden-brown color, spinach is bright green	
	Sauce has smooth, even, nappé texture; cod is opaque, flaky, moist, and easy to cut	

Additional Instructor's Comments

Lab Activity 35-3: **Poached Salmon à la Nage**

Name _____ **Date** _____ **Period** _____

Group Members _____

À la nage is a French phrase that means "to swim." In this recipe, the salmon is "swimming" in the poaching liquid. The poaching liquid used in this recipe is court bouillon and becomes the finished liquid with which the poached salmon is served.

Objectives

After completing this lab, you will be able to

- produce a court bouillon for poaching liquid.
- execute poaching method for fish.

Mise en Place

1. Carefully read through the recipe before starting production. Adjust the yield as needed. Review how to convert recipe yields in text Chapter 15.
2. Review the sections *Poaching* in text Chapter 18 and *Determining Doneness* and *Moist-Heat Methods* in text Chapter 35.
3. Locate all ingredients and equipment needed. Prepare ingredients as required for assembly.

Sanitation and Safety Reminders

1. Clean and sanitize workstation before beginning to work.
2. Wash hands properly and as often as needed.
3. Thoroughly wash and trim fresh vegetable ingredients prior to cutting.
4. Take appropriate steps to avoid cross-contamination of other ingredients by raw fish.

Key Terms

Define the following terms used in this activity. Some may have been defined in previous chapters.

1. poaching _____

   _____

2. court bouillon _____

   _____

3. mirepoix _____

   _____

4. sachet _____

   _____

(Continued)

Poached Salmon à la Nage

Yield: 10 portions

Ingredients

Court Bouillon (recipe 32.5):

1 gal.	3.8 L	water
8 fl. oz.	240 mL	vinegar
2 oz.	60 g	salt
2 lb.	0.9 kg	mirepoix, thinly sliced

Sachet

2 ea.		bay leaves
2 tsp.	10 mL	dried thyme
2 tsp.	10 mL	parsley stems
1 tsp.	5 mL	black peppercorns

Salmon:

10 ea.		salmon fillets, skinless, 5 oz. (140 g)
4 oz.	115 g	butter
2 Tbsp.	30 mL	parsley, chopped

Method

Court Bouillon:

1. Combine all ingredients
2. Simmer 1 hour.
3. Strain before using as a poaching liquid.

Salmon:

4. Reserve about 8 oz. (225 g) of the vegetables strained from the court bouillon.
5. Preheat an oven to 350°F (176.7°C).
6. Place the salmon fillets in a sautoir and add enough court bouillon to nearly cover the fish.
7. Place the pan on a burner and bring to a simmer.
8. Cover fish with buttered parchment paper. Place the pan in the oven for 10 minutes or until it reaches an internal temperature of 145°F (63°C).
9. Remove the fish from the pan, cover, and keep warm.
10. Put 1 qt. (0.95 L) of the poaching liquid in saucepot. Add the reserved vegetables and bring to a simmer.
11. Whisk in the remaining whole butter and add the chopped parsley.
12. Place the salmon in a soup plate, ladle some of the poaching liquid and vegetables over the top, and serve.

(Continued)

Chef's Journal

Write an evaluation of your lab performance. Would your finished product and performance meet the standards of a professional kitchen? Describe how your recipe turned out and what techniques and procedures you need to improve.

_____

_____

_____

_____

_____

_____

_____

_____

_____

_____

_____

_____

_____

Performance Review: **Poached Salmon à la Nage**

Name _____ **Date**_____

Core knowledge/skills: moist-heat cooking method, poaching, shallow poaching, court bouillon, mirepoix, sachet

Culinary Proficiency	Expectations	Instructor's Review
Professionalism: Demonstrate appropriate workplace hygiene and appearance.	Hair neat and restrained	
	Clean chef uniform and apron; nonslip, closed-toe shoes	
	No nail polish or jewelry	
Sanitation: Wash hands properly. Demonstrate safe food handling.	Display correct handwashing at beginning and throughout production	
	Clean and sanitize workstation before and after work	
	Use separate cleaned and sanitized knives and cutting boards for fish and other ingredients	
Mise en Place: Set up workstation properly. Review recommended reading. Organized recipe method and sequence of work.	Prepare ingredients for assembly	
	Adjust recipe yield as needed	
	Needed equipment available and ready	
	Cut small, uniform mirepoix due to short cooking time	
Cooking Technique: Demonstrate correct poaching technique and doneness of fish.	Produce aromatic court bouillon	
	Use shallow-poaching technique	
	Poach fish until flaky and opaque, broth is clear and not thick	
Product Evaluation: Present on a plain, white soup plate for observation. Taste finished product.	Salmon is light pink, with no caramelized color	
	Fish is moist and easy to cut	
	Broth is slightly rich in taste from butter, has bright green flecks from the parsley and bits of vegetables	
	Salmon has absorbed the flavors from the court bouillon	

Lab Activity 35-4: **Steamed Mussels**

Name _____ **Date** _____ **Period** _____

Group Members _____

In France, steamed mussels can be found on café menus for breakfast, lunch, and dinner. The mussels are often served with a piece of crusty bread, which is used to soak up the rich flavored broth.

Objectives

After completing this lab, you will be able to

- check the quality of fresh mussels.
- execute steaming method for shellfish.

Mise en Place

1. Carefully read through the recipe before starting production. Adjust the yield as needed. Review how to convert recipe yields in text Chapter 15.

2. Review the sections Judging the *Quality of Fresh Shellfish* in text Chapter 34 and *Cleaning Mussels and Steaming* in text Chapter 35.

3. Locate all ingredients and equipment needed. Prepare ingredients as required for assembly.

Sanitation and Safety Reminders

1. Clean and sanitize workstation before beginning to work.

2. Wash hands properly and as often as needed.

3. Thoroughly wash and trim fresh vegetable ingredients prior to cutting.

4. Discard dead mussels and clean those that remain. Ensure seafood tags are filed.

5. Take appropriate steps to avoid cross-contamination of other ingredients by raw fish.

Key Terms

Define the following terms used in this activity. Some may have been defined in previous chapters.

1. steaming _____

_____

2. shellfish _____

_____

3. bivalve _____

_____

4. brunoise _____

_____

(Continued)

Steamed Mussels

Yield: 10 portions

Ingredients

3½ lb.	1.6 kg	mussels
4 oz.	115 g	onion, brunoise
3 Tbsp.	45 mL	garlic, minced
8 fl. oz.	240 mL	water
2 oz.	60 g	butter
1 Tbsp.	15 mL	parsley, chopped

Method

1. Wash mussels in cold water and discard any that are open. Remove any beard or barnacles from the mussels. Place the mussels, onions, garlic, and liquid in a pot with a tight-fitting lid.

Chef's Note: This recipe can also be prepared using littleneck or steamer clams.

2. Place the pot over high heat and cook for 3–4 minutes.
3. Mussels are done when most of the shells have opened. Discard any that have not opened.
4. Place the mussels in serving bowls and hold at or above 135°F (57.2°C).
5. Place the cooking liquid on the stove and bring to a boil. Whisk in the butter and parsley.
6. Ladle the liquid over the mussels and serve.

Chef's Journal

Write an evaluation of your lab performance. Would your finished product and performance meet the standards of a professional kitchen? Describe how your recipe turned out and what techniques and procedures you need to improve.

_____

_____

_____

_____

_____

_____

_____

_____

Performance Review: **Steamed Mussels**

Name _____ Date_____

Core knowledge/skills: shellfish preparation, steaming, bivalves, debearding, knife skills

Culinary Proficiency	Expectations	Instructor's Review
Professionalism: Demonstrate appropriate workplace hygiene and appearance.	Hair neat and restrained	
	Clean chef uniform and apron; nonslip, closed-toe shoes	
	No nail polish or jewelry	
Sanitation: Wash hands properly. Demonstrate safe food handling.	Display correct handwashing at beginning and throughout production	
	Clean and sanitize workstation before and after work	
	Use separate cleaned and sanitized knives and cutting boards for fish and other ingredients	
	File seafood tags	
Mise en Place: Set up workstation properly. Review recommended reading. Organized recipe method and sequence of work.	Prepare ingredients for assembly	
	Adjust recipe yield as needed	
	Needed equipment available and ready	
	Inspect and select only raw mussels with closed shells, remove beard fibers and barnacles	
Cooking Technique: Demonstrate correct steaming technique and correct doneness of mussels.	Cook mussels just long enough for most of the shells to open; discard unopened, cracked, or broken shells	
	Reduce cooking liquid if needed, whisk in butter and parsley	
Product Evaluation: Present on a plain, white soup plate for observation. Taste finished product.	Mussels are firm and plump but not tough, and retain a bright fresh color	
	Mussels are left in shell and served with pan sauce	
	Pan sauce is smooth and rich in flavor	

Additional Instructor's Comments

Lab Activity 36-1: **Hamburger**

Name _____ **Date** _____ **Period** _____

Group Members _____

Considered by many to be American food, the hamburger is the universal symbol of a quick, convenient, tasty meal on-the-go. The key to a great burger is a perfect cooking technique and quality ground beef. The fat content in your ground beef is an important consideration when selecting meat for your hamburger recipe. For example, ground beef that is labeled 80/20 means that it is 80 percent lean meat and 20 percent fat.

Objectives

After completing this lab, you will be able to

- execute griddling method.
- produce a sandwich with a hot filling.

Mise en Place

1. Carefully read through the recipe before starting production. Adjust the yield as needed. Review how to convert recipe yields in text Chapter 15.
2. Review the sections Sandwiches with *Hot Fillings* in text Chapter 36.
3. Locate all ingredients and equipment needed. Prepare ingredients as required.

Sanitation and Safety Reminders

1. Clean and sanitize workstation before beginning to work.
2. Wash hands properly and as often as needed.
3. Thoroughly wash and trim vegetable ingredients. Take appropriate steps to avoid cross-contamination of other ingredients by raw beef.
4. Cook hamburger to appropriate internal temperatures according to local health code. Review the section *Cooking* in text Chapter 8.
5. Wear disposable gloves when handling ready-to-eat ingredients.

Key Terms

Define the following terms used in this activity. Some may have been defined in previous chapters.

1. griddle _____
   _____

2. sandwich _____
   _____

3. condiments _____
   _____

(Continued)

Hamburger

Yield: 10 hamburgers

Ingredients

2½ lb.	1.14 kg	ground beef, 80/20 or 90/10
1 tsp.	5 mL	salt
½ tsp.	2 mL	black pepper
10 ea.		hamburger buns

possible condiments:

tomato slices

thinly sliced onion

ketchup

mustard

lettuce

pickle slices or pickle relish

sautéed onions

Method

1. Mix ground beef with salt and pepper.

Chef's Note: Other flavors can be added to the ground meat such as diced onions, garlic, or other herbs and spices.

2. Form into 4 oz. patties approximately 1 in. thick.
3. Sauté on a griddle. When nicely browned on one side, turn over.
4. Continue cooking until the patty has cooked to an internal temperature of 155°F (68.3°C).
5. Serve the hamburger on the bottom half of a lightly warmed bun. Place the top of the bun on the hamburger and serve with condiments on the side.

Chef's Note: The hot, cooked hamburger can be topped with a sliced cheese such as American, Cheddar, Colby, or mozzarella.

Chef's Journal

Write an evaluation of your lab performance. Would your finished product and performance meet the standards of a professional kitchen? Describe how your recipe turned out and what techniques and procedures you need to improve.

_____

_____

_____

_____

Performance Review: **Hamburger**

Name _____ **Date**_____

Core knowledge/skills: measuring temperature, acidulation, dry-heat cooking method, mincing, knife skills, hot sandwich assembly

Culinary Proficiency	Expectations	Instructor's Review
Professionalism: Demonstrate appropriate workplace hygiene and appearance.	Hair neat and restrained	
	Clean chef uniform and apron; nonslip, closed-toe shoes	
	No nail polish or jewelry	
Sanitation: Wash hands properly. Take precautions to avoid cross-contamination. Demonstrate safe food handling.	Display correct handwashing at beginning and throughout production, disposable gloves used to handle ready-to-eat foods	
	Wash and trim produce before use	
	Use separate cleaned, sanitized knives and cutting boards for beef and other ingredients	
	Clean and sanitize workstation before and after work	
Mise en Place: Set up workstation properly. Review recommended reading. Organized recipe method and sequence of work.	Prepare ingredients for assembly, adjust recipe yield as needed	
	Shape patties evenly for consistent cooking	
	Needed equipment available and ready	
	Maintain orderly, efficient workflow and follow recipe	
Cooking Technique: Demonstrate correct griddle technique and doneness of ground beef.	Caramelize hamburger on both sides	
	Cook burger to internal temperature of 155°F (68.3°C), but not dry or overcooked	
Product Evaluation: Cut hamburger sandwich in half and display on a plate. Taste finished product.	Layers of ingredients should be roughly equal on each sandwich half	
	Hamburger has nice caramelized rich flavor, without other ingredients being too strong	
	Meat is hot, condiments are appropriate temperature	
	Bun is fresh and moist	

Additional Instructor's Comments

Lab Activity 36-2: **Grilled Chipotle Chicken Sandwich**

Name _____ **Date** _____ **Period** _____

Group Members _____

Grilled sandwiches have experienced increased popularity in recent years. This sandwich recipe features a rich grilled taste with a spicy mayo twist.

Objectives

After completing this lab, you will be able to

- execute grilling method for poultry.
- produce a sandwich with a hot filling.

Mise en Place

1. Carefully read through the recipe before starting production. Adjust the yield as needed. Review how to convert recipe yields in text Chapter 15.

2. Review the sections *Acidulating Fruits* in text Chapter 21, *Grilling and Broiling* in text Chapter 32, and *Sandwiches with Hot Fillings* in text Chapter 36.

3. Locate all ingredients and equipment needed. Prepare ingredients as required.

Sanitation and Safety Reminders

1. Clean and sanitize workstation before beginning to work.

2. Wash hands properly and as often as needed.

3. Thoroughly wash and trim vegetable ingredients. Take appropriate steps to avoid cross-contamination of other ingredients by raw chicken.

4. Make sure grilled chicken is cooked to appropriate internal temperatures according to local health code. Review the section *Cooking* in text Chapter 8.

5. Wear disposable gloves when handling ready-to-eat ingredients.

Key Terms

Define the following terms used in this activity. Some may have been defined in previous chapters.

1. cross-contamination _____

   _____

2. sandwich _____

   _____

3. grilling _____

   _____

4. acidulation _____

   _____

(Continued)

5. mincing _____

_____

Grilled Chipotle Chicken Sandwich

Yield: 10 sandwiches

Ingredients

1 c.	240 mL	mayonnaise
¼ c.	60 mL	chipotle in adobo sauce (canned), minced
¼ c.	60 mL	green onion, minced
3 Tbsp.	45 mL	lime juice
6 Tbsp.	90 mL	cilantro, chopped
10 ea.		chicken breasts, boneless, skinless, 6 oz. (170 g)
to taste		salt and white pepper
as needed		olive oil
10 ea.		hamburger buns
20 sl.		tomato slices
30 sl.		avocados, thinly sliced

Method

1. Mix the mayonnaise, chipotle, green onion, lime juice, and cilantro.

Chef's Note: Be sure to wear gloves when handling chiles as they can burn your skin. A suitable substitute is 2 Tbsp. (30 mL) chile powder.

2. Season the chicken breasts with salt and pepper. Lightly coat the chicken breasts with olive oil.

Chef's Note: Don't season with salt too far in advance. The salt pulls the juices out of the chicken and to the surface. This results in a dry product even if properly cooked.

3. Grill the chicken breasts over high heat until they reach an internal temperature of 165°F (74°C). This should take about 10 minutes.

4. Spread the chipotle mayonnaise on the bottom of the bun. Top with a chicken breast. Top the chicken breast with tomato and avocado slices. Finish by placing the top of the bun on each sandwich. Serve.

Chef's Journal

Write an evaluation of your lab performance. Would your finished product and performance meet the standards of a professional kitchen? Describe how your recipe turned out and what techniques and procedures you need to improve.

_____

_____

Performance Review: **Grilled Chipotle Chicken Sandwich**

Name _____ **Date**_____

Core knowledge/skills: measuring temperature, grilling, acidulation, dry-heat cooking method, mincing, knife skills, hot sandwich assembly

Culinary Proficiency	Expectations	Instructor's Review
Professionalism: Demonstrate appropriate workplace hygiene and appearance.	Hair neat and restrained	
	Clean chef uniform and apron; nonslip, closed-toe shoes	
	No nail polish or jewelry	
Sanitation: Wash hands properly. Take precautions to avoid cross-contamination. Demonstrate safe food handling.	Display correct handwashing throughout production, disposable gloves used to handle ready-to-eat foods	
	Wash and trim produce before use	
	Use separate cleaned, sanitized knives and cutting boards for chicken and other ingredients	
	Clean and sanitize workstation before and after work	
Mise en Place: Set up workstation properly. Review recommended reading. Organized recipe method and sequence of work.	Prepare ingredients for assembly, adjust recipe yield as needed	
	Needed equipment available and ready	
	Preserve avocado slices' appealing color; finely mince chipotles and green onions	
	Maintain orderly, efficient workflow, follow recipe	
Cooking Technique: Demonstrate correct grilling technique and doneness of chicken.	Cook chicken to minimum internal temperature of 165°F (73.9°C) with appealing grill marks	
	Produce moist, tender chicken with good flavor	
Product Evaluation: Cut sandwich in half and display on a plate. Taste finished product.	Layers of ingredients are evenly distributed over both halves	
	Chicken is hot and has a caramelized, rich flavor	
	Chipotle is not overpowering	
	Tomatoes and avocado are cold, avocado is an attractive green	
	Bun is fresh and moist	

Additional Instructor's Comments

Lab Activity 36-3: **Monte Cristo**

Name _____ **Date** _____ **Period** _____

Group Members _____

Though no one is certain of the origins of the Monte Cristo sandwich, it is believed to be a variation of a popular French sandwich called *croque monsieur*. When prepared properly, this unique sandwich is crisp on the outside and soft on the inside.

Objectives

After completing this lab, you will be able to

- execute sauté method for a hot sandwich.
- produce a whole cooked sandwich.

Mise en Place

1. Carefully read through the recipe before starting production. Adjust the yield as needed. Review how to convert recipe yields in text Chapter 15.
2. Review the sections *Sautéing* in text Chapter 18 and *Sautéed or Griddled Whole Cooked Sandwiches* in text Chapter 36.
3. Locate all ingredients and equipment needed. Prepare ingredients as required.
4. Prepare clarified butter if necessary. Review the section *Clarified Butter* in text Chapter 16.

Sanitation and Safety Reminders

1. Clean and sanitize workstation before beginning to work.
2. Wash hands properly and as often as needed.
3. Inspect eggs and discard any broken or cracked eggs. Store egg mixture on ice during this activity.

Key Terms

Define the following terms used in this activity. Some may have been defined in previous chapters.

1. sauté _____

_____

2. sandwich _____

_____

3. clarified butter _____

_____

4. griddle _____

_____

(Continued)

Monte Cristo

Yield: 10 portions

Ingredients

20 sl.		white bread
20 oz.	560 g	cooked turkey breast, thinly sliced
12 oz.	340 g	ham, thinly sliced
12 oz.	340 g	Swiss cheese, sliced
4 ea.		eggs, beaten
12 fl. oz.	360 mL	milk
as needed		clarified butter
as needed		strawberry jam

Method

1. Lay out 10 slices of bread on a work surface. Put a slice of cheese on each piece of bread. Reserve half of the cheese.
2. Top the cheese with 1¼ oz. (35 g) of ham and 2 oz. (55 g) of turkey. Top with remaining cheese and then the remaining bread slice.
3. Mix the eggs and milk together until homogenous.
4. Dip the prepared sandwiches briefly in the egg and milk mixture.
5. Immediately cook the sandwiches on a well-greased (preferably with clarified butter) griddle or sauté pan.

Chef's Note: Traditionally, the Monte Cristo is a deep-fried sandwich, but it is easier to prepare as a griddled or sautéed sandwich.

6. Once the first side is browned, turn the sandwich over and continue cooking. Sandwich should reach an internal temperature of 145°F (63°C).
7. Hold at or above 135°F (57.2°C) until service. It is traditional to serve a side of strawberry jam with the Monte Cristo.

Recipe courtesy of Chef Mike Artlip CEC, CCE

Chef's Journal

Write an evaluation of your lab performance. Would your finished product and performance meet the standards of a professional kitchen? Describe how your recipe turned out and what techniques and procedures you need to improve.

_____

_____

_____

_____

_____

Performance Review: **Monte Cristo**

Name _____ **Date** _____

Core knowledge/skills: dry-heat cooking method, sautéing, clarified butter, whole cooked sandwich assembly

Culinary Proficiency	Expectations	Instructor's Review
Professionalism: Demonstrate appropriate workplace hygiene and appearance.	Hair neat and restrained	
	Clean chef uniform and apron; nonslip, closed-toe shoes	
	No nail polish or jewelry	
Sanitation: Wash hands properly. Take precautions to avoid cross-contamination. Demonstrate safe food handling.	Display correct handwashing throughout production, disposable gloves used to handle ready-to-eat foods	
	Hold egg mixture on ice or stored at or below 41°F (5°C)	
	Clean and sanitize workstation before and after work	
Mise en Place: Set up workstation properly. Review recommended reading. Organized recipe method and sequence of work.	Prepare ingredients for assembly, adjust recipe yield as needed	
	Produce clarified butter containing little or no milk solids or water	
	Needed equipment available and ready	
	Maintain orderly, efficient workflow, follow recipe	
Cooking Technique: Demonstrate correct sauté technique and doneness of egg product.	Preheat sauté pan or griddle and fat before cooking	
	Caramelize both sides of sandwich	
	Cook sandwich to internal temperature of 145°F (63°C) or higher	
Product Evaluation: Cut sandwich in half and display on a plate. Taste finished product.	Layers of ingredients are evenly distributed over both halves, served with strawberry jam	
	Sandwich is warm and crispy on the outside, soft and melted on the inside	
	Egg has a light caramelized flavor	

Additional Instructor's Comments

Lab Activity 36-4: **Indian-Style Meatballs with Raita Appetizer**

Name _____ **Date** _____ **Period** _____

Group Members _____

Meatballs are a popular appetizer that is easy to make and serve. This recipe employs spices commonly used in Indian cuisine for a new take on meatball appetizers. The raita is used as a dip for the meatball.

Objectives

After completing this lab, you will be able to

- execute fine dice and mince.
- apply uniform, accurate portioning.

Mise en Place

1. Carefully read through the recipe before starting production. Adjust the yield as needed. Review how to convert recipe yields in text Chapter 15.
2. Review the sections *Peeling an Onion, Dicing Onions* and *Peeling and Mincing Garlic* in text Chapter 16.
3. Locate all ingredients and equipment needed. Prepare ingredients as required.

Sanitation and Safety Reminders

1. Clean and sanitize workstation before beginning to work.
2. Wash hands properly and as often as needed.
3. Inspect eggs and discard any broken or cracked eggs.

Key Terms

Define the following terms used in this activity. Some may have been defined in previous chapters.

1. mince _____

    _____

2. dice _____

    _____

3. sheet pan _____

    _____

(Continued)

Indian-Style Meatballs with Raita Appetizer

Yield: 30 ½-oz. meatballs

Ingredients

Meatballs:

1 lb.	450 g	ground beef
1 ea.		egg
½ oz.	15 g	breadcrumbs
1½ tsp.	8 mL	ginger, fine mince
3 oz.	85 g	onion, small dice
2 ea.		garlic cloves, fine mince
¼ tsp.	1 mL	whole fennel seed
1 tsp.	5 mL	turmeric
¼ tsp.	1 mL	cayenne pepper
¼ tsp.	1 mL	ground cumin
1 tsp.	5 mL	garam masala or curry powder
1¼ tsp.	6 mL	salt
¼ tsp.	1 mL	pepper
20 oz.	560 g	pineapple, canned, diced, drained

Raita:

8 oz.	225 g	Greek yogurt, nonfat, plain
2 tsp.	10 mL	lemon juice
2½ oz.	70 g	cucumber, fine dice
¼ tsp.	1 mL	ground cumin

Method

1. Preheat oven to 350°F (177°C).
2. Combine all meatball ingredients except pineapple in a large bowl and mix well.
3. Use a #40 scoop to portion meat mixture and roll to form small meatballs
4. Place meatballs on sheet pan prepared with nonstick cooking spray.
5. Place in oven and bake for 15 minutes or until they reach an internal temperature of 155°F (71°C) or higher.
6. Use a frill pick to skewer a piece of pineapple to each meatball.
7. Combine raita ingredients and mix well.
8. Serve meatball skewers with raita.

(Continued)

Chef's Journal

Write an evaluation of your lab performance. Would your finished product and performance meet the standards of a professional kitchen? Describe how your recipe turned out and what techniques and procedures you need to improve.

_____

_____

_____

_____

_____

_____

_____

_____

_____

_____

_____

_____

_____

Performance Review: **Indian-Style Meatballs with Raita Appetizer**

Name _____ **Date**_____

Core knowledge/skills: dry-heat cooking method, knife skills, dicing, mincing, measurement

Culinary Proficiency	Expectations	Instructor's Review
Professionalism: Demonstrate appropriate workplace hygiene and appearance.	Hair neat and restrained	
	Clean chef uniform and apron; nonslip, closed-toe shoes	
	No nail polish or jewelry	
Sanitation: Wash hands properly. Take precautions to avoid cross-contamination. Demonstrate safe food handling.	Display correct handwashing throughout production, disposable gloves used to handle ready-to-eat foods	
	Ensure meatballs reach 155°F (68.3°C) or higher	
	Clean and sanitize workstation before and after work	
Mise en Place: Set up workstation properly. Review recommended reading. Organized recipe method and sequence of work.	Prepare ingredients for assembly, adjust recipe yield as needed	
	Needed equipment available and ready	
	Maintain orderly, efficient workflow, follow recipe	
Cooking Technique: Demonstrate correct dry heat cooking method.	Portion meatballs uniformly for even cooking and attractive presentation	
	Cook meatballs to internal temperature of 155°F (68.3°C) or higher	
Product Evaluation: Present on a plain, white plate for observation. Taste finished product.	Meatballs have nice caramelized rich flavor, without other ingredients being too strong	
	Meatballs are uniformly garnished with pineapple and frill pick	
	Cucumber is finely minced in raita, flavors are balanced	

Lab Activity 38-1: Scrambled Eggs

Name _____ **Date** _____ **Period** _____

Group Members _____

Preparing scrambled eggs may sound easy, but carryover cooking from the heat of the pan can quickly change a perfectly cooked egg to one that is overcooked and tough. A skilled chef is able to control the cooking method to create the desired final product. In fact, the skill level required to prepare eggs is acknowledged symbolically in the chef's toque. Traditionally, each pleat in a chef's toque represents a different egg preparation the chef has mastered.

Objectives

After completing this lab, you will be able to

- execute scrambled egg preparation.
- recognize protein coagulation.

Mise en Place

1. Carefully read through the recipe before starting production. Adjust the yield as needed. Review how to convert recipe yield in text Chapter 15.

2. Review the sections *Proteins Coagulate* in text Chapter 18 and *Scrambled Eggs* in text Chapter 38.

3. Gather all ingredients and equipment required.

Sanitation and Safety Reminders

1. Clean and sanitize workstation before beginning to work.

2. Inspect eggs and discard any broken or cracked eggs.

3. Thoroughly wash and trim vegetable ingredients.

4. Wash hands properly and as often as needed.

Key Terms

Define the following terms used in this activity. Some may have been defined in previous chapters.

1. carryover cooking _____

_____

2. concassé _____

_____

(Continued)

Scrambled Eggs

Yield: 4 portions

Ingredients

8 ea.		eggs
2 fl. oz.	60 mL	heavy cream
1 tsp.	5 mL	chives, finely chopped
1 tsp.	5mL	Dijon mustard
1 oz.	30 g	butter
to taste		salt and pepper

Method

1. Break the eggs into a mixing bowl and whisk in the heavy cream until it begins to increase in volume.

2. Add the Dijon mustard and chives and briefly mix. Keep on ice until ready to cook.

Chef's Note: If desired, add finely diced tomato concassé. Add near the end of cooking so the tomato doesn't release too much liquid and make the eggs soggy.

3. Preheat a sauté pan over low heat and add the butter. Once melted, add the egg mixture and cook, stirring constantly with a silicone spatula.

4. When the eggs are creamy and slightly thickened, remove the pan from the heat and continue to stir. The carryover cooking from the heat of the pan will finish cooking the eggs.

Chef's Note: When eggs are overcooked, the protein continues to coagulate and cause "weeping." This is the moisture being squeezed from the eggs, making them dry and tough.

5. Plate and serve immediately.

Chef's Note: Try scrambling eggs in a double boiler. It takes longer to cook, but the reward is a delicate and fluffy scrambled egg. The indirect heat decreases the possibility of overcooking.

Recipe courtesy Chef David Ross (not available on website)

Chef's Journal

Write an evaluation of your lab performance. Would your finished product and performance meet the standards of a professional kitchen? Describe how your recipe turned out and what techniques and procedures you need to improve.

_____

_____

_____

_____

_____

Performance Review: **Scrambled Eggs**

Name _____ **Date**_____

Core knowledge/skills: breakfast cookery, coagulation, carryover cooking, concassé, mincing

Culinary Proficiency	Expectations	Instructor's Review
Professionalism: Demonstrate appropriate workplace hygiene and appearance.	Hair neat and restrained	
	Clean chef uniform and apron; nonslip, closed-toe shoes	
	No nail polish or jewelry	
Sanitation: Wash hands properly. Demonstrate safe food handling.	Display correct handwashing throughout production	
	Inspect and discard any cracked eggs	
	Clean and sanitize workstation before and after work	
Mise en Place: Set up workstation properly. Review lab recommended reading. Organized recipe method and sequence of work.	Prepare ingredients for assembly, adjust recipe yield as needed	
	Mince chives, prepare tomato concassé	
	Needed equipment available and ready	
Cooking Technique: Demonstrate correct scrambled egg technique and doneness of eggs.	Use low to moderate heat to cook eggs	
	Remove eggs from heat before fully cooked to accommodate carryover cooking	
	Use silicone spatula or wooden spoon to avoid possible reaction with some metals	
Product Evaluation: Present on a plain, white plate for observation. Taste finished product.	Eggs are pale yellow, not caramelized or green	
	Texture is light, fluffy, and moist	
	Egg is not weeping, no water is on the plate	
	Eggs are well seasoned, no sulfurlike flavor	

Additional Instructor's Comments

Lab Activity 38-2: **Frittata**

Name _____ **Date** _____ **Period** _____

Group Members _____

Frittatas can take many variations. A great number of vegetables and even cured meats can be combined to create a flavorful frittata.

Objectives

After completing this lab, you will be able to

- execute frittata technique.
- recognize protein coagulation.
- apply knife skills.

Mise en Place

1. Carefully read through the recipe before starting production. Adjust the yield as needed. Review how to convert recipe yield in text Chapter 15.

2. Review the sections *Proteins Coagulate* in text Chapter 18 and *Frittata* in text Chapter 38.

3. Gather all ingredients and equipment required.

Sanitation and Safety Reminders

1. Clean and sanitize workstation before beginning to work.

2. Inspect eggs and discard any broken or cracked eggs.

3. Thoroughly wash and trim vegetable ingredients.

4. Wash hands properly and as often as needed.

Key Terms

Define the following terms used in this activity. Some may have been defined in previous chapters.

1. sautéing _____

_____

2. small dice _____

_____

3. mincing _____

_____

4. chiffonade _____

_____

5. concassé _____

_____

(Continued)

Frittata

Yield: 2 portions

Ingredients

8 ea.		eggs
2 fl. oz.	60 mL	heavy cream
2 Tbsp.	30 mL	olive oil
¼ c.	60 mL	onion, small dice
¼ c.	60 mL	red peppers, small dice
¼ c.	60 mL	green peppers, small dice
2 cloves		garlic, finely minced
½ c.	120 mL	tomatoes, concassé
6 leaves		basil, chiffonade
4 oz.	115 g	goat cheese, crumbled
to taste		salt and black pepper (freshly ground)

Method

1. Preheat the oven to 275°F–300°F (135°C–149°C).
2. Break the eggs into a large bowl and add cream. Season with salt and pepper and whisk until they begin to increase in volume. Hold eggs at 41°F (5°C) or below until ready to use.
3. Heat a medium sauté pan over medium heat. When the pan is hot, add the olive oil.
4. Add the onions and sauté until they start to caramelize, or about 5 minutes. Add both peppers and cook for another 3 minutes.
5. Add the tomatoes and garlic, and sauté for 3 minutes more.
6. Pour the egg mix on the pepper mixture and stir constantly until small curds start to form, or about 2–3 minutes.
7. Sprinkle basil and goat cheese on top.

Chef's Note: Try adding any type of pitted olive and thin slices serrano or prosciutto ham.

8. Place pan in oven and bake until the mixture has just set in the middle. Test with a toothpick.
9. Remove from the oven and let rest for 5 minutes before cutting and serving.

Recipe courtesy Chef David Ross (not available on website)

Chef's Journal

Write an evaluation of your lab performance. Would your finished product and performance meet the standards of a professional kitchen? Describe how your recipe turned out and what techniques and procedures you need to improve.

_____

_____

_____

_____

Performance Review: **Frittata**

Name _____ **Date**_____

Core knowledge/skills: breakfast cookery, coagulation, frittata, knife skills, concassé, mincing, small dice, chiffonade

Culinary Proficiency	Expectations	Instructor's Review
Professionalism: Demonstrate appropriate workplace hygiene and appearance.	Hair neat and restrained	
	Clean chef uniform and apron; nonslip, closed-toe shoes	
	No nail polish or jewelry	
Sanitation: Wash hands properly. Demonstrate safe food handling.	Display correct handwashing throughout production	
	Inspect and discard any cracked or broken eggs	
	Clean and sanitize workstation before and after work	
Mise en Place: Set up workstation properly. Review lab recommended reading. Organized recipe method and sequence of work.	Prepare ingredients for assembly, adjust recipe yield as needed	
	Perform neat, uniform vegetable cuts	
	Needed equipment available and ready	
Cooking Technique: Demonstrate correct frittata technique and doneness of eggs.	Sauté vegetables until lightly caramelized	
	Whip eggs to incorporate air	
	Assemble frittata correctly	
	Place frittata in oven just after curds begin to form, and bake just long enough for middle to set	
Product Evaluation: Present on a plain, white plate for observation. Taste finished product.	Color is light caramelized golden-brown	
	Frittata is light and fluffy and has increased volume	
	Texture of eggs is soft and delicate	
	Vegetables and other fillings are tender, with no excessive color	

Additional Instructor's Comments

Lab Activity 38-3: **Chicken-Fried Steak**

Name _____ Date_____ Period _____

Group Members _____

Chicken-fried steak is a popular breakfast food in the south and southwest regions of the United States. In these areas, a restaurant's reputation is sometimes based on the quality of the chicken-fried steak it serves.

Objectives

After completing this lab, you will be able to

- apply a tenderizing technique to meat.
- apply dredging and breading techniques.
- execute panfrying method of meat.

Mise en Place

1. Carefully read through the recipe before starting production. Adjust the yield as needed. Review how to convert recipe yield in text Chapter 15.

2. Review the section *Panfrying* in text Chapter 18, the *Hints from the Chef: Tenderizers* in text Chapter 30, and the discussion about dredging in text Chapter 32.

3. Gather all ingredients and equipment required.

Sanitation and Safety Reminders

1. Clean and sanitize workstation before beginning to work.

2. Wash hands properly and as often as needed.

3. Inspect eggs and discard any broken or cracked eggs. Store egg mixture on ice during this activity.

Key Terms

Define the following terms used in this activity. Some may have been defined in previous chapters.

1. dredging _____

   _____

2. panfrying _____

   _____

3. caramelization _____

   _____

(Continued)

Chicken-Fried Steak

Yield: 4 portions

Ingredients

1 lb.	450 g	beef top round, trimmed of silver skin and fat
4 oz.	115 g	all-purpose flour
2 tsp.	10 mL	salt
1 tsp.	5 mL	fresh ground black pepper
3 fl. oz.	90 mL	whole milk
3 ea.		eggs
3½ oz.	100 g	bread crumbs
3 fl. oz.	90 mL	vegetable oil

Method

1. Cutting across the grain, cut meat into ½-inch thick slices.
2. Tenderize using a meat mallet with spiked ends until the meat is ¼-inch thick.

Chef's Note: This breaks down the connective tissue of the meat fibers.

3. Combine flour, salt, and pepper.
4. Dredge each piece of meat on both sides with the flour mix.
5. Mix the eggs and milk in a small bowl.
6. Dip each piece of meat in the egg mixture and then coat both sides in bread crumbs.

Chef's Note: If fresh herbs are to be added to the recipe, they must be minced and mixed with the flour dredge. If mixed in the bread crumbs, the herbs will burn during panfrying.

7. Place oil in sauté pan over medium-high heat and preheat.
8. Place breaded steak into pan. Oil should only cover steak about halfway. Caramelize both sides, then remove and place on grate to drain off fat.
9. Hold at or above 135°F (57.2°C) until service.

Recipe courtesy Chef David Ross (not available on website)

Chef's Journal

Write an evaluation of your lab performance. Would your finished product and performance meet the standards of a professional kitchen? Describe how your recipe turned out and what techniques and procedures you need to improve.

_____

_____

_____

_____

Performance Review: **Chicken-Fried Steak**

Name _____ Date_____

Core knowledge/skills: dry-heat cooking method, panfrying, knife skills, tenderizing, dredging, breading

Culinary Proficiency	Expectations	Instructor's Review
Professionalism: Demonstrate appropriate workplace hygiene and appearance.	Hair neat and restrained	
	Clean chef uniform and apron; nonslip, closed-toe shoes	
	No nail polish or jewelry	
Sanitation: Wash hands properly. Demonstrate safe food handling.	Display correct handwashing throughout production	
	Inspect and discard any cracked or broken eggs	
	Hold egg mixture on ice	
	Clean and sanitize workstation before and after work	
Mise en Place: Set up workstation properly. Review lab recommended reading. Organized recipe method and sequence of work.	Prepare ingredients for assembly, adjust recipe yield as needed	
	Set up breading station before beginning work	
	Needed equipment available and ready	
Cooking Technique: Demonstrate correct panfrying technique and doneness of steak.	Pound out meat pieces evenly and consistently for even cooking	
	Preheat pan and oil before adding product	
	Sauté until breaded meat is light golden, caramelized color on both sides	
	Apply breading evenly and so it clings to meat	
Product Evaluation: Present on a plain, white plate for observation. Taste finished product.	Breading is golden brown, not burned or undercooked	
	Breading is crunchy-crisp, not soggy and greasy, meat is juicy and tender	
	Breading is well seasoned and does not overpower the beef	

Additional Instructor's Comments

Lab Activity 38-4: **Grated Hash Browns**

Name _____ **Date** _____ **Period** _____

Group Members _____

This recipe takes advantage of a potato's natural starch to bind the hash browns together. If you grate potatoes and allow them to sit, water and a white substance begins to collect in the bottom of the bowl. The white substance is potato starch that you can recycle back into your hash browns to act as a binder.

Objective

After completing this lab, you will be able to

- execute sautéing method of a starch.

Mise en Place

1. Carefully read through the recipe before starting production. Adjust the yield as needed. Review how to convert recipe yield in text Chapter 15.

2. Review the section *Sautéed and Panfried Potatoes* in text Chapter 29.

3. Gather all ingredients and equipment required.

Sanitation and Safety Reminders

1. Clean and sanitize workstation before beginning to work.

2. Wash hands properly and as often as needed.

3. Wash, trim, and peel potatoes as needed before preparation.

Key Terms

Define the following terms used in this activity. Some may have been defined in previous chapters.

1. waxy potatoes _____

_____

2. sautéing _____

_____

3. caramelization _____

_____

4. acidulation _____

_____

5. oxidation _____

_____

(Continued)

Grated Hash Browns

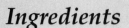

Yield: 8 3-oz. portions

Ingredients

2 lb.	900 g	waxy potatoes
2 fl. oz.	60 mL	vegetable oil
to taste		salt and pepper

Method

1. Wash and peel potatoes.
2. Use the large (coarse grate) side of a box grater to grate potatoes into a bowl.
3. Squeeze the grated potatoes and cover them with a damp paper towel for a few minutes. If the potatoes are not going to be cooked shortly, place them in acidulated water to prevent oxidation.
4. Pour off the water that has collected in the bowl while preserving the white starch substance. Mix the starch back into the grated potato. Season with salt and pepper.
5. Heat a medium sauté pan over high heat. Place oil in pan.
6. Take handful of potato and form it into a thin pancake about 6 inches in diameter. Sauté for 3 minutes.

Chef's Note: If you prefer a thicker pancake, turn the heat down slightly to allow potatoes to fully cook. You could also create a thicker pancake by filling with cheese or ham.

7. Turn hash browns over once starches are caramelized and sauté other side.
8. When cooked, drain on paper towel.

Chef's Note: Hash browns are best served immediately. If they must be held, do not cover or they will become soft and soggy very quickly.

Recipe courtesy Chef David Ross (not available on website)

Chef's Journal

Write an evaluation of your lab performance. Would your finished product and performance meet the standards of a professional kitchen? Describe how your recipe turned out and what techniques and procedures you need to improve.

_____

_____

_____

_____

_____

_____

_____

Performance Review: **Grated Hash Browns**

Name _____ Date_____

Core knowledge/skills: starch cookery, sautéing, caramelization, acidulation, oxidation

Culinary Proficiency	Expectations	Instructor's Review
Professionalism: Demonstrate appropriate workplace hygiene and appearance.	Hair neat and restrained	
	Clean chef uniform and apron; nonslip, closed-toe shoes	
	No nail polish or jewelry	
Sanitation: Wash hands properly. Demonstrate safe food handling.	Display correct handwashing throughout production	
	Wash potatoes	
	Clean and sanitize workstation before and after work	
Mise en Place: Set up workstation properly. Review lab recommended reading. Organized recipe method and sequence of work.	Prepare ingredients for assembly, adjust recipe yield as needed	
	Peel, trim, and grate potatoes	
	Pour water off grated potatoes, while reserving starch	
	Needed equipment available and ready	
Cooking Technique: Demonstrate correct sauté technique and doneness of potato.	Mix reserved starch back in with potatoes	
	Preheat pan before adding oil	
	Potatoes cooked to light caramelized color on both sides	
Product Evaluation: Present on a plain, white plate for observation. Taste finished product.	Hash browns are rich golden-brown on both sides	
	Exterior is crispy and inside is slightly lighter and softer	
	Hash browns have potato flavor with light seasoning, no flavor from the frying oil or fat is present	
	Hash browns hold together in a pancake shape	

Additional Instructor's Comments

Lab Activity 38-5: **Whole Wheat Waffles**

Name _____ **Date** _____ **Period** _____

Group Members _____

While serving as Minister to France, Thomas Jefferson traveled to Holland where he discovered and developed a taste for waffles. When he returned to America, Jefferson introduced waffles—along with other novel dishes and ingredients—to dinner guests at his home and later at the White House.

Objectives

After completing this lab, you will be able to

- prepare a breakfast batter.
- use a waffle iron to cook using conduction.

Mise en Place

1. Carefully read through the recipe before starting production. Adjust the yield as needed. Review how to convert recipe yield in Chapter text 15.

2. Review the sections *Conduction* in text Chapter 18 and *Breakfast Batters* in text Chapter 38.

3. Gather all ingredients and equipment required.

Sanitation and Safety Reminders

1. Clean and sanitize workstation before beginning to work.

2. Wash hands properly and as often as needed.

3. Inspect eggs and discard any broken or cracked eggs. Store batter on ice during this activity.

Key Terms

Define the following terms used in this activity. Some may have been defined in other chapters.

1. conduction _____

   _____

2. batter _____

   _____

(Continued)

Whole Wheat Waffles

Yield: 16 portions

Ingredients

10 oz.	280 g	whole wheat flour
6 oz.	170 g	all-purpose flour
1 tsp.	5 mL	salt
1 Tbsp.	15 mL	baking powder
1 ea		egg
6 oz.	170 g	sugar
2 fl. oz.	60 mL	canola oil
20 fl. oz.	600 mL	milk
¼ tsp.	1 mL	vanilla extract

Method

1. Combine dry ingredients except sugar.
2. In a separate bowl, beat the egg. Add the sugar and oil, and mix with an electric mixer until smooth. Mix in milk and vanilla.
3. Add the dry mixture to the wet mixture while beating. Mix until smooth.
4. Cover and refrigerate at or below 41°F (5°C). Allow the batter to rest at least 1 hour before using.
5. Apply a light coating of vegetable oil on a waffle iron and preheat.
6. Ladle 2 ²/₃ fl. oz. of batter onto the waffle iron and close the lid. Cook according to manufacturer's directions or until steam is no longer released. Serve hot.

Chef's Journal

Write an evaluation of your lab performance. Would your finished product and performance meet the standards of a professional kitchen? Describe how your recipe turned out and what techniques and procedures you need to improve.

_____

_____

_____

_____

_____

_____

_____

_____

_____

_____

Performance Review: **Whole Wheat Waffles**

Name _____ **Date**_____

Core knowledge/skills: dry-heat cooking method, batter, leavening, measurement and scaling techniques

Culinary Proficiency	Expectations	Instructor's Review
Professionalism: Demonstrate appropriate workplace hygiene and appearance.	Hair neat and restrained	
	Clean chef uniform and apron; nonslip, closed-toe shoes	
	No nail polish or jewelry	
Sanitation: Wash hands properly. Demonstrate safe food handling.	Display correct handwashing throughout production	
	Discard any broken or cracked eggs	
	Clean and sanitize workstation before and after work	
Mise en Place: Set up workstation properly. Organized recipe method and sequence of work.	Prepare ingredients for assembly, adjust recipe yield as needed	
	Needed equipment available and ready	
Cooking Technique: Demonstrate correct mixing of batter and use of waffle iron.	Lightly oil and preheat waffle iron	
	Mix batter just long enough to combine ingredients	
	Remove waffle when steam is no longer released	
Product Evaluation: Present on a plain, white plate for observation. Taste finished product.	Waffle has a crisp, golden brown exterior	
	Waffle is light and tender with good flavor	

Additional Instructor's Comments

Lab Activity 41-1: **Biscuits**

For centuries, biscuits have been used as a quick, cheap replacement for bread. Biscuits are found on breakfast menus, accompanying stews and soups, and as ingredients in desserts.

Chef's Note: In England and much of Europe, the word "biscuit" refers to the food item that is known as a "cookie" in the United States.

Objectives

After completing this lab, you will be able to

- implement rolling and cutting to portion biscuits.
- implement a chemical leavening agent.
- execute the biscuit method.

Mise en Place

1. Carefully read through the recipe before starting production. Adjust the yield as needed. Review how to convert recipe yield in text Chapter 15.
2. Review the sections *Units of Weight* and *Measuring Ingredients* in text Chapter 15 and *Biscuits* in text Chapter 41.
3. Gather all ingredients and equipment required.
4. Preheat oven to desired temperature.

Sanitation and Safety Reminders

1. Clean and sanitize workstation before beginning to work.
2. Review *Safety Savvy: Mixer Safety* in text Chapter 40.
3. Wash hands properly and as often as needed.

Key Terms

Define the following terms used in this activity. Some may have been defined in previous chapters.

1. leavening _____

    _____

2. quick bread _____

    _____

3. biscuit method _____

    _____

4. baking powder _____

    _____

(Continued)

5.   shortening _____

_____

Biscuits

Yield: 24 2-in. biscuits

Ingredients

1¼ lb.	560 g	all-purpose or pastry flour
½ oz.	15 g	salt
1 oz.	30 g	sugar
1 oz.	30 g	baking powder
7 oz.	200 g	solid shortening
12 oz.	360 g	milk

Method

1. Sift the dry ingredients together.
2. Using a mixer with a paddle attachment or by hand, cut the shortening into the dry ingredients until it resembles a coarse meal.
3. Add the milk and mix briefly to create dough.
4. On a floured surface, roll the dough into an even sheet 1 inch (2.5 cm) thick.
5. Cut with a round pastry cutter about 2 in. diameter.

Chef's Note: Alternately, biscuits can be formed by scooping dough with a #20 scoop and dropping dough directly on the baking sheet. These are called drop biscuits.

6. Leftover dough can be rolled out to cut more biscuits. Take care not to overwork the dough or the biscuits will be tough.
7. Place the biscuits on a sheet pan lined with parchment.
8. Bake 425°F (218°C) for 15–20 minutes.
9. When removed from the oven, biscuits may be brushed with melted butter for a richer, moister product.

Chef's Note: Substitute buttermilk for the milk in the recipe to create buttermilk biscuits or add 6 oz. of grated cheese (Cheddar, Parmesan, etc.) to create cheese biscuits.

Chef's Journal

Write an evaluation of your lab performance. Would your finished product and performance meet the standards of a professional kitchen? Describe how your recipe turned out and what techniques and procedures you need to improve.

_____

_____

Performance Review: **Biscuits**

Name _____ **Date**_____

Core knowledge/skills: dry-heat cooking method, quick breads, biscuit method, leavening, shortening, cutting in, measurement and scaling techniques

Culinary Proficiency	Expectations	Instructor's Review
Professionalism: Demonstrate appropriate workplace hygiene and appearance.	Hair neat and restrained	
	Clean chef uniform and apron; nonslip, closed-toe shoes	
	No nail polish or jewelry	
Sanitation: Wash hands properly. Demonstrate safe food handling.	Display correct handwashing throughout production	
	Clean and sanitize workstation before and after work	
Mise en Place: Set up workstation properly. Review lab recommended reading. Organized recipe method and sequence of work.	Prepare ingredients for assembly, adjust recipe yield as needed	
	Preheat oven	
	Weigh both dry and liquid ingredients accurately	
	Needed equipment available and ready	
Cooking Technique: Demonstrate correct biscuit method.	Mix dough briefly	
	Place product in oven once appropriate temperature is reached	
	Bake until biscuit is very lightly caramelized on top	
Product Evaluation: Present on a plain, white plate for observation. Taste finished product.	Biscuits are light golden color	
	Texture is soft and moist, not tough	
	Biscuit has doubled in size and almost breaks when picked up	

Additional Instructor's Comments

Lab Activity 41-2: **Corn Bread**

Name _____ **Date** _____ **Period** _____

Group Members _____

Corn bread helped to sustain the early settlers to America. Wheat flour was often in short supply, so they learned to cook with cornmeal. Although the corn bread nourished them, they preferred their lighter, finer wheat flour to the heavy, coarse cornmeal. Today, people enjoy many delicious variations of corn bread.

Objectives

After completing this lab, you will be able to

- execute corn bread preparation using muffin technique.
- implement a chemical leavening agent.

Mise en Place

1. Carefully read through the recipe before starting production. Adjust the yield as needed. Review how to convert recipe yield in text Chapter 15.

2. Review the sections *Units of Weight* and *Measuring Ingredients* in text Chapter 15 and *Muffins* in text Chapter 41.

3. Gather all ingredients and equipment required.

4. Preheat oven to desired temperature.

Sanitation and Safety Reminders

1. Clean and sanitize workstation before beginning to work.

2. Inspect eggs and discard any broken or cracked eggs.

3. Review *Safety Savvy: Mixer Safety* in text Chapter 40.

4. Wash hands properly and as often as needed.

Key Terms

Define the following terms used in this activity. Some may have been defined in previous chapters.

1. leavening _____

   _____

2. quick bread _____

   _____

3. batter _____

   _____

4. baking powder _____

   _____

(Continued)

5. baking soda _____

_____

6. shortening _____

_____

Corn Bread

Yield: 16 2-oz. muffins

Ingredients

½ oz.	15 g	salt
1 oz.	30 g	sugar
8 oz.	225 g	flour
10 oz.	280 g	cornmeal
½ oz.	15 g	baking powder
10 oz.	280 g	eggs (about 5 large eggs)
12 oz.	360 g	buttermilk
2 oz.	60 g	shortening or butter, melted

Method

1. Beat the eggs and mix with the milk.
2. Sift the dry ingredients together.

Chef's Note: If baking powder is not available, you can substitute baking soda. However, you must also add an acid ingredient to react with the baking soda and initiate leavening.

3. Add the eggs, milk, and shortening to the dry ingredients and mix until all ingredients are combined. Do not overmix.
4. Portion the batter into greased muffin tins or a shallow pan.
5. Bake muffins at 400°F (204°C) for about 15 minutes. Bake shallow pan at 350°F (177°C) for about 30 minutes.

Chef's Note: In this recipe, the acidic taste in the buttermilk complements the corn flavor.

Chef's Journal

Write an evaluation of your lab performance. Would your finished product and performance meet the standards of a professional kitchen? Describe how your recipe turned out and what techniques and procedures you need to improve.

_____

_____

_____

_____

Performance Review: **Corn Bread**

Name _____ **Date**_____

Core knowledge/skills: dry-heat cooking method, quick breads, batter, leavening, shortening, measurement and scaling techniques

Culinary Proficiency	Expectations	Instructor's Review
Professionalism: Demonstrate appropriate workplace hygiene and appearance.	Hair neat and restrained	
	Clean chef uniform and apron; nonslip, closed-toe shoes	
	No nail polish or jewelry	
Sanitation: Wash hands properly. Demonstrate safe food handling.	Display correct handwashing throughout production	
	Discard any broken or cracked eggs	
	Clean and sanitize workstation before and after work	
Mise en Place: Set up workstation properly. Review lab recommended reading. Organized recipe method and sequence of work.	Prepare ingredients for assembly, adjust recipe yield as needed	
	Preheat oven	
	Weigh both dry and liquid ingredients accurately	
	Needed equipment available and ready	
Cooking Technique: Demonstrate the correct corn bread preparation using the muffin technique.	Place product in oven once appropriate temperature is reached	
	Mix cornmeal batter just long enough to combine ingredients	
	Bake until corn bread is very lightly caramelized on top	
Product Evaluation: Present on a plain, white plate for observation. Taste finished product.	Corn bread is pale yellow (depending on using white or yellow cornmeal) to very light golden color. Texture is soft and moist. Corn bread has doubled in size.	

Additional Instructor's Comments

Lab Activity 41-3: **Pâte à Choux**

Name _____ **Date** _____ **Period** _____

Group Members _____

Pâte à choux is crunchy-crisp on the outside and empty on the inside. The hollow air pockets are formed when steam is produced during cooking. When the product cools, caverns are left behind just right for sweet or savory fillings. This technique must be followed precisely or your puffs may collapse.

Objectives

After completing this lab, you will be able to

- implement steam as a leavening agent.
- execute pâte à choux technique.

Mise en Place

1. Carefully read through the recipe before starting production. Adjust the yield as needed. Review how to convert recipe yield in text Chapter 15.
2. Review the sections *Units of Weight* and *Measuring Ingredients* in text Chapter 15 and *Pâte à Choux* in text Chapter 41.
3. Gather all ingredients and equipment required.
4. Preheat oven to desired temperature.

Sanitation and Safety Reminders

1. Clean and sanitize workstation before beginning to work.
2. Inspect eggs and discard any broken or cracked eggs.
3. Review *Safety Savvy: Mixer Safety* in text Chapter 40.
4. Wash hands properly and as often as needed.

Key Terms

Define the following terms used in this activity. Some may have been defined in previous chapters.

1. leavening _____

_____

2. pâte à choux _____

_____

3. batter _____

_____

4. shortening _____

_____

(Continued)

Pâte à Choux

Yield: 12 4-oz. pastries

Ingredients

8 oz.	225 g	all-purpose or bread flour
16 oz.	480 g	water or milk
8 oz.	225 g	butter or shortening
pinch		salt
½ oz.	15 g	sugar
1 lb.	450 g	eggs (about 8 large eggs)

Method

1. Sift the flour and set aside.
2. Combine the liquid, butter or shortening, sugar, and salt in a saucepot and bring to a boil.
3. Add the flour all at once and stir immediately.
4. Cook over moderate heat while stirring until the dough forms a ball and pulls away from the sides of the pot.
5. Transfer the dough to the bowl of a mixer.
6. On medium speed, use the paddle attachment to mix eggs in one at a time. Continue to add the eggs in this manner until all the eggs are incorporated into the batter.
7. When batter cools, place into a pastry bag and pipe into desired shape.
8. Bake at 400°F (204°C) until pastry is evenly brown with a rigid, hollow structure.

Chef's Note: To make churros, carefully pipe the dough into hot oil. Once the dough is golden brown, remove from fryer, drain, and coat with cinnamon sugar. Serve with warm chocolate sauce for dipping.

Chef's Journal

Write an evaluation of your lab performance. Would your finished product and performance meet the standards of a professional kitchen? Describe how your recipe turned out and what techniques and procedures you need to improve.

_____

_____

_____

_____

_____

_____

_____

Performance Review: **Pâte à Choux**

Name _____ **Date**_____

Core knowledge/skills: dry-heat cooking method, pâte à choux, batter, leavening, shortening, measurement and scaling techniques

Culinary Proficiency	Expectations	Instructor's Review
Professionalism: Demonstrate appropriate workplace hygiene and appearance.	Hair neat and restrained	
	Clean chef uniform and apron; nonslip, closed-toe shoes	
	No nail polish or jewelry	
Sanitation: Wash hands properly. Demonstrate safe food handling.	Display correct handwashing throughout production	
	Discard any broken or cracked eggs	
	Clean and sanitize workstation before and after work	
Mise en Place: Set up workstation properly. Review lab recommended reading. Organized recipe method and sequence of work.	Prepare ingredients for assembly, adjust recipe yield as needed	
	Preheat oven	
	Weigh both dry and liquid ingredients accurately	
	Needed equipment available and ready.	
Cooking Technique: Demonstrate correct pâte à choux technique.	Place product in oven once appropriate temperature is reached	
	Pipe out batter into consistent size and shape for even baking and professional appearance	
	Bake until a light, high puff with a lightly caramelized top is produced	
Product Evaluation: Present on a plain, white plate for observation. Taste finished product.	Pâte à choux is light golden color	
	Texture is crispy on outside	
	Puffs have doubled in size and hold shape, inside is nearly hollow and very slightly moist	
	Pastries are consistent size and shape	

Additional Instructor's Comments

Lab Activity 42-1: **Chocolate Chip Cookies**

Name _____ **Date**_____ **Period** _____

Group Members _____

Proper creaming method is essential for producing quality cookies. The first step of the creaming method involves mixing the sugar with the fat (normally butter) until smooth. If the fat and sugar are not mixed correctly, the result is a lumpy dough in which the ingredients are unevenly distributed.

Objectives

After completing this lab, you will be able to

- implement creaming method.
- execute drop cookie preparation.

Mise en Place

1. Carefully read through the recipe before starting production. Adjust the yield as needed. Review how to convert recipe yield in text Chapter 15.
2. Review the sections *Units of Weight* and *Measuring Ingredients* in text Chapter 15 and *Creaming Method* in text Chapter 42.
3. Gather all ingredients and equipment required.
4. Preheat oven to desired temperature.

Sanitation and Safety Reminders

1. Clean and sanitize workstation before beginning to work.
2. Inspect eggs and discard any broken or cracked eggs.
3. Review *Safety Savvy: Mixer Safety* in text Chapter 40.
4. Wash hands properly and as often as needed.

Key Terms

Define the following terms used in this activity. Some may have been defined in previous chapters.

1. drop cookies _____

   _____

2. creaming method _____

   _____

3. baking soda _____

   _____

(Continued)

Chocolate Chip Cookies

Yield: 24 3-in. cookies

Ingredients

12 oz.	340 g	butter or shortening
5 oz.	140 g	sugar
5 oz.	140 g	light brown sugar
0.12 oz. (½ tsp.)	4 g	salt
2 oz.	60 g	eggs
1 fl. oz.	30 g	water
0.16 oz. (1 tsp.)	5 g	vanilla extract
10 oz.	280 g	all-purpose or pastry flour
0.1 oz. (½ tsp.)	3 g	baking soda
8 oz.	225 g	chocolate chips
4 oz.	115 g	walnuts or pecans, chopped

Method

1. Cream the butter, sugar, brown sugar, and salt until smooth.
2. Incorporate the eggs, water, and vanilla.
3. Sift the flour and baking soda, and add to the other ingredients. Mix long enough to create a smooth dough.
4. Add the chocolate chips and nuts and mix in at a low speed until evenly distributed.

Chef's Note: Since many people are allergic to nuts, nuts can either be omitted from the recipe or used as a garnish on the top of each cookie. This clearly indicates to customers that the cookies contain nuts.

5. Portion onto a sheet pan lined with parchment.
6. Bake at 375°F (190°C) for approximately 18 minutes. Baking time will vary depending on size.

Chef's Journal

Write an evaluation of your lab performance. Would your finished product and performance meet the standards of a professional kitchen? Describe how your recipe turned out and what techniques and procedures you need to improve.

_____
_____
_____
_____
_____
_____

Performance Review: **Chocolate Chip Cookies**

Name _____ Date_____

Core knowledge/skills: drop cookies, creaming method, baking soda, measurement and scaling techniques

Culinary Proficiency	Expectations	Instructor's Review
Professionalism: Demonstrate appropriate workplace hygiene and appearance.	Hair neat and restrained	
	Clean chef uniform and apron; nonslip, closed-toe shoes	
	No nail polish or jewelry	
Sanitation: Wash hands properly. Demonstrate safe food handling.	Display correct handwashing throughout production	
	Discard any broken or cracked eggs	
	Clean and sanitize workstation before and after work	
Mise en Place: Set up workstation properly. Review lab recommended reading. Organized recipe method and sequence of work.	Prepare ingredients for assembly, adjust recipe yield as needed	
	Preheat oven	
	Weigh both dry and liquid ingredients accurately	
	Needed equipment available and ready	
Cooking Technique: Demonstrate correct creaming method. Demonstrate proper drop cookie technique.	Place product in oven once appropriate temperature is reached	
	Portion cookie dough uniformly for even cooking	
	Bake cookies until lightly caramelized	
	Allow cookies to firm up on cookie sheet before moving	
Product Evaluation: Present on a plain, white plate for observation. Taste finished product.	Cookies are golden brown and have the desired texture (crunchy or chewy)	
	Cookies are consistent size and spread, not torn or broken	
	If used, nuts are visible for those who have allergic reactions to nuts	

Additional Instructor's Comments

Lab Activity 42-2: **Sugar Cookies**

Name _____ Date _____ Period _____

Group Members _____

This recipe is simple but when properly prepared, results in a great product. A sugar cookie is like a blank canvas—decorate it to celebrate a holiday, advertise your business, or with a simple sprinkle of sugar.

Objectives

After completing this lab, you will be able to

- implement creaming method.
- execute rolled cookie preparation.

Mise en Place

1. Carefully read through the recipe before starting production. Adjust the yield as needed. Review how to convert recipe yield in text Chapter 15.
2. Review the sections *Units of Weight* and *Measuring Ingredients* in text Chapter 15 and *Creaming Method* in text Chapter 42.
3. Gather all ingredients and equipment required.
4. Preheat oven to desired temperature.

Sanitation and Safety Reminders

1. Clean and sanitize workstation before beginning to work.
2. Inspect eggs and discard any broken or cracked eggs.
3. Review *Safety Savvy: Mixer Safety* in text Chapter 40.
4. Wash hands properly and as often as needed.

Key Terms

Define the following terms used in this activity. Some may have been defined in previous chapters.

1. rolled cookies _____

   _____

2. creaming method _____

   _____

3. baking powder _____

   _____

(Continued)

Sugar Cookies

Yield: 24 3-in. cookies

Ingredients

8 oz.	225 g	butter or shortening
10 oz.	280 g	sugar
0.24 oz. (1 tsp.)	7 g	salt
2 oz.	60 g	egg (about 1 large)
2 oz.	60 g	milk
0.16 oz. (1 tsp.)	5 g	vanilla extract
1¼ lb.	560 g	all-purpose or pastry flour
0.5 oz. (1 Tbsp.)	15 g	baking powder

Method

1. Cream the shortening, sugar, and salt until smooth.
2. Incorporate the egg, milk, and vanilla.
3. Sift the flour and baking powder and add to the other ingredients.

Chef's Note: Make chocolate sugar cookies by replacing 2 oz. flour with 2 oz. cocoa powder.

4. Roll dough out on a floured surfaced to about ¼ inch (0.5 cm) thickness, cut and decorate as desired.
5. Place on a sheet pan lined with parchment.

Chef's Note: Sheet trays designed for baking cookies are composed of two layers with an air pocket in the middle. This double layer insulates and prevents the bottom of your cookies from burning. If you don't have a cookie sheet tray, improvise by doubling up two single-layer sheet pans.

6. Bake 375°F (190°C) for approximately 15 minutes.

Chef's Journal

Write an evaluation of your lab performance. Would your finished product and performance meet the standards of a professional kitchen? Describe how your recipe turned out and what techniques and procedures you need to improve.

_____

_____

_____

_____

_____

_____

_____

Performance Review: **Sugar Cookies**

Name _____ **Date**_____

Core knowledge/skills: rolled cookies, creaming method, baking powder, measurement and scaling techniques

Culinary Proficiency	Expectations	Instructor's Review
Professionalism: Demonstrate appropriate workplace hygiene and appearance.	Hair neat and restrained	
	Clean chef uniform and apron; nonslip, closed-toe shoes	
	No nail polish or jewelry	
Sanitation: Wash hands properly. Demonstrate safe food handling.	Display correct handwashing throughout production	
	Discard any broken or cracked eggs	
	Clean and sanitize workstation before and after work	
Mise en Place: Set up workstation properly. Review lab recommended reading. Organized recipe method and sequence of work.	Prepare ingredients for assembly, adjust recipe yield as needed	
	Preheat oven	
	Weigh both dry and liquid ingredients accurately	
	Needed equipment available and ready	
Cooking Technique: Demonstrate correct rolled cookie technique.	Place product in oven once appropriate temperature is reached	
	Portion cookie dough uniformly for even cooking	
	Bake cookies until lightly caramelized	
	Allow cookies to firm up on cookie sheet before moving	
Product Evaluation: Present on a plain, white plate for observation. Taste finished product.	Cookies are light golden brown and have the desired texture (crunchy or chewy), sugar granules are visible on top	
	Cookies are not overly sweet	
	Cookies are consistent size and not broken or torn	

Additional Instructor's Comments

Lab Activity 42-3: **Brownies**

Name _____ **Date** _____ **Period** _____

Group Members _____

Everyone enjoys a soft, rich, warm brownie. Brownies are not difficult to make and can be made in any number of variations. For example, by substituting white chocolate for semi-sweet chocolate in the brownies recipe, you can make blondies. Be creative and make a half recipe of each brownies and blondies, then gently swirl the two batters together in the pan before baking. You have just created a marble brownie!

Objectives

After completing this lab, you will be able to

- implement a double boiler.
- execute sheet cookie preparation.

Mise en Place

1. Carefully read through the recipe before starting production. Adjust the yield as needed. Review how to convert recipe yield in text Chapter 15.

2. Review the sections *Units of Weight* and *Measuring Ingredients* in text Chapter 15 and *Hints from the Chef: Melting Chocolate* in text Chapter 47.

3. Gather all ingredients and equipment required.

4. Preheat oven to desired temperature.

Sanitation and Safety Reminders

1. Clean and sanitize workstation before beginning to work.

2. Inspect eggs and discard any broken or cracked eggs.

3. Wash hands properly and as often as needed.

Key Terms

Define the following terms used in this activity. Some may have been defined in previous chapters.

1. sheet cookies _____

   _____

2. sheet pan _____

   _____

(Continued)

Brownies

Yield: 24 3 x 3 in. brownies

Ingredients

8 oz.	225 g	semi-sweet chocolate
12 oz.	340 g	butter
10 oz.	280 g	eggs (about 5 large)
24 oz.	670 g	sugar
0.24 oz. (1 tsp.)	7 g	salt
0.48 oz. (1 Tbsp.)	14 g	vanilla extract
8 oz.	225 g	cake or all-purpose flour
8 oz.	225 g	nuts, chopped
6 oz.	170 g	semi-sweet chocolate chips

Method

1. Melt chocolate and butter together in a double boiler.

Chef's Note: Never place a lid over melting chocolate. Water condenses on the lid and drips back into the chocolate causing it to turn into a stiff mass.

2. Whip the eggs, sugar, and vanilla with a whip until foamy.
3. Mix in the chocolate.
4. Sift the flour and fold it in by hand using a spatula.
5. Fold the nuts and chocolate chips into the mixture.
6. Grease a half-size sheet pan and dust it with flour. Remove excess flour.
7. Pour the batter into the sheet pan.
8. Bake at 350°F (177°C) for 30 minutes.

Chef's Journal

Write an evaluation of your lab performance. Would your finished product and performance meet the standards of a professional kitchen? Describe how your recipe turned out and what techniques and procedures you need to improve.

_____

_____

_____

_____

_____

_____

Performance Review: **Brownies**

Name _____ **Date**_____

Core knowledge/skills: sheet cookies, brownies, double boiler, pan preparation, measurement and scaling techniques

Culinary Proficiency	Expectations	Instructor's Review
Professionalism: Demonstrate appropriate workplace hygiene and appearance.	Hair neat and restrained	
	Clean chef uniform and apron; nonslip, closed-toe shoes	
	No nail polish or jewelry	
Sanitation: Wash hands properly. Demonstrate safe food handling.	Display correct handwashing throughout production	
	Discard any broken or cracked eggs	
	Clean and sanitize workstation before and after work	
Mise en Place: Set up workstation properly. Review lab recommended reading. Organized recipe method and sequence of work.	Prepare ingredients for assembly, adjust recipe yield as needed	
	Preheat oven	
	Weigh both dry and liquid ingredients accurately	
	Needed equipment available and ready, sheet pan is greased and floured	
Cooking Technique: Demonstrate correct use of double boiler. Demonstrate proper sheet cookie technique.	Melt chocolate until smooth, incorporate fully into batter	
	Place product in oven once appropriate temperature is reached	
Product Evaluation: Present on a plain, white plate for observation. Taste finished product.	Brownies are uniform color showing correct mixing	
	Brownies are neatly cut in consistent size, hold their shape when cut but have a slight crumble	
	Texture is somewhat dense, but soft and slightly springy	
	Brownies are moist with rich flavor	

Additional Instructor's Comments

Lab Activity 42-4: **Almond Biscotti**

Name _____ **Date** _____ **Period** _____

Group Members _____

Biscotti are Italian cookies that are often served with espresso coffee. What makes biscotti unique is that they are baked twice. This technique is the secret to the extremely crunchy finished product that has been an Italian favorite for centuries.

Objectives

After completing this lab, you will be able to

- implement a chemical leavening agent.
- execute biscotti preparation.

Mise en Place

1. Carefully read through the recipe before starting production. Adjust the yield as needed. Review how to convert recipe yield in text Chapter 15.
2. Review the sections *Units of Weight* and *Measuring Ingredients* in text Chapter 15.
3. Gather all ingredients and equipment required.
4. Preheat oven to desired temperature.

Sanitation and Safety Reminders

1. Clean and sanitize workstation before beginning to work.
2. Inspect eggs and discard any broken or cracked eggs.
3. Review *Safety Savvy: Mixer Safety* in text Chapter 40.
4. Wash hands properly and as often as needed.

Key Terms

Define the following terms used in this activity. Some may have been defined in previous chapters.

1. leavening _____

   _____

2. creaming method _____

   _____

3. baking soda _____

   _____

4. baking powder _____

   _____

(Continued)

Almond Biscotti

Yield: 24 cookies

Ingredients

12 oz.	340 g	all-purpose flour
0.17 oz. (1 tsp.)	5 g	baking powder
0.1 oz. (½ tsp.)	3 g	baking soda
0.24 oz. (1 tsp.)	7 g	salt
8 oz.	225 g	eggs (about 4 large)
4 oz.	115 g	sugar
0.16 oz. (1 tsp.)	5 g	vanilla extract
0.08 oz. (½ tsp.)	2 g	almond extract
4 oz.	115 g	almonds, toasted and coarsely chopped

Method

1. Beat the eggs and sugar in a bowl until light and foamy. Add extracts.
2. Sift the flour, baking powder, baking soda, and salt. Add flour mixture to the eggs and mix to incorporate ingredients.
3. Fold the almonds in by hand with a spatula.
4. Shape the dough into a log about 12 inches long.
5. Place the log on a sheet pan lined with parchment.
6. Flatten the log slightly using a spatula.
7. Bake for 30 minutes at 325°F (163°C).
8. Remove the log from the oven and lower the temperature to 275°F (135°C).
9. Cut each log diagonally into ½-inch slices.
10. Separate and lay out the slices on the sheet pan.
11. Return the biscotti to the oven for an additional 30 minutes until lightly toasted and crunchy.

Chef's Journal

Write an evaluation of your lab performance. Would your finished product and performance meet the standards of a professional kitchen? Describe how your recipe turned out and what techniques and procedures you need to improve.

_____

_____

_____

_____

_____

_____

Performance Review: **Almond Biscotti**

Name _____ **Date**_____

Core knowledge/skills: cookies, biscotti, creaming method, leavening, measurement and scaling techniques

Culinary Proficiency	Expectations	Instructor's Review
Professionalism: Demonstrate appropriate workplace hygiene and appearance.	Hair neat and restrained	
	Clean chef uniform and apron; nonslip, closed-toe shoes	
	No nail polish or jewelry	
Sanitation: Wash hands properly. Demonstrate safe food handling.	Display correct handwashing throughout production	
	Discard any broken or cracked eggs	
	Clean and sanitize workstation before and after work	
Mise en Place: Set up workstation properly. Review lab recommended reading. Organized recipe method and sequence of work.	Prepare ingredients for assembly, adjust recipe yield as needed	
	Preheat oven	
	Weigh both dry and liquid ingredients accurately	
	Needed equipment available and ready	
Cooking Technique: Demonstrate correct biscotti technique.	Place product in oven once appropriate temperature is reached	
	Bake until biscotti are lightly caramelized	
Product Evaluation: Present on a plain, white plate for observation. Taste finished product.	Biscotti are dark golden-brown color with crunchy texture	
	Almonds are apparent and visible for those who have allergic reactions to nuts	
	Cookie snaps when broken	

Additional Instructor's Comments

Lab Activity 43-1: **Yeast Activation**

Name _____ **Date** _____ **Period** _____

Group Members _____

Yeast is used as a leavening agent for breads. Leavening results when the yeast consumes carbohydrates and carbon dioxide is produced. This is also known as *fermentation*. The process of activating yeast is a basic skill required for great bread making. Fermentation happens most quickly in a warm, moist environment.

Objectives

After completing this lab, you will be able to

- execute the activation of yeast.
- recognize the signs of fermentation.

Preparation

1. Read Lab Procedure and gather the following supplies:
    - 1 Tbsp. active dry yeast
    - 1 Tbsp. honey or sugar
    - 8 fl. oz. water
    - small mixing bowl
    - thermometer
2. Review the section *Yeast* in text Chapter 40.

Key Terms

Define the following terms used in this activity. Some may have been defined in previous chapters.

1. yeast _____

   _____

2. fermentation _____

   _____

3. leavening _____

   _____

Lab Procedure

1. Place water in microwavable container and microwave for a few seconds. Test temperature and repeat process until water reaches 110°F (43°C). If the water is too hot, it will kill the yeast. If the water is too cold, the yeast won't activate.

2. Add the sugar (or honey) and yeast to the water. Stir until yeast has completely dissolved.

(Continued)

3. Allow the mixture to stand at room temperature for 5–10 minutes. Observe the mixture as fermentation begins and record your observations in the Observations/Questions section that follows.

4. Thick foam should build on top of the water mix. Once the foam is about one inch thick, it is ready to be incorporated into most bread recipes that require activated yeast.

Chef's Note: Yeast can be bought in several different forms. Most common are active dry yeast and fresh yeast. Fresh yeast is a moist, ivory-colored block and is most commonly found in commercial kitchen where bread is baked.

Observations/Questions

1. What was the first change you observed that made you think fermentation had begun?

_____

_____

_____

2. Record any visual changes you observed in the mixture.

_____

_____

_____

3. Record any smells you noted as the mixture changed.

_____

_____

_____

Lab Activity 43-2: French Bread

Name _____ **Date** _____ **Period** _____

Group Members _____

French bread makers, called *boulangers*, rise at 2 a.m. to start baking the morning's bread followed by a second batch for lunch. In France, this bread is eaten three times a day and is as popular today as it was centuries ago.

Objectives

After completing this lab, you will be able to

- implement yeast as a leavening agent.
- execute French bread preparation.

Mise en Place

1. Carefully read through the recipe before starting production. Adjust the yield as needed. Review how to convert recipe yield in text Chapter 15.
2. Review the sections *Units of Weight* and *Measuring Ingredients* in text Chapter 15.
3. Gather all ingredients and equipment required.
4. Preheat oven to desired temperature.

Sanitation and Safety Reminders

1. Clean and sanitize workstation before beginning to work.
2. Review *Safety Savvy: Mixer Safety* in text Chapter 40.
3. Wash hands properly and as often as needed.

Key Terms

Define the following terms used in this activity. Some may have been defined in previous chapters.

1. fermentation _____

    _____

2. punching _____

    _____

3. scaling _____

    _____

4. proofing _____

    _____

(Continued)

French Bread

Yield: 2 1-lb. loaves

Ingredients

24 oz.	670 g	bread flour
½ oz.	15 g	salt
12 oz.	340 g	water
½ oz.	15 g	active dry yeast

Method

1. Combine flour and salt in the bowl of the electric mixer.
2. Dissolve the yeast in the water and mix into the dry ingredients.
3. Mix at medium speed for 12 minutes. The dough should be smooth and elastic.
4. Place dough in a lightly oiled bowl and loosely cover. Allow the dough to ferment in a warm place approximately 1 hour, until it has doubled in size.
5. Punch the dough and scale according to use. Shape into rolls and place on a sheet pan lined with parchment paper. If loaves are made, place in lightly greased loaf pans.
6. Proof dough in a warm place until dough has doubled in size.
7. Bake at 400°F (204°C). If using an oven equipped with steam, inject steam for the first 10 minutes. Bake rolls 15–20 minutes, loaves 30–40 minutes.

Chef's Note: French bread gets its crisp crust from steam injected into the oven during the first stage of baking. If your oven does not have injected steam, place a sheet pan in the bottom of the oven while it is preheating. Pour 1 c. (240 mL) hot water onto the sheet pan at the beginning of the baking process.

Chef's Journal

Write an evaluation of your lab performance. Would your finished product and performance meet the standards of a professional kitchen? Describe how your recipe turned out and what techniques and procedures you need to improve.

_____

_____

_____

_____

_____

_____

_____

_____

_____

Performance Review: **French Bread**

Name _____ **Date**_____

Core knowledge/skills: dry-heat cooking method, yeast-raised breads, fermentation, leavening, proofing, punching, measurement and scaling techniques

Culinary Proficiency	Expectations	Instructor's Review
Professionalism: Demonstrate appropriate workplace hygiene and appearance.	Hair neat and restrained	
	Clean chef uniform and apron; nonslip, closed-toe shoes	
	No nail polish or jewelry	
Sanitation: Wash hands properly. Demonstrate safe food handling.	Display correct handwashing throughout production	
	Clean and sanitize workstation before and after work	
Mise en Place: Set up workstation properly. Review lab recommended reading. Organized recipe method and sequence of work.	Prepare ingredients for assembly, adjust recipe yield as needed	
	Preheat oven	
	Weigh both dry and liquid ingredients accurately	
	Needed equipment available and ready	
Cooking Technique: Demonstrate correct yeast-raised bread technique.	Activate and grow yeast successfully	
	Mix or knead dough until smooth and elastic	
	Lightly oil bowl, place dough in bowl and cover with clean cloth to avoid drying out	
	Allow dough to double in size	
	Employ steam during baking process	
Product Evaluation: Cut slices from finished bread and present on a plain, white plate for observation. Taste finished product.	Crust has good caramelized brown color, inside is white	
	Bread has good structure with a crisp crust and soft texture inside	
	Bread has pleasant residual smell from yeast	

Additional Instructor's Comments

Lab Activity 43-3: Soft Rolls/White Bread

Name _____ **Date** _____ **Period** _____

Group Members _____

The finished texture of this bread is slightly springy and moist due to the relatively high level of water used. The outside should not be crunchy or hard. Many different bread products, such as hamburger and hot dog buns, can be made using this white bread recipe.

Objectives

After completing this lab, you will be able to

- implement yeast as a leavening agent.
- execute white bread preparation.

Mise en Place

1. Carefully read through the recipe before starting production. Adjust the yield as needed. Review how to convert recipe yield in text Chapter 15.
2. Review the sections *Units of Weight* and *Measuring Ingredients* in text Chapter 15.
3. Gather all ingredients and equipment required.
4. Preheat oven to desired temperature.

Sanitation and Safety Reminders

1. Clean and sanitize workstation before beginning to work.
2. Review *Safety Savvy: Mixer Safety* in text Chapter 40.
3. Wash hands properly and as often as needed.

Key Terms

Define the following terms used in this activity. Some may have been defined in previous chapters.

1. fermentation _____

   _____

2. punching _____

   _____

3. scaling _____

   _____

4. proofing _____

   _____

(Continued)

Soft Rolls/White Bread

Yield: 2 30-oz. loaves, 40 1½-oz. rolls

Ingredients

32 oz.	900 g	bread flour
4 oz.	115 g	sugar
¾ oz.	20 g	salt
1½ oz.	40 g	milk powder (nonfat dried milk)
20 oz.	560 g	water
1½ oz.	40 g	active dry yeast
1 oz.	30 g	shortening or butter, melted

Method

1. Combine dry ingredients in the mixer bowl.
2. Dissolve the yeast in the water and mix into the dry ingredients along with the shortening.
3. Mix at medium speed for 12 minutes.
4. Place dough in a lightly oiled bowl and loosely cover. Allow the dough to ferment in a warm place approximately 1 hour, until it has doubled in size.
5. Punch the dough and scale according to use. Shape into rolls or loaves.
6. Proof dough in a warm place until dough has doubled in size.
7. Bake at 400°F (204°C). Bake rolls for 12–15 minutes, loaves for 45 minutes.

Chef's Journal

Write an evaluation of your lab performance. Would your finished product and performance meet the standards of a professional kitchen? Describe how your recipe turned out and what techniques and procedures you need to improve.

_____

_____

_____

_____

_____

_____

_____

_____

_____

Performance Review: **Soft Rolls/White Bread**

Name _____ **Date**_____

Core knowledge/skills: dry-heat cooking method, yeast-raised breads, fermentation, leavening, proofing, punching, measurement and scaling techniques

Culinary Proficiency	Expectations	Instructor's Review
Professionalism: Demonstrate appropriate workplace hygiene and appearance.	Hair neat and restrained	
	Clean chef uniform and apron; nonslip, closed-toe shoes	
	No nail polish or jewelry	
Sanitation: Wash hands properly. Demonstrate safe food handling.	Display correct handwashing throughout production	
	Clean and sanitize workstation before and after work	
Mise en Place: Set up workstation properly. Review lab recommended reading. Organized recipe method and sequence of work.	Prepare ingredients for assembly, adjust recipe yield as needed	
	Preheat oven	
	Weigh both dry and liquid ingredients accurately	
	Needed equipment available and ready	
Cooking Technique: Demonstrate correct yeast-raised bread technique.	Activate and grow yeast successfully	
	Mix or knead dough until smooth and elastic	
	Lightly oil bowl, place dough in bowl and cover with clean cloth to avoid drying out	
	Allow dough to double in size	
Product Evaluation: Cut slices from finished bread and present on a plain, white plate for observation. Taste finished product.	Bread has light caramelized brown crust and soft and white inside	
	Crust has soft texture	
	Bread has pleasant residual smell from yeast	

Additional Instructor's Comments

Lab Activity 43-4: **Whole Wheat Bread**

Name _____ **Date** _____ **Period** _____

Group Members _____

When flour is ground using the entire wheat grain, it is called whole wheat flour. This flour contains all three parts of the grain—the bran, endosperm, and germ. When bread is made with this flour, it is called whole wheat bread. In addition to having great flavor and texture, whole wheat bread offers many health benefits.

Objectives

After completing this lab, you will be able to

- implement yeast as a leavening agent.
- execute whole wheat bread preparation.

Mise en Place

1. Carefully read through the recipe before starting production. Adjust the yield as needed. Review how to convert recipe yield in text Chapter 15.
2. Review the sections *Units of Weight* and *Measuring Ingredients* in text Chapter 15.
3. Gather all ingredients and equipment required.
4. Preheat oven to desired temperature.

Sanitation and Safety Reminders

1. Clean and sanitize workstation before beginning to work.
2. Review *Safety Savvy: Mixer Safety* in text Chapter 40.
3. Wash hands properly and as often as needed.

Key Terms

Define the following terms used in this activity. Some may have been defined in previous chapters.

1. fermentation _____

   _____

2. punching _____

   _____

3. scaling _____

   _____

4. proofing _____

   _____

(Continued)

5. yeast _____

_____

Whole Wheat Bread

Yield: 2 1¾-lb. loaves, 3 dozen 1½-oz. rolls

Ingredients

32 oz.	900 g	whole wheat flour
¾ oz.	20 g	salt
1½ oz.	45 g	milk powder (nonfat dried milk)
1 oz.	30 g	active dry yeast
4 oz.	115 g	honey
20 oz.	560 g	water
3 oz.	85 g	shortening, melted

Method

1. Combine dry ingredients in the bowl of the electric mixer.
2. Dissolve the yeast and honey in the water and mix into the dry ingredients along with the shortening.

Chef's Note: Whole wheat flour tends to be a heavier flour, so activation of the yeast is important. Dissolve the yeast in water that is 110°F (43°C) to ensure the yeast is activated.

3. Mix at medium speed for 12 minutes.
4. Place dough in a lightly oiled bowl and loosely cover. Allow the dough to ferment in a warm place approximately 1 hour, until it has doubled in size.
5. Punch the dough and scale according to use. Shape into rolls or loaves.
6. Proof dough in a warm place until dough has doubled in size.
7. Bake at 400°F (204°C). Bake rolls for 12–15 minutes, loaves for 45 minutes.

Chef's Journal

Write an evaluation of your lab performance. Would your finished product and performance meet the standards of a professional kitchen? Describe how your recipe turned out and what techniques and procedures you need to improve.

_____
_____
_____
_____
_____

Performance Review: **Whole Wheat Bread**

Name _____ **Date**_____

Core knowledge/skills: dry-heat cooking method, yeast-raised breads, fermentation, leavening, proofing, punching, measurement and scaling techniques

Culinary Proficiency	Expectations	Instructor's Review
Professionalism: Demonstrate appropriate workplace hygiene and appearance.	Hair neat and restrained	
	Clean chef uniform and apron; nonslip, closed-toe shoes	
	No nail polish or jewelry	
Sanitation: Wash hands properly. Demonstrate safe food handling.	Display correct handwashing throughout production	
	Clean and sanitize workstation before and after work	
Mise en Place: Set up workstation properly. Review lab recommended reading. Organized recipe method and sequence of work.	Prepare ingredients for assembly, adjust recipe yield as needed	
	Preheat oven	
	Weigh both dry and liquid ingredients accurately	
	Needed equipment available and ready	
Cooking Technique: Demonstrate correct yeast-raised bread technique.	Activate and grow yeast successfully	
	Mix or knead dough until smooth and elastic	
	Lightly oil bowl, place dough in bowl and cover with clean cloth to avoid drying out	
	Allow dough to double in size	
Product Evaluation: Cut slices from finished bread and present on a plain, white plate for observation. Taste finished product.	Bread has crisp, caramelized brown crust and soft inside	
	Bread has pleasant residual smell from yeast	
	General texture of bread is more dense due to whole wheat flour	

Additional Instructor's Comments

Lab Activity 44-1: **Mealy Pie Dough**

Name _____ **Date** _____ **Period** _____

Group Members _____

The difference between flaky and mealy pie dough is how the fat is cut into the flour mixture. To achieve a flaky crust, the fat should be cut to about pea-size pieces before mixing. For mealy crusts, the fat is cut into much smaller pieces—about the size of grains of cornmeal—before mixing begins.

Objective

After completing this lab, you will be able to

- execute a mealy pie dough.

Mise en Place

1. Carefully read through the recipe before starting production. Adjust the yield as needed. Review how to convert recipe yield in text Chapter 15.

2. Review the sections *Dough* and *Mixing* in text Chapter 44.

3. Gather all ingredients and equipment required.

Sanitation and Safety Reminders

1. Clean and sanitize workstation before beginning to work.

2. Wash hands properly and as often as needed.

Key Terms

Define the following terms used in this activity. Some may have been defined in previous chapters.

1. mealy pie dough _____

_____

2. flaky pie dough _____

_____

(Continued)

Mealy Pie Dough

Yield: 2 lb. (900 g)

Ingredients

1 lb.	450 g	pastry flour
0.24 oz. (1 tsp.)	7 g	salt
10 oz.	280 g	vegetable shortening
5 oz.	140 g	cold water

Method

1. Combine the flour and salt in a mixing bowl.
2. Cut the shortening into nut-size pieces and add to the flour.

Chef's Note: Chill the vegetable shortening before starting the recipe. The quality of the dough is better if the shortening is still firm and chilled at the end of mixing.

3. Use the paddle attachment to mix in the shortening until the flour and fat mixture takes on a mealy appearance.
4. Add the cold water and mix just until the dough comes together in a cohesive mass. Do not overmix.
5. Refrigerate at or below 41°F (5°C) and reserve for use in Lab Activity 44-2: Pecan Pie.

Chef's Journal

Write an evaluation of your lab performance. Would your finished product and performance meet the standards of a professional kitchen? Describe how your recipe turned out and what techniques and procedures you need to improve.

_____
_____
_____
_____
_____
_____
_____
_____
_____
_____
_____
_____

Performance Review: **Mealy Pie Dough**

Name _____ **Date**_____

Core knowledge/skills: mealy pie dough, crust preparation, cutting in, recipe yield conversion

Culinary Proficiency	Expectations	Instructor's Review
Professionalism: Demonstrate appropriate workplace hygiene and appearance.	Hair neat and restrained	
	Clean chef uniform and apron; nonslip, closed-toe shoes	
	No nail polish or jewelry	
Sanitation: Wash hands properly. Demonstrate safe food handling.	Display correct handwashing throughout production	
	Clean and sanitize workstation before and after work	
Mise en Place: Set up workstation properly. Review lab recommended reading. Organized recipe method and sequence of work.	Prepare ingredients for assembly, adjust recipe yield as needed	
	Weigh both dry and liquid ingredients accurately	
	Chill both fat and liquid ingredients prior to mixing	
	Needed equipment available and ready	
Cooking Technique: Demonstrate flaky pie dough preparation.	Cut cold fat into flour until approx. the size of cornmeal	
	Mix in ice cold water	
	Mix dough just long enough to combine ingredients, do not overwork	
	Wrap dough to prevent drying out, label and place in refrigerator	
Product Evaluation:	Crust will be evaluated in Activity 44-2: Pecan Pie	

Additional Instructor's Comments

Lab Activity 44-2: **Pecan Pie**

Name _____ **Date** _____ **Period** _____

Group Members _____

Pecan pie is a rich, sweet dessert. Pecans are typically grown in the south and offer a rich nutty taste that is perfectly balanced by the dark corn syrup. This dish originates in the south where pecan trees were abundant, which would have made pecan pie an inexpensive dish to prepare.

Objectives

After completing this lab, you will be able to

- implement a liquid pie filling.
- implement a mealy pie dough.
- execute a pecan pie.

Mise en Place

1. Carefully read through the recipe before starting production. Adjust the yield as needed. Review how to convert recipe yield in text Chapter 15.

2. Review the sections *Rolling and Forming* and *Liquid Fillings* in text Chapter 44.

3. Gather all ingredients and equipment required.

4. Preheat oven to desired temperature.

Sanitation and Safety Reminders

1. Clean and sanitize workstation before beginning to work.

2. Wash hands properly and as often as needed.

Key Term

Define the following term used in this activity. It may have been defined in a previous chapter.

1. mealy pie dough _____

_____

(Continued)

Pecan Pie

Yield: 1 9-in. pie

Ingredients

Filling:

6 oz.	170 g	eggs (about 3 large)
0.16 oz. (1 tsp.)	5 g	vanilla extract
16 oz.	480 g	dark corn syrup
½ oz.	15 g	flour
1 oz.	30 g	butter, melted

Assembly:

8 oz.	225 g	pecans, chopped
10 oz.	280 g	mealy pie dough (prepared in Lab Activity 44-1)

Method

1. Combine all filling ingredients and mix well.
2. Roll out pie dough and line the bottom of a 9-inch pie pan.
3. Add the pecans to the shell and pour the filling in the pie pan.

Chef's Note: If other nut varieties are used in place of pecans, consider using a lighter corn syrup. Dark corn syrup has a strong flavor that may overpower other nuts.

4. Bake the pie at 425°F (218°C) for 10 minutes. Lower heat to 350°F (177°C) and continue baking for 35 minutes.

Chef's Note: The oven temperature is reduced to avoid burning the sugar, which will leave your pie with a bitter taste.

Chef's Journal

Write an evaluation of your lab performance. Would your finished product and performance meet the standards of a professional kitchen? Describe how your recipe turned out and what techniques and procedures you need to improve.

_____

_____

_____

_____

_____

_____

_____

_____

_____

Performance Review: **Pecan Pie**

Name _____ **Date**_____

Core knowledge/skills: dry-heat cooking method, mealy pie dough, crust preparation, liquid pie filling, recipe yield conversion

Culinary Proficiency	Expectations	Instructor's Review
Professionalism: Demonstrate appropriate workplace hygiene and appearance.	Hair neat and restrained	
	Clean chef uniform and apron; nonslip, closed-toe shoes	
	No nail polish or jewelry	
Sanitation: Wash hands properly. Demonstrate safe food handling.	Display correct handwashing throughout production	
	Discard any broken or cracked eggs	
	Clean and sanitize workstation before and after work	
Mise en Place: Set up workstation properly. Review lab recommended reading. Organized recipe method and sequence of work.	Prepare ingredients for assembly, adjust recipe yield as needed	
	Preheat oven, ensure pie dough is appropriate temperature to achieve workable consistency	
	Weigh both dry and liquid ingredients accurately	
	Needed equipment available and ready	
Cooking Technique: Demonstrate rolling and forming a piecrust. Demonstrate preparation of pie with liquid filling.	Roll crust out evenly to approx. 1/8-inch thickness	
	Arrange dough neatly in pie pan with edges trimmed off and crimped	
	Mix filling ingredients until smooth and well blended	
	Bake until pie achieves caramelized color	
Product Evaluation: Cut a piece out of pie and present on a plain, white plate for observation. Taste finished product.	Color is rich golden brown	
	Filling is firm enough to hold together during cutting, but not too heavy or hard	
	Nuts are evenly distributed in filling	
	Piecrust is even thickness and not soggy, tender but holds together when handled	
	No bitter flavor from burnt sugar	

Additional Instructor's Comments

Lab Activity 44-3: **Sweet Dough**

Name _____ **Date**_____ **Period** _____

Group Members _____

Sweet dough contains three ingredients that other pie dough recipes do not—sugar, eggs, and milk. These ingredients produce a crust that is slightly richer and sweeter than other crusts. The French word for sweet dough is *pâte sucrée*. This dough is typically used with sweet fillings such as fruits and pastry cream.

Objective

After completing this lab, you will be able to

• execute a sweet dough.

Mise en Place

1. Carefully read through the recipe before starting production. Adjust the yield as needed. Review how to convert recipe yield in text Chapter 15.

2. Review the sections *Mixing* and *Tarts* in text Chapter 44.

3. Gather all ingredients and equipment required.

Sanitation and Safety Reminders

1. Clean and sanitize workstation before beginning to work.

2. Wash hands properly and as often as needed.

3. Inspect eggs and discard any broken or cracked eggs.

Key Term

Define the following term used in this activity. It may have been defined in a previous chapter.

1. sweet dough _____

_____

(Continued)

Sweet Dough (Pâte Sucrée)

Yield: 2½ lb. (1.14 kg)

Ingredients

1 lb.	450 g	pastry flour
0.24 oz. (1 tsp.)	7 g	salt
7 oz.	200 g	sugar
8 oz.	225 g	butter, softened
6 oz.	170 g	egg yolks (about 4 ea.)
3 oz.	90 g	milk

Method

1. Combine flour, salt, and sugar in mixing bowl and cut in butter.
2. Mix with the paddle to blend butter and dry ingredients well.
3. Add yolks and milk and mix to form a smooth dough. Do not overmix.
4. Refrigerate at or below 41°F (5°C) and reserve for use in Lab Activity 44-4: Fruit Tart.

Chef's Journal

Write an evaluation of your lab performance. Would your finished product and performance meet the standards of a professional kitchen? Describe how your recipe turned out and what techniques and procedures you need to improve.

_____

_____

_____

_____

_____

_____

_____

_____

_____

_____

_____

_____

_____

_____

Performance Review: **Sweet Dough**

Name _____ **Date** _____

Core knowledge/skills: sweet dough, crust preparation, cutting in, recipe yield conversion

Culinary Proficiency	Expectations	Instructor's Review
Professionalism: Demonstrate appropriate workplace hygiene and appearance.	Hair neat and restrained	
	Clean chef uniform and apron; nonslip, closed-toe shoes	
	No nail polish or jewelry	
Sanitation: Wash hands properly. Demonstrate safe food handling.	Display correct handwashing throughout production	
	Discard any broken or cracked eggs	
	Clean and sanitize workstation before and after work	
Mise en Place: Set up workstation properly. Review lab recommended reading. Organized recipe method and sequence of work.	Prepare ingredients for assembly, adjust recipe yield as needed	
	Weigh both dry and liquid ingredients accurately	
	Needed equipment available and ready	
Cooking Technique: Demonstrate sweet dough preparation.	Cut fat into flour until approx. pea size	
	Use ice cold milk	
	Mix dough just long enough to combine ingredients, do not overwork	
	Wrap dough to prevent drying out, label and refrigerate	
Product Evaluation:	Crust will be evaluated in Activity 44-4: Fruit Tart	

Additional Instructor's Comments

Lab Activity 44-4: **Fruit Tart**

Name _____ **Date** _____ **Period** _____

Group Members _____

Chefs have been preparing tarts for hundreds of years. Since tarts have no top crust, chefs can use a variety of fruits or fillings to create visual, as well as tasty, treats.

Objectives

After completing this lab, you will be able to

- execute fruit tart preparation.
- apply blind baking technique.
- implement pastry cream preparation.

Mise en Place

1. Carefully read through the recipe before starting production. Adjust the yield as needed. Review how to convert recipe yield in text Chapter 15.

2. Review the sections *Rolling and Forming* and *Tarts* in text Chapter 44 and *Pastry Cream* in text Chapter 46.

3. Gather all ingredients and equipment required.

4. Preheat oven to desired temperature.

Sanitation and Safety Reminders

1. Clean and sanitize workstation before beginning to work.

2. Wash hands properly and as often as needed.

3. Wash and trim fruits before preparing.

4. Wear disposable gloves when handling ready-to-eat ingredients.

Key Terms

Define the following terms used in this activity. Some may have been defined in previous chapters.

1. blind baking _____

   _____

2. pastry glaze _____

   _____

3. sweet dough _____

   _____

4. pastry cream _____

   _____

(Continued)

Fruit Tart

Yield: 1 10-in. tart

Ingredients

as needed		softened butter
12 oz.	340 g	sweet dough (prepared in Lab Activity 44-3)
16 oz.	480 g	pastry cream (recipe 46.2)
as needed		assorted fresh berries and sliced fruits
8 oz.	240 g	apricot pastry glaze

Method

1. Grease a tart pan with softened butter.
2. Roll out the sweet dough and line the tart pan. Trim the edges of the dough.
3. Place a piece of parchment paper over the dough and fill the tart with baking weights.
4. Bake the tart shell at 425°F (218°C) for 25 minutes. Remove weights and cool.
5. Spread an even layer of pastry cream over the surface of the tart shell.
6. Arrange berries and fruit in an attractive pattern.
7. Melt the apricot glaze over low heat.
8. Gently coat the fruit with the glaze using a pastry brush.
9. Refrigerate at or below 41°F (5°C) until chilled.

Chef's Journal

Write an evaluation of your lab performance. Would your finished product and performance meet the standards of a professional kitchen? Describe how your recipe turned out and what techniques and procedures you need to improve.

_____

_____

_____

_____

_____

_____

_____

_____

_____

_____

Performance Review: **Fruit Tart**

Name _____ Date_____

Core knowledge/skills: dry-heat cooking method, blind baking, crust preparation, cutting in, pastry cream, knife skills, fruit preparation, pastry glaze, recipe yield conversion

Culinary Proficiency	Expectations	Instructor's Review
Professionalism: Demonstrate appropriate workplace hygiene and appearance.	Hair neat and restrained	
	Clean chef uniform and apron; nonslip, closed-toe shoes	
	No nail polish or jewelry	
Sanitation: Wash hands properly. Demonstrate safe food handling.	Display correct handwashing throughout production	
	Discard any broken or cracked eggs, wash and trim fruit	
	Clean and sanitize workstation before and after work	
Mise en Place: Set up workstation properly. Review lab recommended reading. Organized recipe method and sequence of work.	Prepare ingredients for assembly, adjust recipe yield as needed	
	Preheat oven	
	Weigh both dry and liquid ingredients accurately	
	Produce uniform, neat fruit cuts	
	Needed equipment available and ready	
Cooking Technique: Demonstrate blind baking of tart shell. Demonstrate tart preparation.	Roll crust out evenly and neatly fit into tart pan	
	Place baking weights in tart shell to prevent bubbling or buckling during baking	
	Cool tart shell before filling with pastry cream	
	Demonstrate correct technique for making pastry cream	
Product Evaluation: Cut a piece out of tart and present on a plain, white plate for observation. Taste finished product.	Crust is even and pastry cream is evenly distributed across crust	
	Fruit is attractive and appealing, pastry glaze is neatly and evenly applied	
	Pastry cream is rich yellow color and soft	
	Tart shell tastes sweet and breaks easily in mouth, but holds together when picked up	

Additional Instructor's Comments

Lab Activity 45-1: **Old Fashioned Pound Cake**

Name _____ **Date**_____ **Period** _____

Group Members _____

The name of this cake is a clue to its recipe. The original recipe called for one pound of each of the four major ingredients—butter, sugar, eggs, and flour. Believed to date back to a time when few people could read, this recipe was easy to remember.

Objectives

After completing this lab, you will be able to

- execute creaming method for pound cake preparation.
- recognize when a cake is fully cooked.

Mise en Place

1. Carefully read through the recipe before starting production. Adjust the yield as needed. Review how to convert recipe yield in text Chapter 15. If necessary, adjust recipe for altitude.
2. Review the sections *Creaming Method*, *Pan Preparation*, and *Baking* in text Chapter 45.
3. Gather all ingredients and equipment required.
4. Preheat oven to desired temperature.

Sanitation and Safety Reminders

1. Clean and sanitize workstation before beginning to work.
2. Inspect eggs and discard any broken or cracked eggs.
3. Review *Safety Savvy: Mixer Safety* in text Chapter 40.
4. Wash hands properly and as often as needed.

Key Term

Define the following term used in this activity. It may have been defined in a previous chapter.

1. creaming method _____

_____

(Continued)

Old Fashioned Pound Cake

Yield: 1 2-lb. loaf

Ingredients

8 oz.	225 g	butter
8 oz.	225 g	sugar
0.06 oz. (¼ tsp.)	2 g	salt
0.16 oz. (1 tsp.)	5 g	vanilla or lemon extract
8 oz.	225 g	cake flour, sifted
8 oz.	225 g	eggs (about 4 large)

Method

1. Preheat oven to 325°F (163°C).
2. Grease a 2-pound loaf pan.
3. Combine the butter with the sugar, salt, and extract in the mixer. Mix with the paddle attachment until well creamed.
4. Add the eggs and mix until well incorporated.
5. Add the sifted flour and mix to form a smooth batter. Do not overmix.
6. Portion the dough into pans and immediately bake at 325°F (163°C) until golden brown, about 1 hour and 15 minutes. Test with skewer.

Chef's Journal

Write an evaluation of your lab performance. Would your finished product and performance meet the standards of a professional kitchen? Describe how your recipe turned out and what techniques and procedures you need to improve.

_____

_____

_____

_____

_____

_____

_____

_____

_____

_____

_____

_____

Performance Review: **Old Fashioned Pound Cake**

Name _____ **Date**_____

Core knowledge/skills: dry-heat cooking method, pound cake, creaming method, cake pan preparation, measurement and scaling

Culinary Proficiency	Expectations	Instructor's Review
Professionalism: Demonstrate appropriate workplace hygiene and appearance.	Hair neat and restrained	
	Clean chef uniform and apron; nonslip, closed-toe shoes	
	No nail polish or jewelry	
Sanitation: Wash hands properly. Demonstrate safe food handling.	Display correct handwashing throughout production	
	Discard any broken or cracked eggs	
	Clean and sanitize workstation before and after work	
Mise en Place: Set up workstation properly. Review lab recommended reading. Organized recipe method and sequence of work.	Prepare ingredients for assembly, adjust recipe for yield and altitude if necessary	
	Preheat oven, prepare cake pan	
	Weigh both dry and liquid ingredients accurately	
	Needed equipment available and ready	
Cooking Technique: Demonstrate correct creaming method. Demonstrate technique to determine doneness of cake.	Cream butter, sugar, salt, and vanilla, gradually add eggs and mix well	
	Add dry ingredients and mix until smooth	
	Bake cake until light golden brown, test with skewer	
Product Evaluation: Cut a piece out of cake and present on a plain, white plate for observation. Taste finished product.	Cake is light golden brown, releases from pan easily, not torn or broken	
	Texture is soft, yet firm enough to hold together when picked up	
	Sponge is cooked throughout, no liquid batter in middle	
	Taste is even, rich, and moist	

Additional Instructor's Comments

Lab Activity 45-2: Basic Yellow Sponge Cake

Name _____ **Date** _____ **Period** _____

Group Members _____

Once you understand and master the preparation of a basic yellow sponge cake, you can apply the technique to other sponges such as red velvet cake or black forest cake. Mise en place is important with this recipe because once the sponge batter is prepared, it must be placed in the oven immediately. Any delays could result in a lower quality finished cake.

Objectives

After completing this lab, you will be able to

- implement cake pan preparation technique.
- recognize when a cake is fully cooked.
- execute sponge cake preparation.

Mise en Place

1. Carefully read through the recipe before starting production. Adjust the yield as needed. Review how to convert recipe yield in text Chapter 15. If necessary, adjust recipe for altitude.
2. Review the sections *Sponge Method*, *Pan Preparation*, and *Baking* in text Chapter 45.
3. Gather all ingredients and equipment required.
4. Preheat oven to desired temperature.

Sanitation and Safety Reminders

1. Clean and sanitize workstation before beginning to work.
2. Inspect eggs and discard any broken or cracked eggs.
3. Review *Safety Savvy: Mixer Safety* in text Chapter 40.
4. Wash hands properly and as often as needed.

Key Terms

Define the following terms used in this activity. Some may have been defined in previous chapters.

1. sponge cake _____

_____

2. baking powder _____

_____

3. gluten _____

_____

(Continued)

Basic Yellow Sponge Cake

Yield: 2 10-in. cakes

Ingredients

8 oz.	225 g	cake flour
0.17 oz. (1 tsp.)	5 g	baking powder
10 oz.	280 g	sugar
8 oz.	225 g	eggs (about 4 large)
1 oz.	30 g	egg yolks
0.08 oz. (½ tsp.)	3 g	vanilla extract
0.12 oz. (½ tsp.)	4 g	salt
4 oz.	120 g	milk
2 oz.	60 g	butter

Method

1. Preheat oven to 375°F (190°C).
2. Prepare cake pans by greasing and dusting with flour.
3. Sift the cake flour and baking powder. Set aside.

Chef's Note: Cake flour is recommended because it contains less protein (gluten) and will produce a more delicately textured cake.

4. Heat the milk, salt, and butter until the butter is melted. Set aside.
5. Combine eggs, yolks, vanilla, and sugar in the bowl of the mixer.
6. Beat the eggs and sugar with the whip attachment until they are thick and ribbonlike.
7. With a spatula, alternately fold in the dry ingredients and the milk.
8. Scale into prepared pans and bake immediately for 20–25 minutes until done when tested with a skewer.

Chef's Journal

Write an evaluation of your lab performance. Would your finished product and performance meet the standards of a professional kitchen? Describe how your recipe turned out and what techniques and procedures you need to improve.

_____

_____

_____

_____

_____

_____

_____

Performance Review: **Basic Yellow Sponge Cake**

Name _____ **Date**_____

Core knowledge/skills: dry-heat cooking method, sponge cake, cake pan preparation, leavening, gluten

Culinary Proficiency	Expectations	Instructor's Review
Professionalism: Demonstrate appropriate workplace hygiene and appearance.	Hair neat and restrained	
	Clean chef uniform and apron; nonslip, closed-toe shoes	
	No nail polish or jewelry	
Sanitation: Wash hands properly. Demonstrate safe food handling.	Display correct handwashing throughout production	
	Discard any broken or cracked eggs	
	Clean and sanitize workstation before and after work	
Mise en Place: Set up workstation properly. Review lab recommended reading. Organized recipe method and sequence of work.	Prepare ingredients for assembly, adjust recipe for yield or altitude if necessary	
	Preheat oven, prepare cake pans	
	Weigh both dry and liquid ingredients accurately	
	Needed equipment available and ready	
Cooking Technique: Demonstrate correct sponge method. Demonstrate technique to determine doneness of cake.	Whip eggs and sugar until mixture becomes thick	
	Fold in dry ingredients and milk carefully	
	Place batter in prepared pans and into preheated oven immediately	
	Bake cake until light golden brown, test with skewer	
Product Evaluation: Cut a piece out of cake and present on a plain, white plate for observation. Taste finished product.	Cake is light golden brown, releases from pan easily, not torn or broken	
	Texture is light and airy, yet firm enough to hold together when picked up	
	Sponge is cooked throughout, no liquid batter in middle	
	Taste is even, moist, and sweet	

Additional Instructor's Comments

Lab Activity 45-3: **Genoise**

Name _____ **Date** _____ **Period** _____

Group Members _____

Genoise preparation is often regarded as a benchmark by which to judge the skills, knowledge, and aptitude of aspiring pastry chefs. This classic method requires close attention to detail.

Objectives

After completing this lab, you will be able to

- execute genoise preparation.
- implement a double boiler.
- recognize when a cake is fully cooked.

Mise en Place

1. Carefully read through the recipe before starting production. Adjust the yield as needed. Review how to convert recipe yield in text Chapter 15. If necessary, adjust recipe for altitude.
2. Review the sections *Sponge Method*, *Pan Preparation*, and *Baking* in text Chapter 45.
3. Gather all ingredients and equipment required.
4. Preheat oven to desired temperature.

Sanitation and Safety Reminders

1. Clean and sanitize workstation before beginning to work.
2. Inspect eggs and discard any broken or cracked eggs.
3. Review *Safety Savvy: Mixer Safety* in text Chapter 40.
4. Wash hands properly and as often as needed.

Key Terms

Define the following terms used in this activity. Some may have been defined in previous chapters.

1. genoise _____

   _____

2. sponge cake _____

   _____

(Continued)

Genoise

Yield: 1 10-in. cake

Ingredients

12 oz.	340 g	eggs (about 6 large)
6 oz.	170 g	sugar
0.08 oz. (½ tsp.)	3 g	vanilla extract
6 oz.	170 g	cake flour
1 oz.	30 g	butter, melted

Method

1. Preheat oven to 375°F (190°C).
2. Prepare cake pan by greasing and dusting with flour.
3. Sift the cake flour. Set aside.
4. Combine eggs and sugar in the bowl of the mixer.
5. Place the bowl over a double boiler and stir continually until sugar dissolves and mixture reaches 100°F (37.7°C).

Chef's Note: The water in the bottom pan of a double boiler should not come in contact with the top pan. The top pan and its contents are heated by steam produced in the bottom pan.

6. Beat the eggs and sugar with the whip attachment until they are thick and ribbonlike.
7. With a spatula, fold in the flour and then the melted butter.
8. Scale into prepared pan and bake immediately for 20–25 minutes until done when tested with a skewer.

Chef's Journal

Write an evaluation of your lab performance. Would your finished product and performance meet the standards of a professional kitchen? Describe how your recipe turned out and what techniques and procedures you need to improve.

_____

_____

_____

_____

_____

_____

_____

_____

_____

Performance Review: **Genoise**

Name _____ **Date**_____

Core knowledge/skills: dry-heat cooking method, genoise, sponge cake, cake pan preparation, double boiler, temperature measurement

Culinary Proficiency	Expectations	Instructor's Review
Professionalism: Demonstrate appropriate workplace hygiene and appearance.	Hair neat and restrained	
	Clean chef uniform and apron; nonslip, closed-toe shoes	
	No nail polish or jewelry.	
Sanitation: Wash hands properly. Demonstrate safe food handling.	Display correct handwashing throughout production	
	Discard any broken or cracked eggs	
	Clean and sanitize workstation before and after work	
Mise en Place: Set up workstation properly. Review lab recommended reading. Organized recipe method and sequence of work.	Prepare ingredients for assembly, adjust recipe for yield or altitude if necessary	
	Preheat oven, prepare cake pan	
	Weigh both dry and liquid ingredients accurately	
	Needed equipment available and ready	
Cooking Technique: Demonstrate correct sponge method. Demonstrate technique to determine doneness of cake.	Heat eggs and sugar to 100°F, then whip until mixture becomes thick	
	Carefully fold in dry ingredients and butter	
	Place batter in prepared pan and place in preheated oven immediately	
	Bake cake until light golden brown, test with skewer	
Product Evaluation: Cut a piece out of cake and present on a plain, white plate for observation. Taste finished product.	Color is light golden brown and cake is cooked throughout, no liquid batter in middle	
	Texture is soft, yet firm enough to hold together when picked up	
	Taste is even and moist, but not as sweet as yellow sponge cake	
	Cake has rich, smoothness from eggs	

Additional Instructor's Comments

Lab Activity 46-1: Crème Anglaise

Name _____ **Date** _____ **Period** _____

Group Members _____

Preparing a perfect crème anglaise requires close attention to temperature—too hot and it might break, too cold and it will not thicken. A well-made crème anglaise is a sign of skill, technique, and control of product.

Objectives

After completing this lab, you will be able to

- implement tempering technique.
- execute a crème anglaise preparation.

Mise en Place

1. Carefully read through the recipe before starting production. Adjust the yield as needed. Review how to convert recipe yield in text Chapter 15.

2. Review the section *Crème Anglaise* in text Chapter 46.

3. Gather all ingredients and equipment required.

Sanitation and Safety Reminders

1. Clean and sanitize workstation before beginning to work.

2. Inspect eggs and discard any broken or cracked eggs.

3. Review the section *Cooling* in text Chapter 8.

4. Wash hands properly and as often as needed.

Key Terms

Define the following terms used in this activity. Some may have been defined in previous chapters.

1. tempering _____

   _____

2. crème anglaise _____

   _____

(Continued)

Crème Anglaise

Yield: 1 qt. (0.95 L)

Ingredients

6 oz.	170 g	sugar
9 oz.	255 g	egg yolks
0.32 oz. (2 tsp.)	10 g	vanilla extract
24 oz.	720 g	milk

Method

1. In a bowl, whisk sugar, egg yolks, and vanilla extract until the sugar dissolves and the mixture becomes fluffy and lighter in color.

2. In a saucepan, bring the milk to a boil.

Chef's Note: Do not use high heat or leave milk unattended while bringing it to a boil. Once milk is scorched or burnt, the flavor cannot be covered and makes the product unusable.

3. While whisking constantly, pour half of the milk into the egg yolk and sugar mixture. Pour this mixture in the saucepan with the remaining half of the milk.

4. Over medium heat, cook the sauce while stirring constantly with a wooden spoon or silicone spatula. Cook until the sauce thickens and reaches 185°F (85°C). Immediately pour the sauce through a chinois.

Chef's Note: For variety, try adding 4 oz. (115 g) of melted semi-sweet chocolate or ¼ c. (60 mL) finely chopped fresh mint into the strained, hot crème anglaise.

5. Chill the crème anglaise on ice and store in the refrigerator at or below 41°F (5°C) until needed.

Chef's Note: Before chilling, place plastic wrap directly on top of the crème anglaise so no air is in contact with the sauce. Be sure to label with product name and date. If not wrapped correctly, the custard forms a thick skin that should not be served.

Chef's Journal

Write an evaluation of your lab performance. Would your finished product and performance meet the standards of a professional kitchen? Describe how your recipe turned out and what techniques and procedures you need to improve.

_____

_____

_____

_____

_____

_____

Performance Review: **Crème Anglaise**

Name _____ **Date**_____

Core knowledge/skills: crème anglaise, tempering, thermometer use, cooling food safely

Culinary Proficiency	Expectations	Instructor's Review
Professionalism: Demonstrate appropriate workplace hygiene and appearance.	Hair neat and restrained	
	Clean chef uniform and apron; nonslip, closed-toe shoes	
	No nail polish or jewelry	
Sanitation: Wash hands properly. Demonstrate safe food handling.	Display correct handwashing throughout production	
	Clean and sanitize workstation before and after work	
	Inspect eggs for cracks and discard, cool sauce to 70°F (21°C) or below in two hours or less, and to 41°F (5°C) or below in less than a total of six hours	
Mise en Place: Set up workstation properly. Review lab recommended reading. Organized recipe method and sequence of work.	Prepare ingredients for assembly, adjust recipe yield as needed	
	Weigh both dry and liquid ingredients accurately	
	Needed equipment available and ready	
Cooking Technique: Demonstrate correct tempering technique. Demonstrate preparation of crème anglaise.	Temper egg yolks properly so there is no curdling or breaking	
	Stir sauce continuously and heat to 180°F to thicken	
	Remove sauce from pan immediately and strain	
Product Evaluation: Display crème anglaise in a plain, white bowl for observation. Taste finished product.	Sauce is very light yellow with nappé consistency, no burnt or scorched flavor is detected	
	Sauce is smooth and light with no signs of curdling or separation	
	When warm, sauce is slightly runny; chilled sauce sets up like gelatin	

Additional Instructor's Comments

Lab Activity 46-2: **Raspberry Mousse**

Name _____ **Date** _____ **Period** _____

Group Members _____

Whenever you hear or see the word *mousse*, it should bring to mind something very light, foamy, and delicate. The light texture comes from whipped heavy cream. During the whipping process, enough air is trapped in the cream to double or even triple the volume.

Objectives

After completing this lab, you will be able to

- implement blooming technique.
- recognize whipped cream at firm peak stage.
- execute a mousse preparation.

Mise en Place

1. Carefully read through the recipe before starting production. Adjust the yield as needed. Review how to convert recipe yield in text Chapter 15.

2. Review the sections *Gelatin* in text Chapter 40, *Whipped Cream* and *Mousse and Bavarian Cream* in text Chapter 46.

3. Gather all ingredients and equipment required.

Sanitation and Safety Reminders

1. Clean and sanitize workstation before beginning to work.

2. Review the section *Cooling* in text Chapter 8.

3. Wash hands properly and as often as needed.

Key Terms

Define the following terms used in this activity. Some may have been defined in previous chapters.

1. mousse _____

   _____

2. blooming _____

   _____

(Continued)

Raspberry Mousse

Yield: 3 pt. (1.7 L)

Ingredients

0.6 oz. (2 Tbsp.)	12 g	powdered gelatin
4 oz.	120 g	cold water
16 oz.	480 g	seedless raspberry purée
3½ oz.	100 g	sugar
24 oz.	720 g	heavy cream

Method

1. Combine water and gelatin. Let sit for 5–10 minutes or until the gelatin has absorbed the water and become translucent.

Chef's Note: Use cold water when blooming gelatin to prevent the powder from clumping. Once the gelatin blooms, it should be warmed very slightly. The slight warming acts to clear the liquid.

2. Whip cream until firm peak. Refrigerate at or below 41°F (5°C).

3. In a small saucepan, combine bloomed gelatin mixture and 2 oz. (65 g) raspberry purée. Heat this mixture over low heat while stirring constantly until dissolved. Remove from heat.

4. Stirring constantly with a whisk, add 4 oz. (120 g) raspberry purée to the heated mixture. Pour this new mixture into the remaining raspberry purée while stirring constantly.

5. Add sugar and stir until dissolved.

6. Fold the whipped cream into the raspberry mixture.

7. Taste and add additional sugar if needed. (More may be needed if the raspberries are acidic.) Ladle raspberry mousse into containers. Chill at or below 41°F (5°C) for at least 12 hours before serving.

Chef's Journal

Write an evaluation of your lab performance. Would your finished product and performance meet the standards of a professional kitchen? Describe how your recipe turned out and what techniques and procedures you need to improve.

_____

_____

_____

_____

_____

_____

_____

Performance Review: **Raspberry Mousse**

Name _____ **Date**_____

Core knowledge/skills: mousse, blooming, whipping cream to firm peak stage, folding in

Culinary Proficiency	Expectations	Instructor's Review
Professionalism: Demonstrate appropriate workplace hygiene and appearance.	Hair neat and restrained	
	Clean chef uniform and apron; nonslip, closed-toe shoes	
	No nail polish or jewelry	
Sanitation: Wash hands properly. Demonstrate safe food handling.	Display correct handwashing throughout production	
	Clean and sanitize workstation before and after work	
	Hold heavy cream at or below 41°F (5°C) until needed, cool mousse to 70°F (21°C) or below in two hours or less, and to 41°F (5°C) or below in less than a total of six hours	
Mise en Place: Set up workstation properly. Review lab recommended reading. Organized recipe method and sequence of work.	Prepare ingredients for assembly, adjust recipe yield as needed	
	Weigh both dry and liquid ingredients accurately	
	Purée and strain raspberries	
	Needed equipment available and ready	
Cooking Technique: Demonstrate blooming technique. Demonstrate preparation of mousse.	Dissolve gelatin completely	
	Produce smooth, seedless raspberry purée	
	Whip cream until doubled in volume and stable	
	Fold whipped cream into raspberry-gelatin mixture thoroughly	
Product Evaluation: Display chilled mousse in a plain, white bowl for observation. Taste finished product.	Mousse is an even, bright raspberry-red that is lightened slightly by the whipped cream	
	Whipped cream is thoroughly incorporated with no streaks of light color	
	Mousse is soft but able to hold shape and dissolves in mouth without chewing	
	Mousse has good, sweet berry flavor with little or no acidity	

Additional Instructor's Comments

Lab Activity 46-3: **American Buttercream**

Name _____ **Date**_____ **Period** _____

Group Members _____

American buttercream is typically used for cake fillings, frostings, and decoration. Food coloring can be mixed in to create a nearly limitless palette of colors for decorating. In addition, flavorings can be added to create desired taste profiles.

Objective

After completing this lab, you will be able to

- execute an American buttercream preparation.

Mise en Place

1. Carefully read through the recipe before starting production. Adjust the yield as needed. Review how to convert recipe yield in text Chapter 15.

2. Review the section *Buttercreams* in text Chapter 46.

3. Gather all ingredients and equipment required.

Sanitation and Safety Reminders

1. Clean and sanitize workstation before beginning to work.

2. Review *Safety Savvy: Mixer Safety* in text Chapter 40.

3. Wash hands properly and as often as needed.

Key Term

Define the following term used in this activity. Some may have been defined in previous chapters.

1. extract _____

_____

(Continued)

American Buttercream

Yield: 1 qt. (0.95 L)

Ingredients

8 oz.	225 g	unsalted butter, softened
0.32 oz. (2 tsp.)	10 g	vanilla extract
11¼ oz.	315 g	powdered sugar

Method

1. Mix butter on medium-high speed using the mixer with the paddle attachment.
2. When the butter is very soft, add vanilla extract.
3. Reduce the speed of the mixer to medium. Add the powdered sugar slowly. If the powdered sugar splashes out of the bowl, reduce the speed of the mixer and add the powdered sugar more slowly.

Chef's Note: Powdered sugar is granulated sugar that has been ground to a fine powder. When powdered sugar is graded 6X, it means it is six times finer than granulated sugar.

4. The buttercream is done once all the powdered sugar in combined with the butter. Refrigerate at or below 41°F (5°C) until service.

Chef's Journal

Write an evaluation of your lab performance. Would your finished product and performance meet the standards of a professional kitchen? Describe how your recipe turned out and what techniques and procedures you need to improve.

_____

_____

_____

_____

_____

_____

_____

_____

_____

_____

_____

_____

Performance Review: **American Buttercream**

Name _____ **Date**_____

Core knowledge/skills: buttercream, icing preparation

Culinary Proficiency	Expectations	Instructor's Review
Professionalism: Demonstrate appropriate workplace hygiene and appearance.	Hair neat and restrained	
	Clean chef uniform and apron; nonslip, closed-toe shoes	
	No nail polish or jewelry	
Sanitation: Wash hands properly. Demonstrate safe food handling.	Display correct handwashing throughout production	
	Clean and sanitize workstation before and after work	
Mise en Place: Set up workstation properly. Review lab recommended reading. Organized recipe method and sequence of work.	Prepare ingredients for assembly, adjust recipe yield as needed	
	Weigh both dry and liquid ingredients accurately	
	Needed equipment available and ready	
Product Evaluation: Display buttercream in a plain, white bowl for observation. Taste finished product.	Color is very pale yellow	
	Texture is smooth and fluffy	
	Flavor is buttery sweet with a light mouthfeel	

Additional Instructor's Comments

Lab Activity 47-1: Chocolate Sauce

Name _____ **Date** _____ **Period** _____

Group Members _____

Although chocolate originates in ancient Central America, it was not the sweet chocolate most people are familiar with today. In fact, chocolate was often mixed with water, chile peppers, and other ingredients to form a drink. It was Spanish explorers that brought chocolate back to Europe. Before long, chocolate was being sweetened with sugar and its popularity began to spread. Today, chocolate is used in many bakeshop preparations such as dessert sauces.

Objectives

After completing this lab, you will be able to

- implement a hot liquid to melt chocolate.
- execute chocolate sauce preparation.

Mise en Place

1. Carefully read through the recipe before starting production. Adjust the yield as needed. Review how to convert recipe yield in text Chapter 15.
2. Review the section *Chocolate Sauce* and *Hints from the Chef: Melting Chocolate* in text Chapter 47.
3. Gather all ingredients and equipment required.

Sanitation and Safety Reminders

1. Clean and sanitize workstation before beginning to work.
2. Wash hands properly and as often as needed.
3. Review the section *Cooling* in text Chapter 8.

Key Terms

Define the following terms used in this activity. Some may have been defined in previous chapters.

1. ganache _____

   _____

2. bain marie _____

   _____

(Continued)

Chocolate Sauce

Yield: 1 qt. (0.95 L)

Ingredients

8 oz.	240 g	milk
8 oz.	240 g	cream
7 oz.	200 g	sugar
pinch		salt
2 oz.	60 g	cocoa powder
5 oz.	140 g	semi-sweet chocolate, chopped into small pieces
1 oz.	30 g	butter

Method

1. In a saucepan, bring milk, cream, sugar, and salt to a boil.

Chef's Note: This recipe calls for half milk and half cream. To make a full rich chocolate sauce called ganache, use all heavy cream. Ganache is used for making chocolate truffles or as a silky-smooth cake covering.

2. Remove from heat and add cocoa powder, chocolate, and butter. Stir until completely melted and homogenous.

3. Chill sauce at or below 41°F (5°C) and serve.

Chef's Note: For warm chocolate sauce, double the amount of chocolate and hold in a bain marie until needed. Do not boil the sauce.

Chef's Journal

Write an evaluation of your lab performance. Would your finished product and performance meet the standards of a professional kitchen? Describe how your recipe turned out and what techniques and procedures you need to improve.

_____

_____

_____

_____

_____

_____

_____

_____

_____

_____

Performance Review: **Chocolate Sauce**

Name _____ **Date**_____

Core knowledge/skills: dessert sauces, melting chocolate, ganache, bain marie

Culinary Proficiency	Expectations	Instructor's Review
Professionalism: Demonstrate appropriate workplace hygiene and appearance.	Hair neat and restrained	
	Clean chef uniform and apron; nonslip, closed-toe shoes	
	No nail polish or jewelry	
Sanitation: Wash hands properly. Demonstrate safe food handling.	Display correct handwashing throughout production	
	Clean and sanitize workstation before and after work	
	Cool sauce to 70°F (21°C) or below in two hours or less, and to 41°F (5°C) or below in less than a total of six hours	
Mise en Place: Set up workstation properly. Review lab recommended reading. Organized recipe method and sequence of work.	Prepare ingredients for assembly, adjust recipe yield as needed	
	Weigh both dry and liquid ingredients accurately	
	Needed equipment available and ready	
Cooking Technique: Demonstrate preparation of chocolate sauce.	Remove cream, milk, and sugar mixture from heat before adding chocolate	
	Stir mixture until all chocolate is melted and ingredients are evenly distributed	
Product Evaluation: Display chocolate sauce in a plain, white bowl for observation. Taste finished product.	Sauce is an even, shiny brown with no streaks of light color	
	Texture is silky-smooth with no lumps	
	Taste is a sweet rich chocolate flavor, absence of bitter flavor due to burnt chocolate or cream	

Additional Instructor's Comments

Lab Activity 47-2: **Caramel Sauce**

Name _____ **Date**_____ **Period** _____

Group Members _____

When sugar is cooked, it goes through several stages of color and texture. As the temperature rises, the color progresses from light golden brown to brown to dark brown. As the sugar syrup gets hotter, the water evaporates and the concentration increases. As the concentration increases, the texture of the cooled product changes. A lower concentration produces a cooled product that forms a soft ball; a higher concentration results in a hard, brittle, flat piece.

Objectives

After completing this lab, you will be able to

- implement caramelization of sugar.
- execute caramel sauce preparation.

Mise en Place

1. Carefully read through the recipe before starting production. Adjust the yield as needed. Review how to convert recipe yield in text Chapter 15.

2. Review the section *Caramel Sauce* in text Chapter 47.

3. Gather all ingredients and equipment required.

Sanitation and Safety Reminders

1. Clean and sanitize workstation before beginning to work.

2. Review *Safety Savvy: Danger! Caramel!* in text Chapter 47.

3. Wash hands properly and as often as needed.

Key Terms

Define the following terms used in this activity. Some may have been defined in previous chapters.

1. caramel _____

_____

2. caramelization _____

_____

(Continued)

Caramel Sauce

Yield: 1 pt. (480 mL)

Ingredients

7 oz.	200 g	sugar
4 oz.	120 g	water
8 oz.	240 g	cream

Method

1. Place cream in a saucepan and bring to a boil. Remove from heat and keep warm until needed.

2. In a different saucepan, combine sugar and water. Bring to a boil over high heat. Continue cooking until the sugar turns medium brown. Do not stir the syrup while making caramel. If the syrup is browning unevenly, swirl the pan gently. Be very careful when working with caramel because it is very hot and can cause serious burns.

Chef's Note: If crystals begin to form on the side of the pan, use a pastry brush dipped in water to wash the crystals off. If the crystals are left, they will spread through the rest of the pan and turn the syrup into a solid block.

3. As soon as the caramel turns medium brown, remove from heat and add the hot cream. Add the cream slowly as the sauce will start to boil furiously. If the cream is added too quickly, the sauce can easily boil over. Be careful when adding cream because the steam can cause serious burns.

Chef's Note: One of the wonders of cooking (and science) is the versatility of heavy cream. In this recipe, heavy cream is added into hot caramelized sugar without breaking the cream or turning the sugar into a solid ball!

4. Once all the cream is added to the sauce, bring the sauce to a boil to ensure that the sauce is homogenous.

5. The sauce can be served at room temperature or chilled. If the sauce becomes too thick, thin it with a small amount of water or cream.

Chef's Journal

Write an evaluation of your lab performance. Would your finished product and performance meet the standards of a professional kitchen? Describe how your recipe turned out and what techniques and procedures you need to improve.

_____

_____

_____

_____

_____

Performance Review: **Caramel Sauce**

Name _____ **Date**_____

Core knowledge/skills: dessert sauces, caramelization

Culinary Proficiency	Expectations	Instructor's Review
Professionalism: Demonstrate appropriate workplace hygiene and appearance.	Hair neat and restrained	
	Clean chef uniform and apron; nonslip, closed-toe shoes	
	No nail polish or jewelry	
Sanitation: Wash hands properly. Demonstrate safe food handling.	Display correct handwashing throughout production	
	Clean and sanitize workstation before and after work	
Mise en Place: Set up workstation properly. Review lab recommended reading. Organized recipe method and sequence of work.	Prepare ingredients for assembly, adjust recipe yield as needed	
	Weigh both dry and liquid ingredients accurately	
	Needed equipment available and ready	
Cooking Technique: Demonstrate caramelization of sugar. Demonstrate preparation of caramel sauce.	Heat sugar syrup until mid to dark brown	
	Add warm cream to syrup gradually and mix in thoroughly	
Product Evaluation: Display caramel sauce in a plain, white bowl for observation. Taste finished product.	Color is a shiny, even golden brown with no streaks of light color	
	Texture is silky smooth with no lumps and nappé consistency	
	Taste is sweet and rich with a developed caramel flavor, absence of bitterness due to burnt sugar	

Additional Instructor's Comments

Lab Activity 47-3: **Vanilla Ice Cream**

Name _____ **Date**_____ **Period** _____

Group Members _____

Do you know anyone who does not like ice cream? Ice cream has been eaten and enjoyed for centuries and its popularity is not showing any signs of fading. The base for this preparation is crème anglaise.

Objectives

After completing this lab, you will be able to

- implement tempering technique.
- produce a crème anglaise.
- execute an ice cream preparation.

Mise en Place

1. Carefully read through the recipe before starting production. Adjust the yield as needed. Review how to convert recipe yield in text Chapter 15.

2. Review the sections *Crème Anglaise* in text Chapter 46 and *Ice Cream* in text Chapter 47.

3. Gather all ingredients and equipment required.

Sanitation and Safety Reminders

1. Clean and sanitize workstation before beginning to work.

2. Inspect eggs and discard any broken or cracked eggs.

3. Review the section *Cooling* in text Chapter 8.

4. Wash hands properly and as often as needed.

Key Terms

Define the following terms used in this activity. Some may have been defined in previous chapters.

1. crème anglaise _____

   _____

2. tempering _____

   _____

(Continued)

Vanilla Ice Cream

Yield: 2¼ qt. (2 L)

Ingredients

16 oz.	480 g	cream
24 oz.	720 g	milk
10 oz.	280 g	sugar
6 oz.	180 g	egg yolks
0.48 oz. (1 Tbsp.)	15 g	vanilla extract

Method

1. Place sugar, egg yolks, and vanilla extract in a bowl and whisk until the sugar dissolves and the mixture becomes fluffy and lighter in color.
2. Place the cream and milk in a saucepan and bring to a boil.
3. While whisking constantly, pour half of the cream and milk mixture into the egg yolk and sugar mixture.
4. Pour this mixture back into the saucepan with the remaining cream and milk mixture.
5. Cook the sauce over medium heat while stirring constantly with a wooden spoon or silicone spatula. Cook until the sauce thickens and reaches 185°F (85°C).
6. Immediately pour mixture through a chinois. Chill container with ice-cream mixture in an ice-water bath at or below 41°F (5°C).
7. When the mixture is cold, pour into an ice-cream maker and churn until frozen to a soft ice-cream consistency. Remove from the ice-cream maker and place in a frozen container. Cover well and store in a freezer until needed.

Chef's Note: Many different flavors can be created using this base vanilla flavor. Create the flavor of your choice by adding a fruit purée, chopped nuts, or other flavoring while the ice cream is churning.

Chef's Journal

Write an evaluation of your lab performance. Would your finished product and performance meet the standards of a professional kitchen? Describe how your recipe turned out and what techniques and procedures you need to improve.

_____

_____

_____

_____

_____

_____

_____

Performance Review: **Vanilla Ice Cream**

Name _____ **Date**_____

Core knowledge/skills: frozen desserts, crème anglaise, ice cream, tempering, use of an ice-cream machine, temperature measurement

Culinary Proficiency	Expectations	Instructor's Review
Professionalism: Demonstrate appropriate workplace hygiene and appearance.	Hair neat and restrained	
	Clean chef uniform and apron; nonslip, closed-toe shoes	
	No nail polish or jewelry	
Sanitation: Wash hands properly. Demonstrate safe food handling.	Display correct handwashing throughout production	
	Inspect eggs for cracks and discard; cool sauce to 70°F (21°C) or below in two hours or less, and to 41°F (5°C) or below in less than a total of six hours	
	Clean and sanitize workstation before and after work	
Mise en Place: Set up workstation properly. Review lab recommended reading. Organized recipe method and sequence of work.	Prepare ingredients for assembly, adjust recipe yield as needed	
	Weigh both dry and liquid ingredients accurately	
	Needed equipment available and ready, ice-cream container placed in freezer to chill	
Cooking Technique: Demonstrate correct tempering technique. Demonstrate preparation of ice cream.	Temper egg yolks properly so there is no curdling or breaking	
	Stir sauce continuously and heat to 180°F to thicken	
	Remove sauce from pan immediately and strain	
	Chill mixture before placing in ice-cream machine	
	Churn ice cream continuously and long enough to incorporate sufficient air	
Product Evaluation: Display vanilla ice cream in a plain, white bowl for observation. Taste finished product.	Color is an even, creamy white with no hint of caramelization or darkness	
	Texture is smooth and creamy with no heavy ice crystals or crunch	
	Ice cream is light, not dense	
	Taste is sweet, with a mild vanilla flavor	

Additional Instructor's Comments

Lab Activity 47-4: **Raspberry Sorbet**

Name _____ **Date** _____ **Period** _____

Group Members _____

Sorbet begins with simple syrup, add to that a puréed ingredient (in this case, raspberries), place this mixture in an ice-cream maker, and churn. Nearly any fruit can be puréed and used to flavor a sorbet, so the possible flavor profiles are many. Because sorbet is so light and refreshing, it can be served at the beginning, middle, or end of a meal.

Objectives

After completing this lab, you will be able to

- produce a simple syrup and fruit purée.
- execute sorbet technique.

Mise en Place

1. Carefully read through the recipe before starting production. Adjust the yield as needed. Review how to convert recipe yield in text Chapter 15.
2. Review the sections *Sweeteners* in text Chapter 40 and *Fruit Sauces and Sorbet* in text Chapter 47.
3. Gather all ingredients and equipment required.

Sanitation and Safety Reminders

1. Clean and sanitize workstation before beginning to work.
2. Wash hands properly and as often as needed.
3. Review *Safety Savvy: Blender Safety* in text Chapter 25.

Key Terms

Define the following terms used in this activity. Some may have been defined in previous chapters.

1. sorbet _____

   _____

2. simple syrup _____

   _____

3. coulis _____

   _____

(Continued)

Raspberry Sorbet

Yield: 2½ qt. (2.4 L)

Ingredients

25 oz.	700 g	sugar
22 oz.	660 g	water
32 oz.	960 g	raspberry purée, strained
to taste		lemon juice

Method

1. Combine sugar and water in a saucepan.

Chef's Note: The amount of sugar used affects how smooth or crunchy the final texture of the sorbet will be. Too much sugar prevents the sorbet from setting up. Too little sugar results in a hard, grainy sorbet.

2. Bring to a boil over high heat and simmer just until the sugar is dissolved. Let the simple syrup cool.

3. When the syrup is cold, combine with the raspberry purée. Add lemon juice if additional acidity is necessary.

4. Pour into an ice-cream maker and churn until frozen to a soft consistency.

5. Remove from the ice-cream maker and place in a frozen container. Cover well and store in a freezer until needed.

Chef's Journal

Write an evaluation of your lab performance. Would your finished product and performance meet the standards of a professional kitchen? Describe how your recipe turned out and what techniques and procedures you need to improve.

_____

_____

_____

_____

_____

_____

_____

_____

_____

_____

Performance Review: **Raspberry Sorbet**

Name _____ **Date**_____

Core knowledge/skills: frozen desserts, coulis, simple syrup, puréeing, use of a blender and ice-cream maker

Culinary Proficiency	Expectations	Instructor's Review
Professionalism: Demonstrate appropriate workplace hygiene and appearance.	Hair neat and restrained	
	Clean chef uniform and apron; nonslip, closed-toe shoes	
	No nail polish or jewelry	
Sanitation: Wash hands properly. Demonstrate safe food handling.	Display correct handwashing throughout production	
	Clean and sanitize workstation before and after work	
Mise en Place: Set up workstation properly. Review lab recommended reading. Organized recipe method and sequence of work.	Prepare ingredients for assembly, adjust recipe yield as needed	
	Weigh both dry and liquid ingredients accurately	
	Needed equipment available and ready, ice-cream container placed in freezer to chill	
Cooking Technique: Demonstrate correct sorbet technique.	Boil sugar and water until sugar is dissolved and syrup is clear, not caramelized	
	Allow simple syrup to cool	
	Purée raspberries until smooth and strain through chinois, mix into cooled syrup	
	Churn sorbet until solid	
	Place sorbet in chilled ice-cream container and cover	
Product Evaluation: Display raspberry sorbet in a plain, white bowl for observation. Taste finished product.	Sorbet is bright raspberry-red, color is uniform	
	Texture in mouth is soft with no heavy ice crystals or crunch	
	Taste is sweet but balanced with strong raspberry flavor	

Additional Instructor's Comments

Lab Activity 48-1: **Quality Table Service**

Name _____ **Date** _____ **Period** _____

The service provided to the guest by the front-of-the-house staff is as important as the quality of the food served. The front-of-the-house and back-of-the-house must work together seamlessly to provide the guest with an optimal experience. The quality of service is improved when each area understands the needs and organization of the other area.

Objectives

After completing this lab, you will be able to

- recognize the roles of the front-of-the-house positions.
- demonstrate an understanding of guest service and customer relations.
- apply the general rules of table setting and service.
- respond to customers' special dietary needs and food allergies.

Preparation

1. Create a list of common customer service issues and complaints. (Be sure to include special dietary needs and/or food allergies on the list.) Write each of these issues on a separate 3″ × 5″ card. (**Note:** *Your instructor may already have these cards prepared.*) Place the cards in a basket face down and in no particular order.
2. Create another list of varying customer descriptions such as "family with young children," "older couple one of whom is in a wheelchair," "executives at a business lunch," and write each on a separate 3″× 5″ card. (**Note:** *Your instructor may already have these cards prepared.*). Place the cards in a basket face down and in no particular order.
3. Write each type of table service described in the text on a separate 3″ × 5″ card. (**Note:** *Your instructor may already have these cards prepared.*) Place the cards in a basket face down and in no particular order.

Lab Procedure

1. Working in groups of five to six students, draw one card from each basket. The descriptions on these cards will provide the parameters for each group's role-play.
2. Assign each member of the group one of the following roles as needed to role-play the meal service scenario described by the three cards drawn from the baskets:
   - maître d'hotel or greeter
   - front server
   - back server
   - bus person
   - customers

(Continued)

3. Each group will be responsible for
    *   presetting the table appropriate to the type of meal service
    *   greeting and seating the customers
    *   presenting the menu
    *   demonstrating knowledge of menu and suggestive selling
    *   taking the customers' orders
    *   serving the meals
    *   addressing any customer needs or complaints
    *   presenting checks

4. As each group presents its role-play, other students should observe and prepare critiques. Critiques should identify moments of quality service as well as moments of service that were lacking. Include specific suggestions for improvements to service where appropriate.

Critiques

Group #1 Members _____

1. Table setting _____

    _____

    _____

    _____

    _____

    _____

    _____

    _____

    _____

2. Greet and seat_____

    _____

    _____

    _____

    _____

    _____

    _____

    _____

    _____

(Continued)

3. Menu presentation _____

_____

_____

_____

_____

_____

_____

_____

4. Menu knowledge and suggestive sell _____

_____

_____

_____

_____

_____

_____

_____

5. Order taking _____

_____

_____

_____

_____

_____

_____

_____

6. Serving _____

_____

_____

_____

_____

_____

_____

_____

(Continued)

7. Handling customer needs and complaints _____

_____

_____

_____

_____

_____

_____

_____

8. Presenting check _____

_____

_____

_____

_____

_____

_____

_____

_____

Group #2 Members _____

1. Table setting _____

_____

_____

_____

_____

_____

_____

_____

2. Greet and seat_____

_____

_____

_____

_____

(Continued)

_____

_____

_____

3. Menu presentation _____

_____

_____

_____

_____

_____

_____

_____

4. Menu knowledge and suggestive sell _____

_____

_____

_____

_____

_____

_____

_____

_____

5. Order taking _____

_____

_____

_____

_____

_____

_____

_____

6. Serving _____

_____

_____

_____

_____

_____

(Continued)

_____

_____

_____

7. Handling customer needs and complaints _____

_____

_____

_____

_____

_____

_____

8. Presenting check _____

_____

_____

_____

_____

_____

_____

_____

_____

Group #3 Members _____

1. Table setting _____

_____

_____

_____

_____

_____

_____

_____

2. Greet and seat _____

_____

_____

(Continued)

_____

_____

_____

_____

_____

_____

3. Menu presentation _____

_____

_____

_____

_____

_____

_____

_____

_____

4. Menu knowledge and suggestive sell _____

_____

_____

_____

_____

_____

_____

_____

5. Order taking _____

_____

_____

_____

_____

_____

_____

6. Serving _____

_____

_____

(Continued)

_____

_____

_____

_____

_____

_____

7. Handling customer needs and complaints _____

_____

_____

_____

_____

_____

_____

_____

8. Presenting check _____

_____

_____

_____

_____

_____

_____